Praise for *Going Circular*

"Rich Bulger's book, *Going Circular*, is a commendable and insightful contribution to the field of reverse logistics, brilliantly updating two decades of knowledge in this area. His work skillfully bridges the gap between profitability and sustainability, showcasing a future-forward approach to business practices. Bulger's dedication and expertise shine through in this book, making it an essential read for anyone interested in innovative supply chain and logistics solutions."

—GLENN RICHEY
Harbert Eminent Scholar in
Supply Chain Management, Auburn University

"Sustainable retail requires more sustainable products, more sustainable suppliers, and more sustainable supply chains. The most sustainable supply chains are also the most circular, ensuring that products can be reused, repaired, refurbished, and resold before they are ultimately disassembled and their materials recycled to make new products. Reverse logistics is the backbone of this emerging circular economy. *Going Circular* provides a practitioner's perspective on reverse logistics, circularity, and the future of sustainable retail."

—SCOT CASE
Vice President of Corporate Social Responsibility and
Sustainability, National Retail Federation

"Rich, with his seventeen-year tenure at Verizon, has made significant strides in the field of reverse logistics, developing innovative solutions and initiating the retail trade-in program. His insights into the complexities of both domestic and international logistics led to the creation of RecirQ, a venture aimed at filling gaps in the secondary market. Throughout his journey, Rich has expressed profound gratitude to the Reverse Logistics Association and his family, whose unwavering support has been a pillar of strength, enabling him to share countless lessons with the sustainability leaders of tomorrow in his book."

—DR. OLIVER HEDGEPETH
Professor of Logistics, American Public University

Going Circular

Going Circular

The Evolution of Reverse Logistics into a Competitive Weapon

Rich Bulger

BROWN BOOKS
PUBLISHING GROUP

Going Circular
The Evolution of Reverse Logistics into a Competitive Weapon

Brown Books Publishing Group
Dallas, TX / New York, NY
www.BrownBooks.com
(972) 381-0009

A New Era in Publishing®

Publisher's Cataloging-In-Publication Data

Names: Bulger, Rich, author.
Title: Going circular : the evolution of reverse logistics into a competitive weapon / Rich
    Bulger.
Description: Dallas, TX ; New York, NY : Brown Books Publishing Group, [2024] |
    Includes bibliographical references.
Identifiers: ISBN: 978-1-61254-690-2 (paperback) | 978-1-61254-696-4 (ebook) | LCCN:
    2023952376
Subjects: LCSH: Business logistics. | Industrial management. | Upcycling (Waste, etc.)
    | Manufactures. | Success in business. | BISAC: BUSINESS & ECONOMICS /
    Logistics & Supply Chain. | BUSINESS & ECONOMICS / Structural Adjustment.
Classification: LCC: HD38.5 .B85 2024 | DDC: 658.7--dc23

ISBN 978-1-61254-690-2
LCCN 2023952376

Printed in the United States
10 9 8 7 6 5 4 3 2 1

For more information or to contact the author, please go to
www.RichBulger.com.

To Auburn University, goTRG, and the Reverse Logistics Association for your commitment to Going Circular and helping other companies go circular as well.

Contents in Brief

Table of Contents

List of Illustrations

About the Author

Rich Bulger is the CEO of RecirQ Global, a pioneering sustainability company dedicated to developing strategies that facilitate the profitable and eco-friendly transfer of products from one user to another. His career is a testament to his commitment to sustainable business practices and innovative logistics solutions.

Rich's journey began in the U.S. Army, where he served from 1996 to 1999, laying the groundwork for his disciplined approach to leadership and strategic thinking. Following his military service, he started as a temporary employee and embarked on a remarkable seventeen-year tenure at Verizon. Rich's innate talent and determination saw him rapidly ascend to various roles, including sales, management, and district management. His leadership skills were further recognized in his appointment to three directorial positions, covering operations, marketing, and, notably, reverse logistics.

In 2009, Rich spearheaded Verizon's inaugural store trade-in program, a groundbreaking initiative that transformed the company's approach to product lifecycle management. Under his stewardship, the program flourished, generating $1.6 billion annually from the sale of used handsets. He was instrumental in processing 15 million handsets through a centralized returns and testing center (CRTC), showcasing his expertise in managing complex logistics operations at scale.

Rich's expertise was further honed at Cisco, where he managed global reverse logistics locations. During his tenure at Cisco, the team consistently earned the prestigious Gartner Top Supply Chain award, a recognition of their collective effective leadership and innovative strategies. Rich played a key role in fostering a collaborative and forward-thinking environment that contributed significantly to these achievements.

Apart from his corporate achievements, Rich also contributed his insights and experience as a member of the advisory board for the Reverse Logistics Association. His commitment to continuous learning and professional development culminated in earning a master's degree in Reverse Logistics Management.

Rich Bulger's career is characterized by a relentless pursuit of excellence in sustainability and logistics. His leadership at RecirQ continues to drive positive change, demonstrating that sustainable business practices can also be profitable and efficient.

Rich is happily married to Naomi Bulger, and they live together with their two children, Riley and Bryce, who he proudly acknowledges as being smarter and better looking than himself.

Reverse Logistics Association
Advisory Board

Glenn Richey
Harbert Eminent Scholar in Supply
Chain Management, Auburn University

Troy Campbell
Director RLC Operations,
The Home Depot

Brad Harris
Senior Director Reverse Network,
Circular Commerce, Walmart

Chuck Johnston
Chief Strategy Officer,
goTRG

Jason Maciver
Vice President, Services Procurement at
Dell, Dell Technologies

Sean Magann
Chief Commercial Officer,
Sims Lifecycle Services

Daniel O'Neill
Vice President, Client Solutions,
Liquidity Services

Nikos Papaioannou
Senior Business Manager, Amazon

Christ Rezendes
Chief Customer Officer, OnProcess
Technology

Ian Rusher
Supply Chain Reverse Logistics Global,
Operations Manager, Cisco Systems

Julie Ryan
Senior Manager NA Returns &
Remarketing, HP Inc.

Gregory Skrovan
Senior Manager Global Reverse
Logistics, Intel

Foreword

Tony Sciarrotta

Executive Director and Publisher of RL Magazine

When Philips decided to take me out of my happy space—being a successful sales manager for major accounts of audio and video products for over ten years—and told me to go work on the company's returns problems, I was totally shocked. What returns? They were just a number we estimated would come off the sales line every month, and we never actually saw them in the stores where new Philips goods were stacked and flying out the door. At that time, no one in the sales organization actually looked at any returned goods, and we had no idea most of them worked when they came back. This was the first hint of a need for a circular approach to returns.

The beginning of reverse logistics in the early 2000s included returns management and asset recovery. Rich will often cite *Going Backwards*, which was among the first books I could find in early Google searches. The book was being offered for free! I used a desk printer to download it and start to learn about my new work assignment. Then, like your good author Rich, I quickly became consumed with doing something about the high return rates for my company. At the same time, I began to learn more about recycling as a solution for returned electronics, only to learn much later a slew of related issues.

What I learned in those early years was the need to improve the customer experience and simplify the products. We found ways at Philips to reduce returns with a focus on those aspects: welcome sheets in the box versus stop sheets, quick start guides with clear steps and pictures, instruction books in less languages and bigger fonts—these methods helped reduce return rates for common products like clock radios, portable audio products, and TV sets. Consumers could take products home and easily get them started. In regard to working with major retailers, I remember the words of Chuck Johnston, who was then at Walmart. He said, "Ninety-nine percent of customers do not walk into a store to buy something with plans to take it back." Something was wrong. Granted, unlimited return policies did allow customers to upgrade their digital products as newer, better models came out, and they were becoming savvy enough to have their own circular economy. But it was not all about liberal return policies.

Retailers began to learn that accountability was also needed to reduce unnecessary and unwarranted returns of products that were well past their purchase. As returns began to increase, systems were needed to validate product purchases including receipts, serial-number-capturing technology, and smart serial numbers. Major retailers implemented many systems to enforce gatekeeping on returns, but the customer was still king and often got the refund they wanted. But retail rates at brick-and-mortar stores were stabilized at an estimated 7–8 percent of sales until the 2010s. At Philips, the many steps we took reduced returns from lower double digits to lower single digits—the equivalent of millions of dollars saved for the company.

The beginning of e-commerce changed the retail landscape in many ways. To take business from stores, e-commerce retailers focused on making it easier to buy and then easier to return, as well as free shipping for returns. Some e-commerce retailers began to encourage multiple purchases and allow customers to make their choices at home and send everything else back. Where these returns went never mattered to consumers; it was not their problem. Yet.

Before e-commerce, returns generally went back to the manufacturers for most brand-name goods. Companies like Philips,

Sony, HP, and Dell would often sell the returned products "as-is" and let the buyers do the sorting between the working from the nonworking, so the scrap was less visible to the manufacturers. In some cases, companies did have partners process the returns and create refurbished products that were sold quietly to a secondary channel. But the focus was on financial accountability, and if it was cheaper and faster to sell the goods as-is, many companies did. There were no environment, sustainability, and governance (ESG) reports then, and if a few goods ended up in landfills, companies did not change their liquidation processes except to reduce their losses. Brand protection became less important, and financial predictability became paramount to the revolving CFOs. It became common for companies to provide allowances for retailers to make the issue of product returns just "disappear."

Sustainability became a buzzword in the 2010s as retailers and manufacturers saw many more news reports about returns going to waste. Brands did not want to appear in the news with pictures of their products in landfills. Companies began to focus on ways to recover returns and do something with them. While there were costs associated with processing returns, the growth of the secondary market increased asset recovery, and companies could reduce losses or even begin to show a profit from selling returns, albeit through some creative accounting.

In the late 2010s, the circular economy grew from a buzzword to an end-to-end concept. The Ellen MacArthur Foundation had been pushing the ideas for years, and global companies were starting to pay attention. ESG reports were beginning to be a basis for some in the investment community. While many consumer electronics companies had been focused on asset recovery for returns, the growth of the mobile phone industry and the rapid churn of the newest and latest models produced millions of returns that were often thrown away. Along with the e-commerce return rates at three to four times previous store rates, fashion and electronics returns were out of control, generating millions of tons of waste to landfills and polluting our planet's air, land, and waters.

This important book *Going Circular* is about going back to the beginning. Consumers have become overwhelmingly more entitled than ever in history to buy what they think they want, not just what they need. Yes, sales have increased because online shopping is easy (and was necessary during the pandemic), but so have returns. The circular concept is to start at product creation. Is this product necessary, and does it serve a purpose? If it does, can eventual reuse be part of the design? Is the product simple to use, easy to connect to other products in our new digital universe, and interoperable with other products?

A great example of a company's passion for circular economy is Intel, which created the USB-C standard plug. In the past, every brand of mobile and consumer electronics used their own format for plugs and powers, leading to billions of discarded cords and chargers in landfills. Today, most brands have agreed to use this format plug, and the future is hopeful to create harmony among products and reduce the throw-away mentality that consumers have learned.

Reduce, reuse, repair, and recycle are part of the mission statement of the Reverse Logistics Association. When I took over this organization in 2016, part of its revitalization included finding members who were focused on going circular. Your author Rich Bulger became an advisory board member while still at Cisco and displayed the highest passion for going circular since then. This book is a much-needed blueprint for companies to join the circular economy and make a difference. The difference is to help the planet and help companies find ways to reduce returns, reuse products for second and third lives, repair them whenever possible, and recycle them back to raw materials. As Rich shows, this can be done. In fact, not only can it be done, but companies can also make a profit and make a difference.

I hope you enjoy reading this book, written from a place of passion that is inside Rich and inside many more of us. We are making a difference by going circular.

Author's Note

I began my career at the age of seventeen as a military enlistee and later embarked on a seventeen-year tenure at Verizon. Starting in a temporary role, I ascended to manage the largest retail district, eventually spearheading a $1.6 billion sales channel that monetized returned products. In 2009 as a newly appointed marketing and operations director, I delved into reverse logistics and pioneered Verizon's first retail trade-in program to grow market shares and introduce a new revenue stream. I was also responsible for traditional reverse logistics metrics like reduction of returns rates. When I was developing the trade-in program, I realized that not all returns were bad, and I needed to increase strategic returns as well. My fall into reverse logistics was more of a necessity than a choice, driven by my relentless pursuit of sales and revenue growth.

Despite skeptics who mockingly labeled Verizon Wireless as a "sell" phone company and not a "buy" phone company and questioned my intent to buy back devices, our focus on sustainability proved profitable as the revenue from returned products eventually exceeded the combined sales of every accessory across all of Verizon's sales channels. Remarkably, our small team of just twelve people was responsible for generating 2 percent of Verizon's total income, operating almost invisibly within the company with products the first customer no longer wanted. Like many of my friends in this space, no one in my company knew how to train us; we had to figure it out as we went.

The moment I was invited to apply for the Director of Reverse Logistics position at Verizon's centralized returns and testing center, I recall asking, "What is reverse logistics, and what is a CRTC?" That was the beginning of a learning journey through trial and error. The shift marked the start of an enlightening path filled with both challenges and discoveries. While serving a three-year rotation on the Reverse Logistics Association (RLA) advisory board, I had the privilege of engaging with professionals across various sectors, which revealed more similarities than differences in our challenges and underlined the importance of knowledge exchange in this exponentially growing industry.

When I was recruited by Jack Allen, a visionary leader and champion of sustainability, to lead Cisco's global reverse logistics operations, I encountered a different corporate landscape compared to my tenure at Verizon. Cisco, primarily a manufacturer of networking gear, presented a unique set of challenges and opportunities distinct from Verizon's focus on mobility and distribution. Despite these differences, I soon realized the substantial overlap in the Venn diagram of our challenges and approaches. Both being Fortune 100 companies, Cisco, like Verizon, lacked formal training programs for reverse logistics. This meant that we had to navigate and innovate in this space with the resources and experience we had, often learning and adapting as we went along.

Likewise, I noticed the knowledge gap in academia for reverse logistics. Recently, I completed my master's degree in Reverse Logistics from American Public University. During my studies, *Going Backwards*, a seminal text in logistics written in 1999, was often referenced. However, with the evolving nature of the field, particularly with the emergence of concepts like the circular economy, it became apparent that updates to this body of scholarship were necessary.

In 2023, I spoke at a leadership conference where I encountered approximately twenty logistics graduates, none of whom had been exposed to reverse logistics in their academic curriculum. Just like every business challenge that arises, you have a choice: wait for someone else to build what you need, or take the initiative to solve it yourself. This proactive approach embodies the spirit of this book. This is an attempt to fill that educational void, combining insights from my academic research, decades of real-world sales and logistics experience, and the collective wisdom of my RLA colleagues.

This book is a practical guide, shaped by my diverse experiences as a sales leader, logistical director, RLA board member, soldier, and student. It aims to be a dynamic learning tool, evolving alongside trends in reverse logistics, including the circular economy and green logistics.

Acknowledgments

I am grateful to numerous individuals who have shaped my journey. Jerry Fountain's faith in my potential was a career-defining catalyst, teaching me the essence of courage and leadership. Another guiding figure in this venture has been Randy Elliott. Initially known as Dr. No during his tenure in finance, he amusingly transformed into Dr. Go as he ventured into reverse logistics alongside me. His decades of unwavering friendship and partnership have been invaluable.

I am thankful to my partners at RecirQ—Reuben, Arthur, Mark, and Noah—for their patience and support as I shared my thoughts on the topic. I extend my gratitude to Scott Wagner from Assurant, who joined me in taking the first steps into the trade-in segment of the circular economy.

Members of the Reverse Logistics Association, especially Tony Sciarrotta, and authors like Dr. Rogers and Dr. Lembke who wrote *Going Backwards* have been instrumental in this project. I am grateful to Dr. Oliver Hedgepath at American Public University for his encouragement to pursue a master's degree. This opportunity not only challenged me but also provided a valuable platform to articulate and delve into my thoughts and research. A special thanks to both Sender Shamiss and goTRG for sponsoring this publication and to Dr. Glenn Richey of

Auburn University for his academic support. A heartfelt thank you to Fara Alexander, goTRG's marketing whiz, for her patience of a saint and her invaluable assistance in moving this project forward. Shout out to Beril Toktay from Georgia Tech for our enlightening conversations about relicensing. I also appreciate Sandra Rhee, a master's student at MIT, for her valuable feedback, and Erika Pollak whose mentorship has been indispensable. I would also like to thank the fantastic team at Brown Books Publishing Group for working on a tight deadline so that this book is ready to meet its audience.

Finally, my deepest gratitude goes to my family: my wife, Naomi, and my sons, Riley and Bryce. Their support and patience have been the bedrock of my journey.

Thank you all for being part of this process.

Introduction

In 1999, Drs. Dale Rogers and Ronald S. Lembke wrote a groundbreaking book, *Going Backwards: Reverse Logistics Trends and Best Practices.*[1] It is one of the only publications that specializes in reverse logistics. The book illustrates the difference between **forward logistics**—moving products from the manufacturer to the customer—and **reverse logistics**—returning products from the customer back to the manufacturer. The goal of optimizing the reverse logistics process at that time was to reduce unwanted returns and protect sales margins.

The traditional linear **supply chain**, characterized by a make-use-dispose approach, fostered a linear return system in which products were processed in a reverse order.[2] This mindset perpetuated the idea that returns followed a straightforward path back to their origin and that all returns were inherently undesirable. Linear financial models were developed with an emphasis on promoting sales while making the return process cumbersome and discouraging. The business dynamics of the late 1990s can be summarized in this way:

- Going forward is selling **Product One** to **Customer One**. Competitors compete to sell Product One to Customer One.
- Going backward is returning Product One to the Source. The

strategy for reverse logistics is driving unwanted returns down to protect sales margin.

Over the past twenty-five years, we have witnessed a significant transformation in the global marketplace, primarily driven by technological advancement. This revolution has fundamentally altered customer shopping habits as more and more consumers have shifted from traditional brick-and-mortar stores to online or omnichannel platforms. This transition has not only opened new sales channels but has also given rise to a burgeoning market for used products. Additionally, these changes have profoundly impacted purchasing and return behaviors, reflecting the evolving landscape of consumerism in the digital age.

This has given rise to the desired outcome of the **circular economy**, in which the focus is on creating value from used products, with or without the supplier's involvement. *Going Circular* explores the evolution of the reverse logistics process and presents updated strategies for managing unwanted returns while increasing some return streams because it is not just right for the environment, it's smart business.

The goal is to create a circular flow of products by recirculating valuable and durable goods, thereby strategically increasing return volume and generating revenue by selling the same product and related services multiple times. The fundamental principles of a mature circular economy program are to prioritize reuse over recycling whenever possible while accomplishing the movement of goods with minimum impact to our environment and society through a **green logistics** strategy.

First, we will discuss an updated view of **best practices** for managing unwanted returns from Customer One. We will then discuss the concept of developing a strategy to service **Customer Two+**. This evolution of the reverse logistics process introduces a different sales, return, and logistics strategy. If **retailers**, distributors, or **manufacturers** do not provide solutions, customers take matters into their own hands and find value for their products on their own. In going circular, the rules of the game are different:

- Going circular is the process of moving Product One from the hands of Customer One into the hands of Customer Two+.
- Competitors in a circular economy compete for the sale and return of Product One.
- Going circular is the realization that customers can bypass the source and find value themselves.
- Not all returns are bad! In fact, a strategy for highly valuable and highly durable goods is to drive some return streams up and make money by selling the same product more than once.
- "Reuse first" and "recycle last" are the foundations of a mature circular economy program.

Reverse logistics and the circular economy are complementary but distinct concepts. Reverse logistics activities can fulfill various corporate desired outcomes beyond the pursuit of the economic framework characterized by the "necessary evil of returns" or "desired outcome" of the circular economy. Some contend that there is a niche for a book on the interplay of the circular economy with a surface-level teaching of reverse logistics. However, reverse logistics is a complicated world of its own and deserves its own literature. Practitioners specializing in reverse logistics routinely face complex challenges in managing the flow of returned products. This includes dealing with items originating from various sources and handling the varying conditions in which these products are received.

Within the scope of the circular economy, numerous books effectively discuss and clarify the concept, capturing the "what" of its vision with precision. However, these often lack depth in addressing the "how," particularly in the critical area of managing returns—an aspect frequently overlooked. The distinction between intent and outcome in the circular economy hinges on the implementation of concrete actions. While this book acknowledges various studies on manufacturing and forward logistics within the circular economy framework, it primarily concentrates on the intricate role of reverse logistics, highlighting its importance in a product's lifecycle.

Professionals in reverse logistics bear the responsibility of fulfilling corporate objectives such as building customer-friendly programs, fraud prevention, implementing green logistics, enhancing customer experience, and reducing unwanted returns. This focused approach offers a detailed understanding of the pivotal role of reverse logistics in ensuring efficient, sustainable, and economically viable product-lifecycle management.

This book is written for those who are positioned to actively manage and drive these processes rather than for leaders seeking a superficial grasp. Many leaders recognize the surface value of reverse logistics but lack the logistical expertise, bandwidth, or passion to immerse themselves in the subject. This is the guide they would pass on to their key personnel to ensure the creation and management of an exemplary reverse logistics division. Our aim is to spotlight state-of-the-art practices, underline the invaluable contributions of reverse logistics experts to sales and the overall supply chain, and empower the next cadre of reverse supply chain specialists with the insights and tactics they need to affect meaningful change from their distinctive perspective within the supply chain. Reverse logistics, when leveraged effectively, serves as a competitive weapon with four desired outcomes:

1. Sales-enablement
2. Return prevention/Cost prevention
3. Green logistics
4. Circular economy

In essence, reverse logistics is not just a cost center but a part of the sales engine. This book expounds upon these goals, providing insights into modern best practices adopted by companies to realize these objectives.

Going Circular methodically breaks down various aspects of the **reverse supply chain** into three fundamental activities related to the products journey: (1) **asset recovery**, (2) operations, and (3) **value generation**. The book contains three Reuse Cases that illustrate how companies have achieved success applying these strategies in real life: Chapter 2 explores Verizon's journey in developing a circular economy program. Chapter 3 includes an invaluable case study on how **goTRG**—a third-party logistics and **re-commerce** provider— is managing complex returns processes for major companies like Walmart. Chapter 5 highlights ACS Clothing's innovative approach to reducing the **environmental impact** of fashion returns while creating a sustainable product-as-a-service model.

The final chapter of this book concludes with a discussion on future trends and findings in the evolving space of reverse logistics. A glossary of terms is included at the end to define key concepts discussed throughout the book.

Chapter 1

Size and Role of Reverse Logistics in the Circular Economy

1.1 Rethinking Reverse Logistics in the Circular Economy Era

Going Backwards was published in 1999 to provide insights into the emerging field of reverse logistics. The book highlighted the primary reasons why products were being returned and outlined the best practices that businesses could adopt to reduce such returns. The findings of the book have served as a guiding framework for reverse supply chain leaders over the past twenty-four years.[1]

Since then, technological advancements, improved communication tools, and evolving sales practices—coupled with a heightened awareness of humanity's impact on the planet—have significantly transformed the landscape of return management. The emergence of the **circular economy** has prompted companies to reevaluate their approach to returns, considering both economic and sustainability factors.

Initially, policies in reverse logistics were primarily focused on limiting the frequency of returns and minimizing associated costs. However, it has become increasingly clear that returns offer substantial economic and environmental opportunities. Returns have become a crucial component of the circular economy, highlighting the importance of waste reduction and the efficient use of resources.

Best practices—guidelines or principles that have proven effective in specific industries or fields—have traditionally been integrated into these policies to establish a structured set of standards for organizations. Yet, as competition dynamics, technological advancements, legislative changes, and customer needs continue to change, these policies, too, must adapt. The shift toward viewing returns not just as a cost center but as a potential source of value illustrates the need for policies that are responsive to the new dynamics in business and the environment.

Professionals in reverse logistics, therefore, face the task of refining their strategies in response to the industry's shifting demands. This necessitates a significant reconsideration of existing norms, including the idea that all returns are unfavorable. In fact, some returns can be beneficial, especially with the growing understanding that returns management should minimize environmental and societal impact. In short, there is an industry-wide need to revisit established policies, ensuring they align more closely with the principles of a circular economy.

1.2 What Is Logistics?

Logistics

The word "logistics" originates from the Greek term *logistikē*, which refers to the art of calculating. It is derived from the Greek word *logos*, meaning "reason" or "speech." In ancient Greece, *logistikē* encompassed the skills of calculation, reasoning, and organizing resources for effective decision-making.

Over time, the meaning of **logistics** expanded to include the management of resources. During ancient wars, logistics involved the planning, coordination, and supply of troops, equipment, and provisions. In *The Art of War* (originally published around 500 BC), Sun Tzu stated, "The line between disorder and order lies in logistics."[2]

The term gained prominence during the Napoleonic era and was further developed in the nineteenth and twentieth centuries as military organizations recognized the crucial role of efficient supply chains in supporting military campaigns.

In a similar vein, the global supply chain is equally susceptible to disruptions, as evinced by the COVID-19 pandemic, ransomware attacks, **labor** shortages, global conflicts like the war in Ukraine, and increasing political pressure to incorporate sustainable alternatives. In light of these challenges, the parallels between the military and civilian sectors become more apparent. Their shared vulnerabilities highlight the need for collaboration and knowledge-sharing to address challenges effectively and maintain robust supply chains across both sectors.

The importance of logistics in both military and civilian supply chains can be seen in the collaboration between Combined Arms Support Command (CASCOM), a major subordinate command of the United States Army responsible for both training and doctrine development related to sustainment and **logistics operations**, and Virginia Commonwealth University (VCU). Each year, army captains are sent to complete a master's degree program in supply chain management at VCU. This partnership facilitates the exchange of best practices between military and civilian supply chain leaders, drawing knowledge from both the battlefield and factory floor.[3]

In the twentieth century, logistics began to find applications beyond the military context, expanding into commercial and industrial domains. Today, logistics refers to the comprehensive process of managing the movement and storage of products or goods from point to point, encompassing activities such as **warehousing**, resource management, systems, packaging, transportation, and services among other efforts. The goal of logistics is to ensure that the right product is in the right place, at the right time, and in the right condition to meet the needs of customers or the desired outcome of the military. Logistics is "how" products move.

LOGISTICS

Systems
Transportation
Resource Management
Receiving
Sortation
Inspection
Testing
Repair
Storage/Warehousing
Packaging
Pick/Pack/Ship

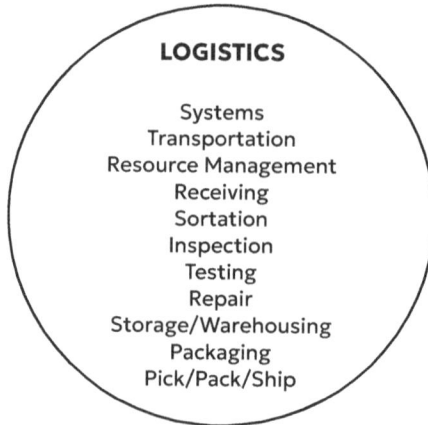

Figure 1.1. "Elements of Logistics" shows the logistical activities that can occur as a product moves from point to point.

Logistics encompasses both forward logistics and reverse logistics, which—though they may be unfamiliar terms—are integral to our daily lives. Forward logistics is a visible and familiar process, involving the purchasing and delivery of a product to a customer for use. It is the journey of goods from **manufacturers** to the end users, ensuring that products reach customers efficiently and effectively.

Reverse logistics, on the other hand, is less visible but equally important. It comes into play when a customer decides to return a product or no longer needs it. This process involves returning the product from its original destination to another point, often for the purpose of reselling, recycling, or properly disposing of the product no longer wanted by the original customer.

Both forward and reverse logistics are essential components of the supply chain, ensuring that products not only reach customers but also that the flow of returned goods is managed in a way that maximizes value and minimizes waste.

Supply Chain

The supply chain consists of multiple points and involves the movement of goods and services. Dr. Wallace Burns, a Transportation and Logistics

Management professor at American Public University, explains that logistics includes storage and distribution and encompasses various customer-tailored elements, such as: schedules, **procurement**, **inventory control**, product lifecycle management, pricing, demand management, forecasts, and partnerships with strategic and tactical enablers.[4]

The **forward supply chain** starts with the acquisition of raw materials needed for manufacturing a product. The manufacturing process involves assembling various parts from different suppliers to create the final product. **Distribution centers** play a role in aggregating products from different manufacturers for sale. Retailers act as distributors, collecting products from distribution centers or receiving direct shipments, and they can cater to other distributors as well as **end customers**.

The assumption is that the reverse supply chain is a one-direction process moving backward from the customer to the manufacturer, but the reality is much more complex. A product can take various paths as it goes from the customer into the hands of the next user. Sometimes, manufacturers may not want to take the product back, but customers still desire value for the product they no longer need. In such cases, customers will seek alternative points to return the product. This creates a scenario in which different organizations compete to offer value to customers, aiming to move the product into the hands of another user for profit.

The logistics involved in the reverse supply chain are like those in the forward supply chain, but the methodologies and competition for maximizing product value differ significantly. In a circular economy, products move backward only when customers perceive value in doing so. This system fosters a competitive environment where customers choose points that benefit them the most, regardless of the concerns of the manufacturer.

The key inference that emerges from this complex interplay is that the reverse supply chain is not just a linear path back to the manufacturer but a multifaceted journey that can lead to various destinations. Thus, organizations within the supply chain must adapt their strategies to this dynamic landscape, recognizing that the flow of returned products can create opportunities for value recovery, **customer satisfaction**, and **sustainability**. Ultimately, success in the reverse supply chain requires a deep understanding of customer needs and the ability to offer appealing solutions for the reprocessing and redistribution of returned products.

Forward Logistics

Forward logistics involves the movement of products from one point to another. Manufacturers often require the transfer of products in large quantities to **distribution points** further down the forward logistics process. These distribution points can be outlets or retailers that break down the products into smaller lots for final sale to end customers. Typically, the path for forward logistics involves the manufacturer, distributors/retailers, and end customers.

Figure 1.2. "Forward Logistics Flow" shows how a product moves from a manufacturer to an end customer.

Forward logistics, at its core, reads left to right like a book: (1) make, (2) distribute, and (3) sell. In traditional cases, forward logistics must occur before the reverse logistics process, because you cannot return what you did not make or sell.

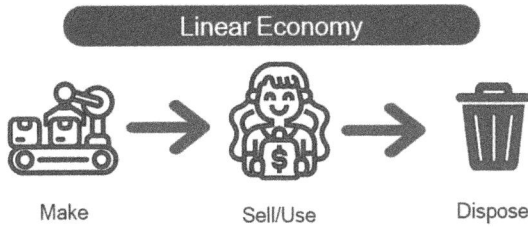

Linear Economy

Make   Sell/Use   Dispose

Figure 1.3. "The Linear Economy Model" depicts the linear process from manufacturing to use to disposal.

The process involving the creation, sale, and eventual **disposal** of products is often termed the linear economy. The concept captures the unidirectional flow of goods from their inception to their termination. This model has been articulated in various ways, including make-use-discard or take-make-dispose, but the underlying mechanism remains consistent across these descriptions.

The linear economy begins with the extraction, or "taking" of raw materials, often through mining or other resource-intensive methods.[5] These materials are then used to "make"—or manufacture—products, which are subsequently bought and "used" by consumers. After a product has served its purpose or is no longer deemed valuable by the consumer, it reaches the end of its life cycle and is "discarded." In most cases, these discarded products end up in landfills, incinerated, or left to deteriorate in the environment. This linear flow emphasizes a one-way trajectory with no meaningful attempt to reintegrate used products back into the production cycle.

However, there is a nuance to this model. Occasionally, before the discard phase, customers choose to return the product due to various reasons such as product defects or dissatisfaction. This process, termed **linear returns**, occurs when a customer sends back a product because it fails to meet their expectations. While it slightly diverges from the traditional linear model, the product is still typically destined for disposal if it cannot be refurbished or resold.

Reverse Logistics

Reverse logistics is the process of managing the movement and disposal of goods from their point of consumption to another point for the purpose of capturing value or proper disposal, not limited to the original manufacturer. This includes returning goods to vendors, recycling or properly disposing of goods that have reached the end of their useful life, and refurbishing and reselling goods. This process also covers third-party entities who offer a benefit that product manufacturers or distributors are not willing to provide. The product moves away from the customer as opposed to the traditional forward logistics process.

In this sense, regardless of where the customer chooses to return products—whether it is back to the manufacturer or to another point— reverse logistics also reads left to right like a book: (1) **asset recovery**, (2) operations, and (3) value generation.

Why do returns occur in the first place? There are many reasons why a customer would want to return a product. They could have purchased the product and decided they did not need it. Others could have encountered a problem and needed to return the product under a warranty claim. **Circular programs** encourage the return of a product, such as a **lease** return or an annual upgrade program, and are crafted with the intention of receiving Product One back as the customer migrates to the next product, **Product Two+**. There are valuated trade programs where a financial incentive is given or free recycling programs, where products can be responsibly disposed of. We will discuss these strategies in detail in chapter 2.

Reverse Logistics Moves a Product FROM Another Point

Recycle — Value Generation with Customer 2 — Operations — Asset Recovery — Return from Customer 1

Figure 1.4. "Reverse Logistics Flow" shows how a product moves from the first customer to the next through reverse logistics.

Many corporate leaders achieved their success because of their ability to generate revenue through product sales. However, few leaders have a deep understanding of the logistics aspects related to the movement of goods, both forward *and* reverse. Most companies hire logistics experts to manage these operations. Reverse logistics is a multifaceted field encompassing various stakeholder expectations, which often, and unknowingly, complement or conflict with each other. Despite its significance, many business leaders have yet to master utilizing reverse logistics effectively to minimize costs or boost revenue. This lack of expertise underscores the necessity for a more sophisticated approach in handling reverse logistics, which takes into account the diverse and occasionally opposing goals of different stakeholders.

The Linear Return Model and Reverse Logistics

The linear return model adopts the principles of reverse logistics in the traditional linear economy and can be summed up in three parts: (1) asset recovery, (2) operations, and (3) value generation. This can be visualized in Figure 1.5, which delineates the process through which products are returned, recovered, and either reintegrated or disposed of.

1. **Asset Recovery.** Once the return request is approved, the product (referred to as the "asset" in this context) is retrieved. This might involve the customer shipping the product back, dropping it off at a designated point, or participating in a pick-up service provided by the returning party.
2. **Processing.** Upon its recovery, the product undergoes a series of **inspections** for defects, damage, or any other issues. Based on this assessment, decisions are made about the next steps.
3. **Value Generation.** If the returned product is deemed fit for **reuse**, it might be refurbished, repaired, or repackaged for resale. If it cannot be restored to a saleable condition, the product is disposed of either through recycling, incineration, or relegation to a landfill.

It is within this context of reverse logistics that the phrase "going backward" finds its origin. The concept highlights the movement against the traditional flow of goods in commerce, retracing steps from the consumer back to the manufacturer or seller. This "backward" movement underscores the importance of efficiently managing product returns to maximize value recovery while minimizing waste. Through the lens of reverse logistics, businesses can uncover opportunities for both economic gains and the promotion of sustainability and responsible consumption.

Similarities and Differences between Forward and Reverse Logistics

Forward and reverse logistics use similar processes, but the **infrastructure** operates differently due to the nature of how products move. Let us break down the similarities and differences between forward logistics and reverse logistics in terms of transportation, warehousing, labor, systems, packaging, and information:

Transportation

- **Forward Logistics. Transportation** focuses on moving goods from the point of origin to the point of consumption. It involves activities such as selecting the appropriate mode of transportation (e.g., trucks, ships, and planes), arranging shipping routes, and coordinating deliveries.
- **Reverse Logistics.** Transportation in reverse logistics is the process of moving products from their point of consumption back to a different location. Unlike new items, these products have discrete conditions and values, which present unique challenges in areas such as tax or tariff declarations. Used products, especially electronics or hazardous materials, often fall under stricter environmental regulations and safety standards during transportation compared to new products. Additionally, the responsibility for compliance changes depending on the product's destination—whether it is being returned to the manufacturer, resold, or recycled. These variances underscore the specialized nature of reverse logistics transportation, which

requires a different approach and expertise than that used for the transportation of new goods.

Warehousing

- **Forward Logistics.** Warehouses are used for inventory management, **order fulfillment,** and timely deliveries. New products are typically identically packaged and easily planned for. In forward logistics, **stock keeping unit (SKU)** management is relatively straightforward, with each product having a single **universal product code (UPC)** corresponding to its new condition.
- **Reverse Logistics.** Warehouses are used to handle returned products. These facilities may involve processes like sorting returned items, assessing their condition, and determining the appropriate disposition (e.g., **repair, refurbishment**, or recycling). The **condition of packaging** may be open, damaged, or nonexistent, requiring different methods of storage or identification.

Reverse logistics complicates SKU management significantly. When products are returned, they can vary in condition. Depending on the range of cosmetic and functional states, a product initially represented by one SKU can multiply. For example, if a company supports one hundred products, this could translate to 500 different SKUs or other identification methods in reverse logistics.[6] These variations might include categories such as: "New," "Like New," "Best," "Better," and "Good." Each condition necessitates its own categorization and management. Thus, the broader the SKU catalog and the more grading conditions applied, the more complex the reverse **logistics operations** become.

Labor

- **Forward Logistics.** Labor is required to handle tasks such as order **picking**, packaging, loading and unloading of goods, and transportation coordination.
- **Reverse Logistics.** Additional labor is necessary to manage activities like inspecting returned items, processing product

returns, repairing or refurbishing products, and handling reverse transportation operations.

Systems

- **Forward Logistics.** Systems like inventory management software, order processing systems, and transportation management systems are used to track and manage the flow of goods, optimize routes, and ensure efficient operations.
- **Reverse Logistics.** Systems that support activities such as return authorization, product tracking, contract management, **quality control**, and disposition management are used to enable the efficient handling and processing of returned products.

Packaging

- **Forward Logistics.** Packaging is designed to protect goods during transportation, ensure their integrity, and facilitate easy handling and storage. Products can be shipped in a similar shape and size and are packaged by the manufacturer.
- **Reverse Logistics.** Packaging involves **repackaging** returned items, especially if they require repairs or refurbishment, or if they need to be prepared for resale or disposal. Acquiring the correct package at scale can be difficult, and the products may need to be stored in an open condition if the original container is discarded.

While packaging is crucial in both forward logistics and reverse logistics, the specific requirements may differ based on the direction of the flow of goods and the purpose of the packaging. This makes **automation** easier for the forward stream than the returned stream, where the product can come back in a variety of functional and **cosmetic conditions**.[7]

Information

- **Forward Logistics.** Accurate and timely information about product availability, order status, delivery schedules, and customer requirements is necessary to ensure smooth operations and customer satisfaction.

- **Reverse Logistics.** Information related to product returns, reasons for return, **customer feedback**, warranty information, and repair or refurbishment instructions is required.

When it comes to the interaction between forward and reverse logistics, data sharing is critical for ensuring efficient and effective operations. Having separate forward and reverse logistics teams that operate in silos can lead to inefficiencies and miscommunication. Building a connection between these two teams by sharing data and working collaboratively is an industry best practice that can help companies streamline their operations, improve customer satisfaction, and increase the overall value of their supply chain. For example, accurate and up-to-date information about the location, condition, and availability of products can help companies plan for the movement of goods and make informed decisions about how the product should be routed before it arrives back at the facility.

While forward logistics and reverse logistics share some similarities in terms of transportation, warehousing, labor, systems, packaging, and information, their specific processes and priorities differ due to the direction of the flow of goods and the nature of the activities involved. Many companies rely on separate forward and reverse teams due to the unique characteristics of each process. The shared and distinct traits of forward and reverse logistics can be seen in the **Venn diagram** below.

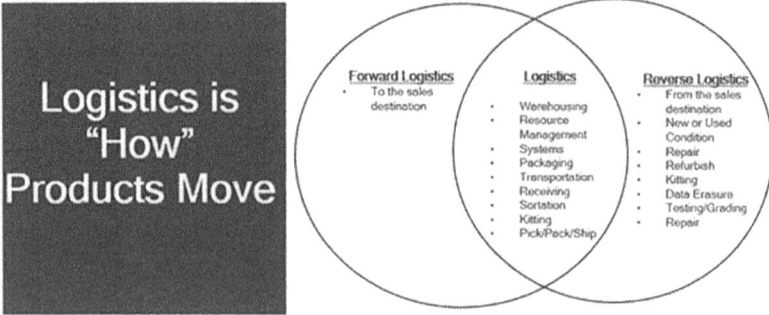

Figure 1.5. "Forward and Reverse Venn Diagram" shows the similar and different activities between forward and reverse logistics.

1.3 Size of Reverse Logistics

Linear Return Impact and the Desire to Drive Down Returns

"Returns have consistently had a negative impact on **retailers**' bottom lines. The cost of reverse logistics in retail returns was $35 billion in 1997, and this figure rose dramatically to an estimated $816 billion in 2022."[8] According to a 2021 study conducted by Appriss Retail on behalf of the National Retail Federation (NRF), for every $1 billion in sales, the average retailer returns about $166 million to the buyer.[9]

The cost of reverse logistics serves as a clear indication of the growing significance of reverse logistics within the contemporary economy. In 2022, the average retail return rate experienced a slight increase from 16.1 percent in 2021 to 16.5 percent.[10] Consequently, the cost associated with reverse logistics has emerged as a substantial factor within the broader supply chain landscape, prompting companies to allocate greater resources toward the efficient management of these expenses.

The Size of the Circular Economy and the Desire to Drive Some Returns Up

The rising costs associated with reverse logistics are fueled by factors extending beyond simply minimizing returns due to **buyer's remorse** or enhancing product quality. Companies are increasingly embracing the concept of a circular economy, augmenting their return flows through **trade-in**, leasing, products-as-a-service, or recycling initiatives. This sustainability-centric shift demands the development of multifaceted strategies for **returns programs**. The goal is to finely balance the reduction of unfavorable returns (i.e., "bad returns") with the promotion of beneficial ones (i.e., "good returns").

However, quantifying the impact of these circular economy initiatives is a complex task. One key challenge is the diverse and fragmented nature of sales data, which is not restricted to a single brand's point-of-sale systems or its authorized channels. The circular economy introduces a fluid movement of products from one owner to another, with the trajectory dictated by maximum consumer value. This includes returning items to the manufacturer, selling to a different, more value-adding company or engaging with third-party marketplaces like Amazon, eBay, Swappa, and Facebook. Other options include donations to charities or personal sales. A significant hurdle in evaluating the **secondary market**'s full scale is the disparate and often unshared transactional data across these varied channels.

In 2022, a study titled "The Importance of Secondary Markets in the Changing Retail Landscape: A Longitudinal Study in the United States and China" sought to estimate the size of the US's secondary market. The research involved informal interviews with senior executives in reverse logistics and corporate inventory from prominent multinational corporations. From this data, the study gauged the secondary market's value from 2008 to 2020, revealing approximately $643 billion in revenue in 2020 and a consistent year-over-year growth.[11]

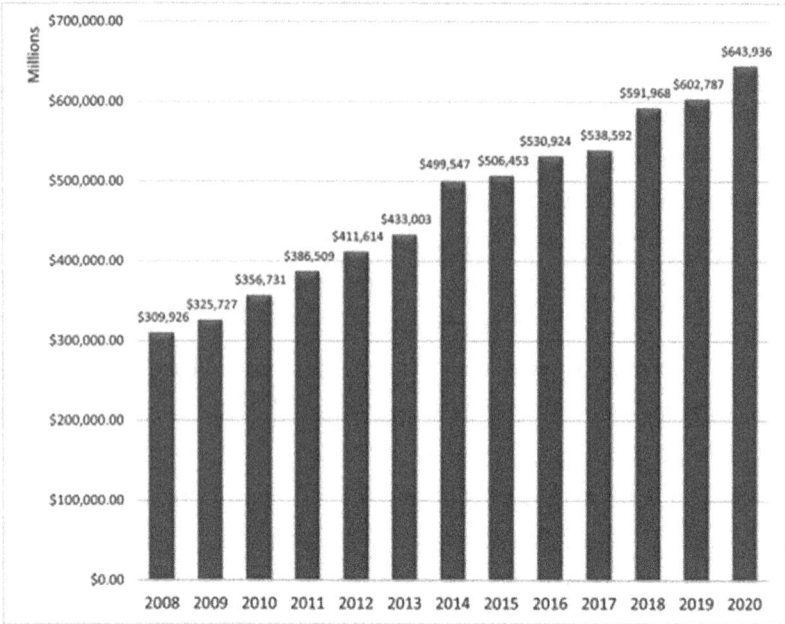

Figure 1.6. "Size of Secondary Market Bar Graph," illustrates the ascending trajectory of the US's secondary market's revenue from 2008 to 2020.

Chapter 6 will offer an in-depth exploration of the secondary market's various segments and forecasted growth trends in popular product categories. It will shed light on how the role of returns teams goes beyond merely reducing costs and reversing revenue in linear returns programs to show that there is an opportunity to increase revenue by reselling the same product to different users at distinct times, facilitated by a circular economy approach, which is underpinned by effective reverse logistics.

By and large, the lifecycle of a product's movement through a circular model can be perceived in three phases: (1) forward logistics moves the product to the original customer, (2) reverse logistics covers the return of the product, and (3) dispatching the product to a new user. For some products, this process may happen more than once. Thus, in today's fast-paced business world, reverse logistics professionals are increasingly vital, not only for driving cost efficiencies and adding value but also for their role in shaping the circular economy by balancing the reduction of unwanted returns with the exploitation of secondary market opportunities.

Companies are finding ways to manage return costs effectively. The same reverse logistics infrastructure used for managing unwanted returns is also proving beneficial in tapping into the burgeoning secondary market. This approach not only addresses return challenges but also capitalizes on new revenue opportunities within the circular economy.

1.4 Brands and Manufacturers: *Steering the Course of Product Creation and Returns*

It is common knowledge that both manufacturing and brand management are pivotal to the creation of products, but their relationship to reverse logistics may not be as immediately obvious. To gain a clearer perspective, we will explore the distinct roles each entity occupies within the supply chain.

The Visibility of Brands

Brands are the faces of products and services in the market. They create a specific image or perception in the minds of consumers, heavily influencing their purchasing decisions. For example, Apple stands as an iconic brand recognized for its innovative designs and exceptional marketing prowess. The brand is what consumers identify with and feel loyalty toward.

The Behind-the-Scenes Role of Manufacturers

While brands like Apple are responsible for **product design** and marketing, they do not always manufacture the products themselves. Instead, they often rely on contract manufacturers—entities tasked with assembling and preparing products based on the brand's designs and specifications. This relationship showcases how the brand guides the product's journey but relies on the manufacturers to physically create the product.

Direction from Brands

Brands have an authoritative role in this partnership. They provide clear directions, design specifics, parts, and packaging requirements. They even decide the sales channels. Their overarching strategy dictates how the product will reach the end customer, ensuring a seamless journey from production to purchase.

Quality Assurance and Returns Protocols

A crucial aspect of the brand-manufacturer relationship is ensuring product quality. Brands typically establish stringent standards, and if a product fails to meet these, they might have the right to return it to the manufacturer. This quality assurance protects the brand's reputation and ensures consumers receive products that align with the brand's promise.

Identifying Respective Roles in the Supply Chain

Both brands and manufacturers are pivotal entities in the creation of products; they stand at the beginning of the supply chain, laying the foundation for a product's journey to the consumer. However, their roles are distinct: brands provide the vision, strategy, and identity, while manufacturers execute the physical production under the guidance of the brand.

Inventory versus Reventory

Manufacturing, sales, and forward and reverse logistics are all interconnected and interdependent processes that play a crucial role in the supply chain management of a company. To build a successful reverse logistics infrastructure, professionals need to understand how each part of the supply chain is connected and how information can be shared between them. This will enable them to make informed decisions and optimize the entire supply chain to maximize efficiency, reduce costs, and improve customer satisfaction. Operations that are built in silos lose the benefit of knowledge-sharing and risk establishing performance metrics that incentivize departments to save money within their own budget at the expense of another. By understanding the cause and effect of sales processes and return policies, teams can work together for the best results.

Manufacturing is the process of converting raw materials into finished goods by using tools, machines, and labor. This can include assembling components, fabricating parts, and applying final touches to create a finished product ready to be sold to customers. The specific manufacturing process used depends on the type of product being produced. This can vary greatly between industries.

Inventory refers to the stock of finished goods or products that a company holds at any given time. It includes items that have been manufactured or remanufactured and are awaiting sale or distribution. Inventory serves as a buffer between the production process and customer demand, ensuring that products are readily available when needed.

When a customer determines they do not want a product and sends a product to another destination, it enters a different phase known as reventory. **Reventory**™ represents products that have been sent back to the company through the reverse logistics flow and is awaiting **disposition**, an industry term indicating that the product is ready to be sent to its next destination.

Once the returned product reaches the company, it goes through a **grading and assessment process**. This involves inspecting the item to determine its condition and potential for reuse. Depending on the assessment, the returned product may undergo refurbishment, repairs, repackaging, or other necessary actions to prepare it for its next use.

After the grading and assessment process, the product transitions from the reventory status back into the inventory status. It is now ready to be reintegrated into the company's supply chain and shipped through the forward logistics process or responsibly recycled.

Benefits of Integrating Reverse Logistics with Manufacturing

Integrating reverse logistics with manufacturing offers a strategic advantage for businesses seeking to optimize their operations and enhance product quality. By tracking the reasons for return, companies can pinpoint patterns and trends in returned products. This invaluable data can then guide improvements in product design, quality control, and customer service, ultimately aiming to diminish future, unwanted-return rates. For instance, should a significant volume of products be returned due to a specific manufacturing flaw, immediate corrective action can be initiated, ensuring both customer satisfaction and reduced wastage. This integration not only streamlines the manufacturing process but also promotes a proactive approach to product excellence.

Customer feedback is also an important factor in reducing unwanted returns. By understanding why customers are returning products, companies can take steps to address their concerns and improve the overall customer experience. For example, if a high number of customers are returning products due to a lack of information on how to use the product, the company can improve its product information and customer support to reduce the number of returns.

With advancements in **artificial intelligence (AI)**, **machine learning (ML)**, and cloud technologies, companies now have the ability to capture and analyze large amounts of data in real time. This data can be used to optimize reverse logistics processes, improve quality, and drive down unwanted returns.

Conventionally, the initial step in establishing a circular economy program is to focus on designing products that are built to last and can be easily refurbished or repaired. This moves away from a concept known in the industry as "induced obsolescence," where some manufacturers intentionally create products that stop functioning properly after a certain period. Getting rid of this practice would be environmentally ideal, as manufacturers can then help to reduce waste and extend the life of their products by using durable materials that are easily repairable, incorporating modular design elements that can be replaced as needed, and ensuring that products can be easily disassembled for repair or refurbishment.

But additionally, designing products with the intention of easy refurbishment and repair implies new business opportunities and revenue streams for manufacturers. For example, by offering repair and refurbishment services, manufacturers can increase customer loyalty, reduce waste, and create new revenue streams. To successfully implement this approach, manufacturers must consider the entire lifecycle of their products from design and production to use, return, and reuse. This includes ensuring that products are made with sustainable materials, **energy consumption** and **greenhouse gas emissions** throughout the supply chain are reduced, and that products are properly disposed of at the end of their life. The key differences between running a manufacturing operation and a reverse logistics operation can be summarized as follows:

Reverse Logistics Operation	Manufacturing Operation
• Move Immediately • Treating Product Within an SLA • Sending Product for Reuse as Quickly As Possible	• Acquire Product • Set Production Schedule • Ship on a Set Pattern

Figure 1.7. "Reverse Logistics and Manufacturing Comparison." Attaining a consistent benefit forecast is possible if returned equipment is held until a building plan can be created. However, moving equipment as it comes in represents a better financial decision.

In manufacturing, the **production schedule** is typically determined by the company based on demand forecasts and sales projections.

The company sources parts and materials and plans their production schedule accordingly. In reverse logistics, the schedule is determined by the customer's desire to return a product, making it difficult to plan and forecast what product will arrive and when it will arrive.

1. **Product Condition.** In manufacturing, the products are made in new condition and are easier to forecast and build plans around. In reverse logistics, the products are returned or traded in, and their condition can vary greatly. This makes it difficult to predict their **residual value** and the processes to improve condition.

2. **Service-Level Agreement (SLA).** In manufacturing, the shipment process is typically synchronized with a production schedule that aligns with sales forecasts. However, in the realm of reverse logistics, products are usually handled within the framework of a **service level agreement**. In this context, service level agreement refers to the ability to meet the terms and conditions specified in the SLA. Essentially, it signifies the commitment to swiftly process returned products to minimize the time elapsed between their return and the realization of their value.

3. **Forecasting.** In manufacturing, **forecasting** is more straightforward because demand forecasts and sales projections can be used to plan production schedules. In reverse logistics, forecasting is different and more complicated because of the unpredictable nature of returns.

4. **Predictability Contrast.** Manufacturing is much more predictable than reverse logistics, which is more reactionary. This is because in reverse logistics, the company must react to the customer's desire to return a product, whereas in manufacturing, the company owns their production schedule.

Manufacturing and reverse logistics share some similarities, such as the need to manage assembly lines, kitting supply, parts' supply chains, and logistics, but they are fundamentally different operations that require different approaches. Manufactured products are typically new and placed in standard packaging, making it easier to control processes like kitting, storage, **shipping**, forecasting, and cost prediction with greater precision. On the other hand, returns present unique challenges, including the possibility that the product may not be in its original packaging, can vary in quantity, and has increased risk of developing discrepancies. It can be difficult to predict what part of the product may become defective and when, complicating the procurement of replacement parts over time.

1.5 Sales and Reverse Logistics

Understanding Sales Channels in the Supply Chain

Central to the supply chain are the **distribution channels**, which act as conduits facilitating the flow of products from one phase of the supply chain to the next. These distribution channels can vary significantly in their operation and structure.[12] Some channels might be directly overseen by the brands/manufacturers while others operate via intermediaries such as retailers or distributors. Regardless of its nature, each channel plays a crucial role in ensuring the product reaches the end customer, comprising elements of the sales process, product movement, and return management.

1. **Direct from the Brand or Vendor.** The brand or manufacturer sells directly to the end consumer, often through its own system or process. This channel offers a direct line of communication with the customer, allowing for personalized experiences.

2. **Brick-and-Mortar Retail Stores.** Physical retail locations remain significant touchpoints where consumers can interact with products firsthand, get immediate possession, and benefit from in-person customer service.

3. **Manufacturer or Retailer's Own ".Com" Website.** Operating through their own website allows brands or retailers to maintain complete control over the user experience, branding, and product presentation. This ensures a consistent brand narrative and can provide customers with a more personalized

shopping journey without paying marketplace commissions for third-party markets.

4. **Third-Party Marketplaces**. Online platforms like Amazon, eBay, and Walmart act as digital storefronts for brands, reaching vast audiences and offering integrated logistical solutions. These platforms have a broad and established user base, allowing brands to tap into a massive audience without investing heavily in customer acquisition. Many third-party platforms offer logistical solutions—such as warehousing, shipping, and returns—simplifying operations for brands. One of the trade-offs for the benefits offered by these platforms is the commission fee. Brands or retailers must pay a certain percentage of each sale to the platform.

5. **Enterprise or Small Business Sales.** Products can also be channeled through business-to-business (B2B) sales, where bulk orders might be placed for office use, resale, or further modification.

Each of these distribution points possesses unique characteristics and operational challenges. Whether it is managing inventory for a physical store, ensuring speedy delivery for direct online sales, or coordinating with third-party platforms for optimal product listing, each channel demands a tailored strategy. Furthermore, they all play a role in the customer's journey, influencing purchasing decisions and ensuring a satisfactory post-purchase experience. Effective management and understanding of these distribution channels are paramount to a brand or retailer's success, since they directly influence product accessibility, brand perception, and overall customer satisfaction.

Bridging Sales and Reverse Logistics: A Partnership for Sustainable Success

It is important for reverse logistics professionals to establish a strong and collaborative relationship with the sales and marketing teams. The strategies for managing returns, which involve reducing unwanted returns while increasing desired ones, are deeply intertwined with sales initiatives. At the same time, there often exists a natural tension between the sales team's desired outcome of boosting revenue and the logistics team's goal of **cost management**. This dynamic can be exacerbated by the misconception held by some sales leaders who believe that high returns are a direct result of high sales figures. In reality, the failure to appropriately qualify or communicate the benefits of products can lead to not just an uptick in sales but a significantly higher return rate as well. This situation can be effectively mitigated through an improved sales process that focuses not only on volume but also on customer satisfaction and long-term value. By working closely with **sales teams**, reverse logistics professionals can ensure that the return strategies are aligned with the goals and the desired outcomes of the organization and that the sales process is designed to minimize unwanted returns while maximizing the potential benefits of circular economy returns. This collaboration can help organizations achieve a balance between reducing costs, enhancing customer satisfaction, and promoting sustainability.

Most sales begin with a promise to the customer. That promise consists of a product, a price, and perhaps a commitment to quality, a return period, and/or a warranty. Organizations that make or sell a product will structure their logistics around their product and the **customer promise** with the desired result of reducing cost and increasing revenue.

One of the first known "100 percent **satisfaction guarantee**" promises was made by a mail-order businessman named Aaron Montgomery Ward in 1875. He offered a 100 percent money-back satisfaction guarantee on all the merchandise he sold. He believed that customers should be able to examine a product before they bought it and that if they were not completely satisfied with their purchase, they should be able to return it for a full refund. [13] This was a revolutionary idea at the time, as most businesses did not offer any kind of satisfaction guarantee. Ward's guarantee helped him to build a successful business and set a standard for customer service in the retail industry.

The adoption of these promises perpetuated the reasons for returns we will explore in detail in chapter 2. To fulfill these customer promises, returns became a "necessary evil" for companies to endure. The impact of returns was often measured in operation cost and revenue erosion. For explanation purposes, let us suppose we have five players in the sales process.

1. **Product One:** The product that is built with the purpose of being sold.
2. **Manufacturers:** An entity that builds the product for the purpose of being sold.
3. **Distributors/Retailers:** An entity that purchases or consigns products from a manufacturer with the purpose of selling for a profit.
4. **Customer One:** The entity or individual who purchases the product for use.
5. **Competitors:** The entity or individual who offers a similar product with a different value proposition to gain market share.

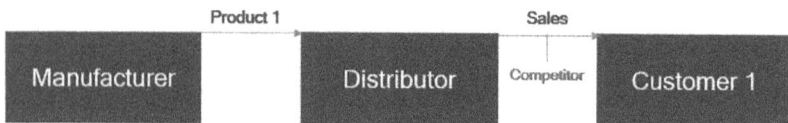

Figure 1.8. "Product One Flow diagram" depicts a product as it moves from manufacture to customer.

In the dynamic landscape of product sales and distribution, a key aspect to understand is the strategic alignment among the main stakeholders—manufacturers, distributors, and customers—when the products are purchased. This alignment leads to the mutual goal of maximizing sales and enhancing the customer experience. However, competitors often try to disrupt this alignment between the manufacturer and the customer.

Sales Racetrack Model

Manufacturers and retailers aim to develop programs that boost demand and stimulate customer purchases by promoting continuous consumption and incentivizing upgrades to newer models, thereby encouraging quicker adoption of the latest offerings. For example:

- **Continuous Consumption.** If you buy a six pack of Coke, Coke would like you to return to the store and purchase that product again.
- **Upgrade Type 1.** If a customer buys the top item in their fall fashion line, the manufacturer would want that customer to come back and purchase the manufacturer's winter wardrobe items.
- **Upgrade Type 2.** If a customer purchases the 2022 Dodge Ram, Dodge will want that customer to purchase the next model as soon as possible.

Sales strategies have been developed to motivate customers to move from Product One to **Product Two+** as fast as possible. One sales model that exists is the Racetrack Model, which is a system that Cisco, a networking gear manufacturer, utilizes.

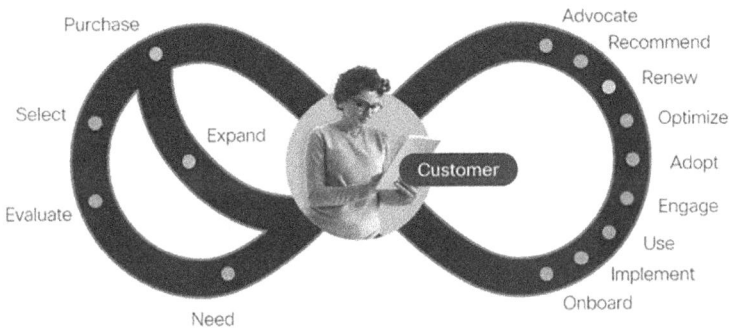

Figure 1.9. "Sales Racetrack Model" is the sales "racetrack" adopted by Cisco Systems as a strategy to sell Product One to Customer One and motivate Customer One to purchase the next product, Product Two+.

The Cisco Racetrack Model offers an insightful perspective into the modern corporate strategy for maintaining long-term customer relationships. It underscores the corporate goal of unending consumption from one model to another. Additionally, marketers strategize on methods to accelerate purchase adoption. (In chapter 4, we will delve into customer purchasing behavior, as this is pivotal for grasping customer-return behavior.) Let us delve into the Racetrack Model's core components:

1. **Shape and Structure.** The model is visually represented as a racetrack in the shape of an infinity loop. The infinity symbol represents the idea of continuous, never-ending consumption. Unlike traditional sales funnels that have a definite beginning and end, this model envisions a customer journey that does not have an exit.

2. **Central Focus—The Customer.** The customer is placed at the center of this model, which highlights their pivotal role in the consumption process. Companies use this model to prioritize the customer's needs, preferences, and behaviors to keep them engaged in the loop.

3. **Desired Corporate Outcome.** The aim is to keep the customer in the consumption loop for as long as possible. This is achieved by making them buy a product and, as soon as that product's cycle ends, entice them to buy the next model or version. The absence of an exit strategy ensures the customer stays loyal and continuously purchases from the brand.

4. **Speeding Up Adoption.** Marketers strategize on ways to reduce the time between purchases. By understanding the factors that influence quicker adoption of new products, companies can drive faster sales cycles and ensure that the customer is always engaged with the latest offerings.

1.6 The Evolution toward a Circular Economy

The Circular Economy Model: A Paradigm Shift

Historically, some manufacturers practiced planned obsolescence, designing products with limited lifespans to promote repeat purchases. The circular economy counters this by fostering markets that match used supply with demand, independent of corporate marketing strategies. It focuses on manufacturing longer-lasting, higher-quality products. In this market dynamic, a product that may no longer be useful to one customer could still hold value for another, necessitating an effective returns process to enable this value exchange.

Interest in the circular economy is growing, driven by the fundamental business objective of increasing profit margins in a responsible way. The lifecycle of a product—from manufacture to sale through various channels—is central to this process. While companies acknowledge the importance of sustainability, the complexity of implementing these practices can be a deterrent without clear economic benefits, hindering investment in necessary talent, tools, and infrastructure.

However, technological advancements, transportation improvements, and the growth of **e-commerce marketplaces** have facilitated the matching of supply and demand for used products. The Internet enables customers to recirculate products themselves or through businesses that transfer products from one user to another. This burgeoning secondary market often surpasses manufacturers' and competitors' participation.

The success of a circular program can be measured by tracking how many returned goods are reintegrated into the forward logistics cycle for reuse or recycling their raw materials for new product production. This aligns with the circular economy's goals of extending product and material lifespans, especially when recirculating items as-is becomes unfeasible, thereby reducing waste. With growing environmental awareness and shifting customer preferences toward sustainability, businesses face increasing pressure to manage products from creation to **end of life** in an environmentally responsible manner.[14] This balance between environmental responsibility and smart business practices is becoming more critical.

Product Lifecycle Loop

Transitioning to a circular economy requires a strategic approach, much like the **Sales Racetrack Model** where each customer interaction is carefully orchestrated. The **Product Lifecycle Loop** places the product at its core, whereas the Sales Racetrack Model focuses on the customer's journey. Shifting from the traditional, linear make-use-dispose model to a circular economy emphasizes the need for product return, repair, and reuse. The Product Lifecycle Loop serves as the foundation of this circular approach, ensuring products are used sustainably. Therefore, it is essential for a supply chain professional to grasp the complete journey of a product from its inception to its end of use.

Visualize the Product Lifecycle Loop as a continuous racetrack: products consistently transition between use and reuse. When they reach the end of their economic life, there is an "off-ramp" guiding them toward responsible recycling. A crucial moment in the circular economy arises when a product, after the reverse logistics phase, reenters the forward logistics stage, signaling its readiness for a new lifecycle.

This evolution from linear to circular thinking emphasizes prolonging product utility and building programs for sales and support over time. The circular economy promotes long-lasting, valuable products; some items, although having surpassed their functional lifespan for the initial user, remain beneficial for another.

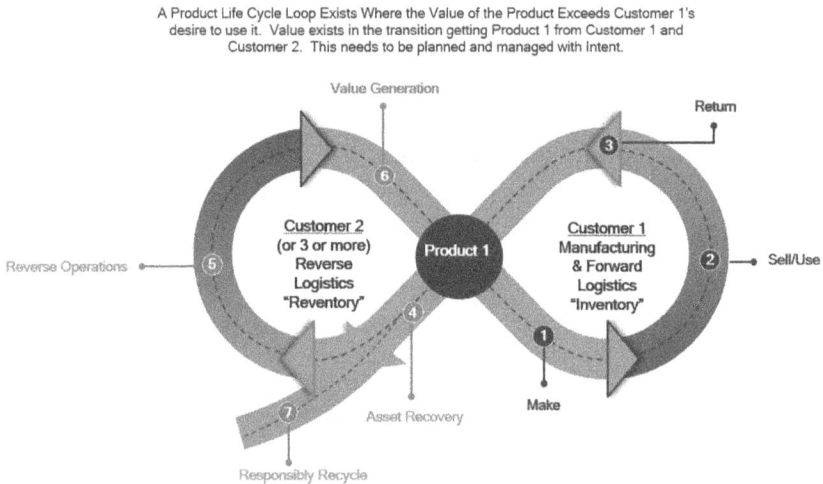

A Product Life Cycle Loop Exists Where the Value of the Product Exceeds Customer 1's desire to use it. Value exists in the transition getting Product 1 from Customer 1 and Customer 2. This needs to be planned and managed with Intent.

Figure 1.10. "Product Life Cycle Loop" maps out the journey of the product as it progresses from Customer One to Customer Two.

The Product Lifecycle Loop aims to reduce waste, save costs, and optimize resources by ensuring that returned goods are either resold, refurbished, or recycled. Here are its core components:

- **Shape and Structure.** The loop, much like the Sales Racetrack Model, is an endless cycle, an infinity sign. This design emphasizes the idea that a returned product does not mark the end of its journey. Rather than dispose of it, companies aim to reintroduce it into the market or extract value from it in other ways. The cycle persists until the product lacks enough value for further use. At this point, a designated off-ramp for responsible recycling comes into play, ensuring sustainable disposal.

- **Central Focus—The Product.** Unlike sales models that center around the customer, here, the returned product takes center stage. The process revolves around assessing the product's condition, understanding the reason for its return, and deciding its next destination.

- **Desired Corporate Outcome.** The desired outcome is to reduce waste while optimizing value. Returned products are assessed for potential resale, refurbishment, or recycling, ensuring multiple-use cycles or the potential for multiple sales. This approach aligns with financial targets and supports environmental sustainability goals.

- **Efficient Reintegration.** Businesses prioritize swiftly processing returned goods. The faster a product is evaluated and—if suitable—reintroduced into the market, the lower the associated holding costs, and the greater its potential resale value.

Decoding the Product Lifecycle Loop: A Circular Economy Perspective

Figure 1.10 offers a visual representation to help companies strategize the lifecycle of a product as it transitions between owners. In a circular economy, it is essential to deliberately plan and manage both sales and logistics based on the product's ownership and service duration.

It is crucial for reverse logistics professionals to shape the product's entire lifecycle management rather than only the logistics of the return journey.

Let us delve into the key components of this model:

- **The Loop's Core.** At its heart lies the product.
- **The Loop's Sides.** The loop has two distinct sides:
  - The *left* side denotes reverse logistics, termed the "reventory" phase.
  - The *right* side represents forward logistics, or the "inventory" phase.
- **Arrows in the Model.** These symbolize the logistical movement either to or from logistical operations. Four arrows are highlighted here, but depending on a company's supply chain, there could be more.
  - Arrows pointing *right* indicate the shipping of a product to a destination.
  - Arrows pointing *left* show a product being dispatched from a point.

Example: On the model's right, one arrow points rightward as products move from the "Make" to the "Sell/Use" phase. Conversely, an arrow pointing left symbolizes the "Return" phase.

- **Lanes in the Process.** Seven lanes interweave the model, illustrating the relationship between the linear economy and its return components.
  - *Manufacturing/Make Phase.* In this foundational phase where products are crafted, the emphasis should be on the durability and longevity of each product. Manufacturers are advised to select renewable, recyclable, or biodegradable materials. Designing products with modularity ensures that components can be easily replaced or repaired, promoting long-term use.
  - *Sell/Use Phase.* As products reach the market or end users, there is an opportunity to reimagine the business model. Instead of the classic sales approach, companies can pivot to

product-as-a-service or leasing models. Here, it is crucial to guide users on proper product care, maintenance, and the advantages of returns, ensuring extended product life and eventual reintroduction into the system.

· *Return Phase.* The journey of products back to their origins must be efficient and incentivized. A systematic approach, complemented by incentives like discounts or loyalty rewards, can foster sustainable product-returns programs.

· *Asset recovery Phase.* Once products are returned, tracking becomes paramount. Implementing robust mechanisms to monitor a product's history, usage, and condition can guide subsequent processes, ensuring maximum value extraction.

· *Reverse-Operations Phase.* This is the assessment or rejuvenation phase. Products may undergo refurbishment, **restoration**, and repair, making them fit for either resale or repurposing, thereby extending their life in the economic system.

· *Value-Generation Phase.* Here, products are prepped for their next cycle of use. By viewing returned products as assets, they can be recirculated to new or previous users, generating additional value.

· *Responsible Recycling.* A product's life is finite. When its reuse becomes economically or environmentally untenable, it exits the loop. Detailed analyses guide whether a product should be responsibly recycled, ensuring materials are reclaimed and waste is minimized.

In conclusion, the Product Lifecycle Loop for returned goods champions a revolutionary approach in modern product management. It reframes returned goods as assets, allowing businesses to tap into enhanced revenue streams, reduce waste, improve brand image by advocating for sustainability, and—potentially—increase profitability. As more companies integrate this approach, the ripple effects can only be positive for both the economy and the environment.

It must be acknowledged, however, that each company crafts distinct strategies and business models based on their position in the supply chain. While the loop's foundational structure remains unchanged, the way each stage is executed depends on a company's goals and priorities. chapter 2 elaborates on these strategic outcomes. For instance, a company might focus on product design to enable easy repair and refurbishment, aiming to extend product lifespan. Conversely, another might highlight the recycling phase to minimize waste and prevent used products from competing with their new offerings.

Chapter 3 explores the logistical measures that businesses can adopt to optimize their Product Lifecycle Loop. A cohesive Product Lifecycle Loop considers each stage, ensuring they are seamlessly linked and well-prepared for. This loop not only represents a meticulous plan for a product's journey but also illustrates the handoff from reverse to forward logistics, epitomizing a genuine circular economy approach. Throughout this book, we will explore both the desired outcomes and the logistical tactics to enhance the reverse dimensions of the Product Lifecycle Loop.

Chapter 2

The Four Desired Outcomes of Reverse Logistics

2.1 Strategy and Execution of Reverse Logistics

This chapter presents the four primary goals of reverse logistics, highlighting the expectations companies set regarding the customer promise and customer journey to achieve their desired outcomes. But before we can talk about desired outcomes, we need to talk about strategy. A strategy is a high-level plan of action or guideline to achieve a specific goal or desired outcome. Strategies are developed based on a comprehensive analysis of the organization's goals, strengths, weaknesses, opportunities, and threats, and they set the goals and desired outcomes that logistics operations must support. Logistics operations, in turn, provide the means to execute the strategy.

Strategy is the desired outcome, or "goal," of **supply chain management**, while logistics operations are the fundamentals of how the supply chain management operates. Strategy and logistics are fundamentally interdependent: a good strategy is essential for effective logistics operations, but without effective logistics operations, the strategy cannot be successfully executed. The company's strategy consisting of culture and capabilities is what sets one company apart from another and is the key reason why some companies engage in the circular economy while others do not.

To craft a successful strategy, businesses should concentrate on four key desired outcomes:

1. **Sales-Enablement.** The goal is to create customer-friendly policies such as return windows, warranty programs, accelerated upgrade cycles, and omnichannel returns. This approach aims to bolster customer confidence in their purchases and stimulate sales.

2. **Returns Management.** The goal is to manage the flow of returned goods, encompassing the collection, repair, transportation, quality control, and storage of products. The aim is to streamline the returns process, reduce unwanted returns, reduce costs, and improve customer satisfaction.

3. **Green Logistics.** The goal is to minimize the environmental impact of reverse logistics operations by utilizing sustainable packaging materials, reducing waste, optimizing transportation routes, and investing in renewable energy sources.

4. **Circular Economy:** The goal is to reduce waste and maximize the value of resources by keeping them in use for as long as possible. It involves designing products that are easy to repair and refurbish, developing take-back programs, and partnering with stakeholders to promote circularity.

These four key desired outcomes require different applications of reverse logistics systems, packaging, transportation, **sortation**, erasure, **testing**/grading, storage, repair, kitting, and shipping. The traditional returns management strategy primarily focused on return prevention, aiming to reduce the volume of returns due to various reasons such as order issues, buyer's remorse, products arriving **dead on arrival (DOA)**, warranty returns, stock rotations, warranty defects, and **failure to deliver**. This approach sought to minimize the impact of returns on business operations and profitability by addressing the root causes that lead to customer returns. Overall, the strategy was to minimize the cost of returns on the organization. The circular economy's returns strategy, on the other hand, aims to increase the trade-in, lease, early upgrade programs, and recycling assistance programs. It is focused on maximizing the value of products and materials by encouraging returns to the source through incentives.

Furthermore, while these four desired outcomes serve a specific purpose, they often overlap, complement, and sometimes conflict with each other when managed under different parts of an organizational chart. For example, a trade-in program can facilitate sales-enablement while promoting circularity by increasing returns and, therefore, increasing costs. A new fuel option for transportation, on the other hand, can serve a green logistics purpose but increase costs in conflict with the cost-avoidant desires of returns management. Reverse logistics professionals should understand the balance between these strategies and how they relate to each other.

Reverse Logistics Desired Outcome

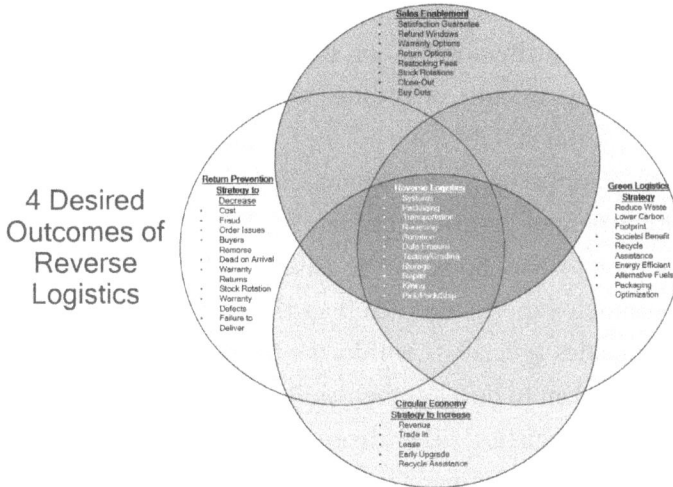

Figure 2.1. The *Four Desired Outcomes of Reverse Logistics* diagram depicts how each strategy relies on the execution of reverse logistics. Desired outcomes are the results that a company is driving toward, and reverse logistics is how the company operates to achieve those goals.

Bridging the Gap between Aspiration and Action

There is a significant disconnect in comprehending the fundamental nature of reverse logistics and its interaction with various segments of organizations. Alarmingly, individuals can earn business and logistics degrees without any exposure to reverse logistics—a complex subject for which specialized courses are notably scarce.

Some advocates suggest shifting the emphasis toward circular economy educational programs, relegating reverse logistics to a minor aspect in the larger picture. This stance, however, overlooks a few crucial points. First, a substantial portion of a product's circular journey involves its departure from the consumption point, a complex process that requires a team adept in managing returns. Second, fostering a circular economy is only one facet of a company's desired outcomes that reverse logistics must enable. The teams responsible for the reverse logistics of a circular economy not only champion sales initiatives and cost reduction but also facilitate green logistics for a myriad of returns programs that companies rely on.

Deborah Dull, a prominent figure in the circular supply chain domain, made a noteworthy observation in her book, *Circular Supply Chain*. After traveling to and attending various circular economy conferences where sustainability was a hot topic, she asked the question: "Where are all the supply chain professionals?"[1] Her remark was about the limited involvement of logistics in advancing the circular economy. Specifically relevant to this book is the absence of reverse logistics professionals and their expertise, which begs the next question: where are the reverse logistics specialists within the supply chain, and what measures are being taken to develop their skills to address the complex demands of reverse logistics? The diverse outcomes managed by different divisions within a company can sometimes align, intersect, or even conflict with one another.

The gap between high-minded aspirations and practical results begs proactive measures. It is crucial for reverse logistics professionals to be thoroughly educated, trained, and equipped to manage a variety of returns programs. Concentrating solely on one desired outcome, without a comprehensive understanding of all four desired outcomes, risks diverting from the aim of a progressive, profitable, and sustainable supply chain. In this chapter, we will take a closer look at the four essential outcomes of reverse logistics and examine how they interrelate and impact the larger framework of a robust and visionary supply chain.

2.2 Desired Outcome 1: *Sales-Enablement*

In the dynamic landscape of retail shopping in 2023, the primary objective is to design compelling offers that not only reinforce customers' purchasing decisions, regardless of where the product was purchased, but also provide them with peace of mind. This could manifest in various forms, such as offering free shipping, uncomplicated return policies, and other commitments which will be explored in this chapter. The customer's journey commences from the moment a customer opts to return a product and culminates when they receive their perceived value. This approach challenges the traditional linear perception of returns as merely a consequence of lost sales.[2] The essence of sales-enablement in this context is to develop programs that delight customers without compromising the business's integrity. Overly lenient **sales-enablement programs** risk revenue loss and fraud, whereas excessively stringent ones may drive customers to competitors. A corporate stance that rigidly views all returns negatively hinders the progression toward a circular economy. By shifting focus and viewing returns not as a loss but as an opportunity to enhance customer loyalty and stimulate repeat business, this section delves into how returns can be strategically used to boost sales and ensure customer retention.[3]

Customer Promise

Montgomery Ward's 100 percent satisfaction guarantee in the late 1800s instilled confidence in customers that they could return any product they were not happy with, reinforcing their buying decision. Over time, additional programs were established to accommodate evolving customer needs and changing buying behaviors. Reverse logistics operations became a necessity to fulfill these customer promises.

The first desired outcome of reverse logistics is primarily a sales activity rather than a logistical one. This desired outcome involves establishing the various scenarios in which returns can occur. These scenarios, in turn, are often designed and implemented by the sales and marketing departments and are communicated to customers during the sales process through their customer promise. A customer promise often includes provisions such as the ability to return the product if unsatisfied, warranty services for product malfunctions, or incentives for product returns through programs like leasing or trade-ins. These customer promise programs provide customers with reassurance that returns will be accepted under certain conditions, and by doing so, implicate the role of reverse logistics.

One pivotal aspect of the sales-enablement strategy is crafting a compelling customer journey that motivates customers to remain loyal to the seller. This foundational step entails identifying potential return scenarios. The creation and implementation of these scenarios are typically the responsibility of sales and marketing teams, aimed at promoting business growth. These defined scenarios are presented to the customers as part of their customer promise in order to bolster the customer's confidence in their purchasing decision by assuring them that returns are manageable and accepted under specified terms.

Hence, the synergy between sales and marketing teams and logistics teams in a company is vital for customer satisfaction and operational efficiency. Sales and marketing teams often set customer commitments, like return windows or warranties, which directly affect logistics operations. While logistics teams usually have an advisory role in these decisions, their input is crucial for practical implementation.

Customer Journey

The **customer journey** is a comprehensive, end-to-end experience in which a customer chooses to exercise the terms laid out in the customer promise.

The journey begins when a customer reaches out to their supplier with a return request. This interaction should be facilitated by user-friendly systems and tools, allowing customers to easily initiate and track their return.[4] Ideally, there would be multiple communication channels available, such as chat, email, or a dedicated phone line, ensuring the customer can choose the method most convenient for them.

Once the return request is made, the customer should receive clear instructions on shipping, including details like packaging, labeling, and drop-off or pickup options. Some advanced systems might offer the option for customers to schedule a pickup directly from their home or workplace, further simplifying the process. Additionally, pre paid shipping labels or discounted return-shipping rates can enhance the customer experience, making it financially feasible for them to return products.

As one can imagine, communication is key during this process. From the moment a product is returned, the customer should be instantly notified and kept in the loop. Well-established companies often have sophisticated dashboards and carefully set the frequency and timing of these notifications. The cadence should not be arbitrary; it is a result of studies regarding the optimization of customer satisfaction and engagement. Moreover, these updates are crucial in maintaining **transparency** and trust with the customer. The modes can vary and include emails, SMS, or even a dedicated online portal. The idea is to not only keep the customer informed but also give them a sense of control over the process, contributing to a positive post-control experience.

Once the product is received and processed, the customer should receive confirmation, acknowledging the completion of the return process. This could be paired with details of the refund, exchange, or any other actions taken in line with the customer promise.

The seamless orchestration of all these steps is what defines the customer journey. Every single touchpoint and interaction should be designed with the customer's ease and convenience in mind, ensuring that they feel valued, respected, and reassured. By meticulously defining and refining this journey, businesses not only fulfill the customer promise but also foster trust, loyalty, and long-term relationships with their customers.

Adapting Reverse Logistics to Evolving Sales Practices and Customer Expectations

Reverse logistics professionals must adapt to the sales practices and customer promises made by the company, considering not just what customers buy but also where they make their purchases. The **sales outlet** can impact return rates, and a surge in revenue from a particular sales channel may lead to an increase in return rates that need to be managed. The shift from brick-and-mortar stores to **e-commerce** significantly alters return behavior, with product return rates rising by nearly 30 percent compared to traditional retail shopping.[5] Consequently, the programs designed to support retail returns have evolved. In-store returns can be aggregated and returned in bulk quantities according to a schedule, while online shoppers may return products individually.

The reverse logistics scene has responded through great **innovation** with practices like virtual returns, which offer customers instant benefits, reshaping their expectations and experiences associated with returns and warranties. One such trend is instant refund, where customers receive credit before the returned product is even received and assessed by the company. This approach prioritizes customer satisfaction by ensuring immediate financial return. However, it carries the risk of the product not being returned or not matching the expected condition. In such cases, companies may implement a chargeback procedure to recover costs.

Another emerging practice is instant exchange. Here, a replacement product is dispatched immediately with the anticipation that the customer will return their original purchase. If the return does not occur, similar chargeback measures may be employed.

Interestingly, some companies are now offering instant refunds with no expectation of the product being returned at all. This decision is often made when the cost and effort of processing a return outweigh the benefits. In such scenarios, customers receive a refund and are allowed to keep the product, which can be particularly relevant for low-value or bulky items where return logistics are complex and expensive.

Of course, these innovative practices are not without risks. Companies are countering this by implementing robust monitoring safeguards to quickly identify and mitigate any fraudulent activities. All things considered, integrating these modern approaches with traditional return and warranty policies highlights a significant shift in how businesses view and handle returns. It reflects an understanding that return and warranty issues are a standard part of doing business as well as an opportunity to enhance customer trust and loyalty through efficient and customer-friendly processes.

The integration of sales, marketing, and logistics is essential in managing customer commitments and efficiently handling various challenges in reverse logistics. These challenges extend beyond typical consumer returns, encompassing a range of issues such as sales failures, over-forecasting, products damaged during shipment, unsold seasonal inventory, restocking due to contractual obligations, recalls, salvage, and excess-inventory management. This aspect of logistics, highlighted by Rogers and Tibben-Lembke, plays a key role in maintaining equilibrium between customer satisfaction and operational effectiveness.[6]

Moving from the general role of reverse logistics to specific customer scenarios, the handling of product failures significantly influences customer trust and the company's reputation. When a warranty claim is made, customer expectations typically include having the product repaired or replaced. The type of return benefit—be it a refund, credit, or replacement—often hinges on the original customer agreement and the promises made by the company. For example, a distributor returning unsold goods to a manufacturer might expect various forms of compensation, such as full refunds, **partial credits**, or credits for future orders. By contrast, end users returning purchased items generally look for benefits like full monetary refunds, partial credits, or credits for their next purchases with the business. This variation in expectations underscores the importance of clear and well-communicated policies, illustrating the interconnectedness of logistics, sales, and marketing in shaping customer experiences.

The linear return flow, intended to go back to the manufacturer, does in fact go backward through a series of returns programs.

Figure 2.2. "Return Flow from Customer to Manufacturer diagram" depicting product as it moves from the customer back to the manufacturer.

How a company sells impacts the nature of returns. Bulk returns to a manufacturer, like a distributor returning unsold items from a winter lineup, differ markedly from individual customer returns focused on processing single items and ensuring proper customer credit. Retailers, facing these varied scenarios, strive to simplify the return process for customers by offering clear terms like free returns, specific return windows, or warranties.

The situation becomes more complex when retailers work with multiple brands, each with its own customer journey and promises, including specialized forms, legitimate **return merchandise authorization (RMA)** reasons, and specific response times outlined in purchase agreements or contracts. Managing returns from different vendors with diverse requirements adds another layer of complexity.

The accounting of returned goods also varies across companies. Some write down the full sale and manufacturing costs to zero, others depreciate the value over time; some maintain the current **market value** of returns, and yet others consider only the marginal value of the product. These varying accounting methods, to be elaborated on in chapter 5, add to the complexity of return management.

Managing returns requires a careful balance between customer expectations, logistical-costs management, and appropriate accounting practices. Companies must make strategic decisions that respect financial considerations and the commitments made to their customers.

Examples of Manufacturer Returns Programs

Manufacturer returns programs are designed to enhance the sales process between manufacturers, retailers, and distributors by providing avenues to recoup value for products that did not reach the end customer or were no longer desired by them. These programs facilitate the movement of products from retailers or distributors to alternative locations, aside from the customer's destination, or enable returns from the end customer to the distributor for appropriate handling. The following are examples of manufacturer's returns programs that allow manufacturers, retailers, and distributors to manage inventory, mitigate financial losses, and maintain positive business relationships within the supply chain.

- **Closeout.** The discontinuation of a specific product by a retailer, distributor, or manufacturer. **Closeout** items are new products that are no longer produced or sold. The reverse logistics process for closeouts entails removing the product from shelves and transferring excess inventory to another location. The value generated from closed-out products may involve soliciting bids from external firms to aid in their removal and **liquidation.**

- **Buyout**. A **buyout** refers to a situation where one manufacturer acquires the entire supply of a competitor's products from a retailer or distributor with the intention of replacing them with their own goods. This allows the retailer to free up shelf space for higher-selling products and reduces the financial risk associated with holding unwanted inventory. The acquired products can be liquidated to offset expenses. Manufacturers may choose to liquidate these competitors' products in an alternate market where they do not directly compete, or they may choose to responsibly recycle the competitor's product to remove it from the market entirely.

- **Job-Out.** A **job-out** return refers to products that are sold within a specific timeframe, such as seasonal clothes, tools, furniture, or holiday items. These products experience heightened demand and popularity for a designated period, but once that time passes and consumer preferences shift, **surplus** products must be cleared from retail shelves to accommodate the arrival of the next seasonal items. For example, during summer, swimwear and beach toys are in high demand, but as the season transitions to fall, customers will seek warmer clothing and back-to-school items instead. Job-out firms are companies that specialize in purchasing and liquidating these products once the peak demand season concludes, assisting retailers in effectively managing inventory turnover by efficiently removing excess stock and creating space for the next batch of seasonal merchandise.

- **Surplus.** Surplus returns refer to products that were originally sent by a manufacturer to a distributor but failed to sell as expected, resulting in excess stock with no demand. These unsold items need to be removed from the shelves. The course of action for handling surplus returns depends on the customer promise made during the purchase. In some cases, the product can be returned to the supply source, while in others, it can be disposed of through alternative channels to generate value.

- **Return Rights**. Return rights are policies implemented by manufacturers or distributors that allow retail outlets to return items that customers have tried and no longer want in exchange for credit. By enabling retailers to return products to the original place of purchase, the risk associated with customer returns is shifted from the retailer to the upstream source. These programs may have limitations, such as a cap on the percentage of returns or offering partial credits for returned items. The guarantee through **return rights** reduces the retailer's risk of selling and experiencing losses on poor-quality items. These types of returns are often received in an open condition, as customers have already tried the product before returning it.

- **Demonstration Devices**. A **demonstration device** return, also known as try-and-buy, is a program that allows customers to receive an item for temporary use or display on a shelf before making a purchase. Unlike a rights return, this program involves providing customers with a device that may or may not be in new condition. For instance, if a customer wishes to try out a tool or equipment before committing to a purchase, they may be provided with a used piece of equipment. Once the customer makes a purchasing decision, the demonstration equipment is returned, and a new item is sent to the customer. This approach ensures that a new product is preserved from being opened, used, and devalued during a trial period. Similarly, for display purposes, used devices may be sourced instead of opening newly manufactured products. When these display devices are no longer needed, they may be returned to the manufacturer as a condition for demonstrating the product's functionality.

- **Failure to Deliver**. A failure-to-deliver return refers to a situation where a product, initially shipped through forward logistics to a designated destination, fails to reach the customer due to reasons such as an incorrect address, customer rejection, or shipping errors. In such cases, the product is returned to the shipper, initiating a reverse logistics process as it moves back from the intended delivery point. During transit, the product may incur damage, resulting in a change in its condition from when it was initially manufactured. As a result, the returned product may require reinspection and repackaging before it can be resold. If the cosmetic damage exceeds the customer promise of new condition, alternative programs indicating that the product is not new or in a used condition may need to be implemented to derive value from the return.

- **Manufacturer Warranty**. A **manufacturer warranty** refers to the guarantee provided with a purchased product, covering any defects or issues outlined in the customer promise. Warranty programs typically offer options such as replacing the faulty unit with a new one or repairing the problem and returning the product. In instances where the defect is due to a manufacturer error, the original builder of the product bears the responsibility for covering the costs associated with refurbishment.

- **Dead-on-Arrival.** A dead-on-arrival return refers to a product that has been sold to an end user, but upon receiving it, the user discovers that the product does not function as intended. This discovery occurs within a specific timeframe specified in the customer promise, such as a failure occurring within thirty days. In such cases, the user is entitled to return the defective unit and have it replaced with a brand-new unit of the same product. The DOA return policy ensures that customers receive functional products and helps address any immediate issues encountered upon purchase.

Examples of Customer Returns Programs

Customer returns programs strengthen the sales process between a business and its end customers by providing avenues to recoup value for returned products. These programs can streamline initial product sales or leverage used products to incentivize future purchases, generate revenue, promote responsible treatment, enhance customer satisfaction, drive repeat business, and foster **sustainable practices** in product-lifecycle management. Some programs follow a circular approach, encouraging returns for further utilization or recycling, which will be explored in detail in Section 2.5, Desired Outcome 4. Examples of customer returns programs include:

- **Satisfaction Guarantee.** A satisfaction-guarantee return ensures that if the customer, for any reason, decides that the product does not meet their expectations, they are eligible for a full or partial refund. The satisfaction-guarantee return policy aims to build trust and confidence in the brand by offering a risk-free purchasing experience. For products purchased through the internet or telesales, customers may be promised free shipping for returns.

- **Customer Warranty.** A **customer warranty** is provided to a customer by a distributor or retailer, enabling the customer to receive a replacement unit or have a defective product repaired. It differs from a manufacturer's warranty in that the customer does not directly return the product to the manufacturer. Instead, the customer leverages the distributor or retailer as the return destination, making them responsible for handling the return process and logistics. In some cases, the distributor or retailer may then ship the product back to the source with a manufacturer's warranty. Furthermore, many companies offer extended warranties that are managed separately from the manufacturer's warranty, typically handled by reverse logistics teams.

- **Trade-In:** A trade-in return refers to the process of returning a used product to receive its residual value, which can be applied toward the customer's next purchase or provided as an alternate form of payment. These programs have a circular nature. They encourage customers to upgrade their products by providing incentives, such as trade-in values, and they can also attract new customers who may be considering switching brands or products. Additionally, trade-in returns create incremental revenue streams if the returned products can be refurbished and resold at a profit to the next customer. Overall, these programs promote both customer satisfaction and business growth.

- **Early Upgrade**: An early-upgrade return program is a customer-oriented initiative that emerges when a customer purchases a device under a contractual agreement, making monthly payments for a predetermined period before becoming eligible for a new device. This program enables customers to exchange their current device for a newer one before the contract ends. The residual value of the returned device is applied toward the remaining payments required to fulfill the customer's contractual obligations. By offering early upgrade programs, companies can generate value from the old product, enhance customer satisfaction by keeping them up-to-date with the latest releases, and extend the duration of their customer base under contract. These programs offer mutual benefits to both the customers and the company, fostering loyalty and continuous engagement.

- **Promotional Trade-In:** A **promotional trade-in** refers to a customer returns program in which the residual value of the old product being returned does not solely cover the value offered to the customer as an incentive to make a purchase. This type of program involves the expense of providing compelling offers to encourage the sale of a new product and the return of the old product. It operates on an if-then basis: *if* the customer makes a purchase and returns their old product, *then* they receive a market offer that exceeds the standard trade-in value of the products. Companies often combine their marketing budget with the inherent value of the old product to present customers with the most attractive offer available in the marketplace. Promotional trade-ins are designed to drive customer acquisition, encourage upgrades, and entice customers to switch brands.

- **Lease.** A lease return refers to the process of returning a product at the end of a lease agreement between a business and a customer. The customer utilizes the product over a specific period in exchange for lower payments compared to purchasing the product outright. The lease agreement considers the forecasted residual value, which reduces the customer's cost of ownership. At the end of the lease term, the customer has three options: (1) making a final payment to purchase the product, (2) continuing to make monthly payments and extend the lease, or (3) returning the product as agreed upon in the lease contract. The returned products are sent back to the source in accordance with the terms outlined in the customer promise and lease agreement. Lease returns allow customers to enjoy the benefits of using a product without the long-term commitment of ownership.

- **Product as a Service (PaaS).** PaaS represents a departure from traditional product-consumption models. Instead of outright purchasing or simply leasing a product, consumers access its functionalities through a subscription basis. Stemming from IT concepts like **software as a service (SaaS)**, this approach has transcended into the realm of tangible products ranging from cars and apparel to household appliances. The model not only offers consumers financial flexibility and continuous access to updated products but it also removes the challenges of direct ownership.

  - While leasing and PaaS may seem similar, they have distinct differences. A lease is typically a contractual agreement where consumers use a product for a set period, after which they can return, purchase, or renew the lease. PaaS, on the other hand, emphasizes a continuous service relationship. Consumers subscribe to the product's benefits, and the service often includes maintenance, updates, and potential upgrades, reflecting a shift from mere temporary possession to an ongoing service provision and value addition.

  - For businesses, PaaS creates an avenue for sustained engagement with customers, allowing for greater opportunities in upselling, cross-selling, and fostering loyalty. This ongoing relationship contrasts with the finite nature of traditional leases. Moreover, by retaining ownership and control over the product lifecycle, businesses can reflect a deeper commitment to environmental responsibility and market adaptability.

- **Recycling/Salvage.** A **recycling or salvage return program** is a customer-oriented initiative that encourages the voluntary return of old products to ensure responsible environmental treatment. In this program, customers are invited to donate their old products without expecting monetary compensation.

The program guarantees proper disposal methods, such as **harvesting**, recycling, or **closed-loop recycling** where the raw materials are reused to make the next product. Customers may expect proof of responsible handling, such as a certificate of destruction or **data destruction**, ensuring that the product is not disposed of in a landfill and their information is secure.

Return Stream: A Conceptual Understanding

In any business operation, especially one that involves sales and customers, a critical aspect to understand and manage is the sales-enablement program. In this context, the concept of **return stream** emerges as an integral part of this program.

Every **sales-enablement** program can be seen as a return stream or inflow source. This implies that the customer expects to receive a certain amount of value when they choose to ship a product back to the company. This expectation of value can be categorized into one or more of the following expectations of value:

- **Refunds.** This involves returning the customer's money in exchange for the product.
- **Exchanges.** This allows the customer to swap the returned product for another one.
- **Discounts.** The customer is provided with a discount on their next purchase.
- **Credits.** The company issues credit to the customer that can be used for future purchases.
- **Goodwill.** The customer chooses to return a product for no value to ensure a product is responsibly handled or used again.

Understanding and managing return streams is a fundamental aspect of any sales-enablement program and is significantly influenced by the type of return, the associated desired outcome, and the level of stakeholder required. It is also contingent upon whether the company's strategic focus is on decreasing or increasing returns. The company might want to decrease returns to minimize costs and resource consumption, or increase returns to build customer trust and satisfaction, which can contribute to long-term customer loyalty.

Figure 2.3 illustrates the correlation between return types, desired outcome, stakeholder levels, and the desire to decrease or increase returns.

Return Product Type	Customer Value Expecation	Desired Outcome	Strategy
Close Out	% Value/Credit	Sales Enablement	Decrease
Buy-Out	% Value/Credit	Sales Enablement	Decrease
Job-Out	% Value/Credit	Sales Enablement	Decrease
Surplus	% Value/Credit	Sales Enablement	Decrease
Buyers Remorse	% Value/Credit	Sales Enablement	Decrease
Defective Upon Arrival	% Value/Credit/Replacement	Sales Enablement	Decrease
Failure to Deliver	% Value/Credit	Sales Enablement	Decrease
Defective In Warranty	Repair or Replacement Value	Sales Enablement	Decrease
Trade-In	Value or Discount	Circular Economy	Increase
Lease	Use of Unit	Circular Economy	Increase
Early Upgrade	Elligible to Move to New Unit	Circular Economy	Increase
PAAS	Use of Unit	Circular Economy	Increase
Demonstration	Trial	Sales Enablement	Increase
Recycle/Salvage	Zero/Reporting	Circular Economy	Increase

Figure 2.3. The "Return Product Type" table outlines returns programs that can be created by sales-enablement programs with the corresponding desired impact to return volumes.

The Evolution of Retail Returns in a Digital Era

Imagine walking into your favorite clothing store. You pick out four shirts, head to the dressing room, and decide that only one truly suits your style. The three you leave behind are promptly returned to their respective racks by a store associate, ready for the next shopper. In this brick-and-mortar environment; the act of trying on items does not alter their status. They remain as new and available for purchase since they were never sold, even though they were tried on.

Now, consider the online shopping experience, which has become increasingly popular. You order those same four shirts, delivered to your doorstep for your convenience. After trying them on, you decide, just as before, to keep only one. But the process of returning the unwanted three is where things diverge significantly. The shirts have left the warehouse, spent days in transit, been handled and perhaps tried on, then repackaged and sent back. Are they still considered new? Is there a criterion that can be achieved so they may be resold at full price without hesitation?

This shift in the shopping paradigm has called for a reevaluation of how retailers classify returned merchandise. While in-store try-ons maintain the integrity of a product's "newness," online purchases present a different challenge. Once an item travels to a customer and back, even if never officially used, its journey has potential implications on its quality, appearance, or even hygiene. The box might be damaged, the item could pick up odors or minor imperfections, or it simply might not be as pristine as something straight off the shelf.

To address this, retailers are adapting. Some are investing in rigorous quality checks for returned items, ensuring they meet standards before reselling. Others offer discounted "open box" or "like-new" categories for items that have made the round trip. There is even a growing market for third-party businesses that refurbish or resell returned goods, making sure they find a home rather than contributing to waste.

In an age where convenience and online shopping reign supreme, the definition of "new" is evolving. As customers change the way they shop, retailers must adapt their return and resale strategies to ensure trust, quality, and sustainability in the e-commerce landscape.

Establishing Clear Guidelines: Aligning Customer Guarantees for the Transition from New to Used Products

Clarifying and aligning the customer guarantee is of utmost importance before initiating the reverse logistics operational process including restoration, refurbishment, or repair. It is crucial that the disposition of value generation and what can be reused as new is clearly communicated among staff and to customers. Many companies rely on corporate policies or past practices to establish these rules.

Therefore, it is imperative for companies to revise their policies in response to evolving consumer behaviors, particularly regarding the impact of online and app-based shopping, and how home delivery is reshaping consumer habits. This could involve redefining what constitutes a used product in the online realm or developing new systems for managing returns and restocking items in a way that reflects the reality of how customers shop online. By acknowledging and adapting to these shifts, companies can better meet customer expectations and manage their inventory more effectively.

Transparent guidelines in line with customer assurances help prevent excessive repairs and keep clarity in the reverse logistics operation. Rules can differ between manufacturers and distributors/retailers and might also fluctuate across different company divisions. Some firms have set up integrated customer fulfillment functions in their reverse logistics hubs to enhance the worth of returned items still in new condition. These smart supply chains, or integrated supply chains, allow for fulfilling subsequent orders from the reverse center once goods are marked as "new." This strategy helps planners avoid buying inventory already present elsewhere in the supply chain and negates the need to merge products into a primary distribution hub.

There are some current best practices adopted by companies to guide the evaluation of whether a returned product can be resold as "new."

1. **Shipment or Sale.** The product is considered "used" once it is sold to a customer and shipped from a facility. The transfer of ownership or possession initiates the change, whether the product has been opened or used.

2. **Delivery and Shipment Rejections.** The product is considered "used" once it is delivered to the customer. Even if the customer rejects the shipment and returns it unopened, the product might still be classified as used due to the handling and logistics involved.

3. **Package Damaged or Opened.** The product is considered "used" once the packaging is damaged or opened. This assumes that the product's integrity or original state has been compromised, even if the item itself remains unused.

4. **Product Opening and Usage.** Opening a product's packaging does not necessarily classify it as used unless there is evidence of handling or environmental factors that diminishes its original condition. Many companies use tamper-proof tape, seals, and

other markers to indicate whether a product has experienced more than superficial handling. If a product can connect to the internet and a server, monitoring its usage or online activity can be a method to ascertain if the product has been utilized.

5. **Tamper-Proof Seal**. A tamper-proof seal serves as an integrity indicator for a product. If removed, the product might not qualify for return. An intact seal can also signify that the item remains in a "new" condition. For instance, a seal might connect two shoes, permitting try-ons but discouraging extensive wear. If this seal is broken, the product may be deemed "used" or could undergo further evaluation to ascertain its condition.

6. **Length of Time from Point of Sale and Return Condition.** If a product is purchased and returned unopened within a specific period, it may be considered new. However, the condition of the returned item should be assessed to ensure it meets new product standards.

7. **Length of Time from Point of Manufacturing.** Products can be refurbished, repaired, or restored from a given period after the manufacturing date and resold as new, provided that **warranty options**, cosmetic condition, and functional condition meet manufacturing standards.

It is crucial to consider the risks inherent to different product categories and values when establishing these policies. Different rules may be established from manufacturers to distributors/retailers and can even vary among departments within a company. Clear guidelines that align with the customer guarantee prevent devaluing perfectly good inventory, **over-repairing** items, and maintain transparency in the reverse logistics process.

Resistance

The objective of implementing resistance strategies in product returns is to minimize the volume of returns, aiming to limit the necessity of issuing credits or refunds. This approach can create a contentious dynamic, positioning the manufacturer and the customer in a seemingly adversarial relationship. The elements of **resistance** are conveyed through the customer promise, establishing the criteria and conditions under which a product can be returned. Marketing and sales teams are typically central in defining these rules, as they are formulated during the purchase phase. Examples of resistance strategies in product returns programs include:

1. **Denial Criteria:** specific conditions or criteria that must be met for a return to be accepted, such as intact packaging or within a certain time frame.

2. **Return Windows:** imposed time limits within which customers are allowed to initiate returns.

3. **Partial Credit:** offering customers only a partial refund or credit for returned products.

4. **Restocking Fees:** charging customers a fee for returning products, intended to offset costs associated with restocking and processing returns.

5. **Commission Chargeback:** reducing or reclaiming commissions paid to sales representatives or distributors when returns occur

6. **Processing Fees:** imposing fees on customers for handling or processing their returns.

7. **Receipt Requirement:** mandating that customers provide the original purchase receipt to initiate a return, ensuring verification of purchase.

8. **No Free Shipping:** returns that requiring customers to bear the cost of sending back items.

9. **Thresholds:** setting specific benchmarks or conditions that must be met for a return to be considered; can include minimum usage levels, specific defect types, or scenarios under which the product can be returned.

10. **Approval Processes:** implementing a multistage approval process for returns, through which the request must undergo several layers of review before being accepted.

11. **Specialized Forms:** mandating the completion of detailed and complex forms to initiate a return process that may ask for

extensive information about the product, its use, and the nature of the issue.

12. **Detailed Instructions:** providing customers with complicated and exhaustive instructions for returning a product, which may involve numerous steps, strict packaging guidelines, or specific carriers to be used.

13. **Evidence Submission:** requiring customers to submit evidence, such as photos or videos, demonstrating the product's condition or the issue faced; evidence must often meet certain criteria to be deemed acceptable.

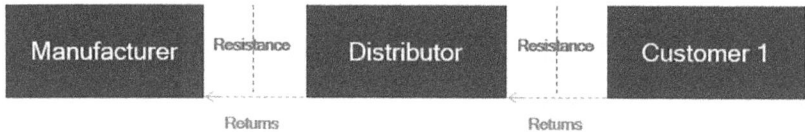

Figure 2.4. Resistance reverse logistics flow diagram depicts a product as it moves from the customer back to the manufacturer with resistance.

These resistance mechanisms discourage return activities and minimize their impact. In other words, resistance stimies the transition from a reverse organization to a circular economy. These countermeasures for return can become obstacles for companies seeking to effectively compete for the market share of Customer Two, who values sustainable and circular practices.

Complexities of Managing Returns for Multibrand Retailers

In the complex world of multibrand retail, not only must outlets maintain a detailed catalog of their products by vendor but they also need to manage the intricacies of returning products to these vendors through various return merchandise authorization protocols. These protocols often involve managing contracts with specific end dates and adhering to different policies for each vendor. While the sales and logistics processes are generally streamlined to facilitate sales, the return process introduces a layer of complexity due to the diverse and sometimes challenging return policies of each vendor.

Advanced retail companies employ sophisticated information exchange methods that provide updates on a weekly, daily, or even a live basis, actively managing and updating their contract management system.[7] This system is integral for feeding information into **decision-support systems**, which then strategically route products through the operation to optimize value.

On the customer-facing side, a retailer might offer a straightforward RMA policy, such as a fifteen-day return window with no shipping charges, creating a customer-friendly environment. However, each brand the retailer stocks usually has its own unique return policy with specific conditions, necessary forms, return-to-sales ratios, defined response times, and other stipulations. This diversity in vendor policies adds another layer of complexity to managing returns, making it a significant operational challenge as the number of brands a retailer offers increases.

Chapter 3 will present the case study of goTRG, examining the tools and strategies they employ to navigate and manage these complexities. The real-world example demonstrates how sophisticated systems and practices can effectively handle the multifaceted nature of returns management in a multibrand retail environment.

Omni-Channel Sales

Omni-channel shopping refers to a retail strategy that provides customers with a seamless shopping experience across various channels—physical stores, online platforms, mobile apps, and social media—allowing them to interact with the brand through multiple touchpoints.[8]

This means that brick-and-mortar retailers have expanded their online presence, and online retailers have ventured into physical stores. One example is Untuckit, which started as a shirt company that manufactured shirts designed to be worn untucked. Customers originally made their purchase online, but their sales strategy expanded to opening retail outlets to give their customers choices of where to shop and not limiting their customers to one channel.[9] The proliferation of omni-channel investments aims to leverage store assets and distribution capabilities, while simultaneously providing customers with expanded service options such as in-store returns, buy online/pick up in-store, and ship from store.

However, these broader service offerings come with additional costs and operational challenges, requiring careful logistical planning and returns management across channels. Many companies have adopted different return policies for purchases made in the store versus purchases made online due to the higher cost of shipping returns individually versus an **aggregate bulk shipment** from a retail outlet. Driving customers to the store also encourages additional purchases to offset the return that an online shopper may not be compelled to make.[10]

2.3 Desired Outcome 2: *Return Prevention and Cost Management*

The essence of the second desired outcome revolves around minimizing return flows of unwanted returns and efficiently managing the expenses of all return initiatives. While sales or marketing departments typically make customer commitments as outlined in the first desired outcome, it is often up to the logistics teams to bring these commitments to fruition. Thus, seamless communication between these departments is imperative. They must work in harmony to ensure successful results.

Profitability beyond the Initial Sale

The primary goal of any for-profit organization is to make a net profit. This is a twofold desired outcome: to generate income and to retain it. The case of forward sales, such as analyzing the cost of product acquisition and the selling price, is a straightforward process and easily understandable for organizational leaders. However, the journey to profitability does not end with the initial sale. The second desired outcome of reverse logistics, **return prevention and cost management (RPCM),** becomes significant at this stage. This desired outcome is about managing the causes of returns and the operational costs associated with product movement, repair, and refurbishment. While sales and marketing focus on generating revenue, effective reverse logistics management is crucial for preserving and maximizing the company's financial resources.

Returns are associated with a multitude of costs that may be difficult to identify and track. These can include **direct costs** such as shipping and handling, tariff or tax reversals, storage, inspection, repackaging, restocking, and even disposal of unsellable goods. There are also **indirect costs** to consider, including administrative workloads, lost sales, potential harm to **brand reputation**, and the need to manage customer relationships and satisfaction during the return process.

While these costs can be significant, they are often spread across various parts of the company's operations and can easily become "hidden" within the larger balance sheet. This obscurity makes it challenging to gain a comprehensive understanding of the true cost of returns, leading many businesses to underestimate their impact.

Thus, it is important that companies actively manage this area of their operations. This involves setting up procedures to accurately track and quantify all return-related costs, including those that may not be immediately apparent.

Desired Outcome of Operational Processing

The primary goal of **operational processing** is to finalize the logistics associated with closing out a return, determine both cosmetic and functional conditions, and ensure products are directed to the appropriate value-generation outlet both cost effectively and efficiently. Areas of focus include:

- **Process Efficiency.** The operational processing workflow should be streamlined to ensure minimal touchpoints, reducing time and costs associated with handling the product. Examples of efficiencies will be discussed in our Reuse Cases later in the book.

- **Accuracy.** Accuracy in identifying the returned product is essential, as it influences order accuracy and communication with the customer regarding the status of their return.
- **Storage and Preparation.** Products should be stored properly to maintain their condition and adequately prepared for the next stage in the value chain, whether it be resale, repair, or disposal.

Desired Outcome of Repair/Refurbishment/ Restoration Operations

The goal of **repair operations** is to improve the cosmetic and/or functional aspects of a returned product or packaging. This process prepares a product for potential resale or supports a warranty program.

Repair operations must strike a balance between cost and quality control to fulfill the customer promise made when a product is returned and reused. The following practices are recommended:

- **Assess before Repair.** Not every component of a product may need repair or replacement. It is essential to pinpoint which parts aren't functioning properly and determine the best solutions, whether through new, refurbished, or salvaged parts.
- **Quality Control.** The repaired product should be thoroughly tested to ensure it performs as expected. This is crucial in preventing a poor customer experience that could negatively impact brand reputation and future revenue.
- **Avoid Over-Repair:** Over-repairing a product, or replacing parts that are not defective, results in unnecessary costs. It is important to identify precisely the repair needs of each product.

Importance of Data in Returns Management

Once a system for tracking these costs is in place, businesses can analyze the data to identify patterns and areas for potential improvement. **Data-driven insights** from the returns management program can be instrumental in identifying areas that contribute most to unwanted returns. Once these areas are identified, corrective measures can be taken to mitigate them. This might involve refining product design, improving product quality, enhancing customer communication, or offering better education about the product, among other initiatives. All these actions are directed towards reducing the rate of returns and the costs associated with them.

- **Operational Cost Control.** This includes labor, materials, transportation, and troubleshooting customer returns to minimize expenses and maximize efficiency.
- **Order Issue Reduction.** Feedback from the reverse logistics teams can help resolve root causes of problems like incorrect item shipment, incorrect delivery, or mismatched products.
- **Failure to Deliver.** Issues where a product is returned to the sender due to customer refusal, incorrect product address, or carrier mistakes need to be identified and addressed.
- **Buyer's Remorse.** Strategies to increase communication with customers can be implemented, such as modifying instructions or improving visibility of size charts, to reduce the frequency and costs associated with remorse returns.
- **Dead on Arrival.** Quality failures resulting in products that do not work upon arrival need to be addressed, including helping customers operate the product if they mistakenly believe it does not work.
- **Warranty Returns.** Management of warranty returns can involve fixing the item or leveraging recovered or refurbished components to reduce costs. In cases where defective products must be replaced with new ones, costs may be higher.
- **Stock Rotations, Job-Outs, and Closeouts.** The cost of return trends like these can vary, and it is the responsibility of reverse logistics teams to manage these to optimize costs and minimize waste.

Warranty Management

A critical function within the second desired outcome of returns management is **warranty management**. It is closely intertwined with return prevention and cost management, given its involvement after a product has completed the cycle of manufacturing, shipping, and returning via reverse logistics.

A fundamental part of warranty management includes the application of repair and refurbishment protocols. In instances where a product's packaging is damaged, but the product remains functional, refurbishing the package can be a more cost-effective alternative to replacing the entire unit. In other cases, when a unit is malfunctioning, companies might choose to extract parts from one unit to repair another. These procedures, known as the **rules of engagement**, are typically stipulated in the customer promise and enacted by the reverse logistics team.

As part of their warranty services, companies may opt to provide a **certified like-new** product instead of a completely new replacement. This strategy can help manage costs more effectively by reutilizing returned units instead of incurring expenses for manufacturing new ones.

Companies might also extend their money-back guarantee window—for example, from thirty to ninety days. This extended period could help circumvent the need for managing a repair operation, thus reducing costs. Other companies might decide to offer a specific part repair service, thereby eliminating the need to refurbish an entire unit and focusing solely on the cost of replacing the defective part. There is also the factor of quality control during warranty and repair operations. A scenario in which products are returned, refurbished, reshipped, and then returned again is termed as a bounce. **Bounces** can inflate costs and decrease customer satisfaction, thus warranting diligent management and prevention strategies.

Warranty management is a vital responsibility of the second desired outcome of returns management, significantly contributing to cost management, return prevention, and the efficient running of reverse logistics operations.

The Power of Transparency

Transparency in cost reporting can bring the **hidden costs** of returns into the light. This increased visibility can lead to more informed decision-making and ultimately to a more profitable and efficient approach to managing returns.

2.4 Desired Outcome 3: *Green Logistics*

Green logistics is a strategic approach to logistics management that aims to achieve desired business outcomes while reducing the carbon footprint, waste, and other adverse effects associated with logistical operations. The reverse logistics desired outcome for green logistics can be summarized as:

- minimizing carbon emissions, energy consumption, and **waste generation** in transportation and reverse operations;
- optimizing repackaging design and materials to reduce environmental impact;
- implementing **reclamation** of parts in the warranty or certified preowned products;
- utilizing energy-efficient facilities and equipment in logistics operations;
- promoting sustainable procurement and supplier management practices;
- optimizing transportation routes to reduce fuel consumption and emissions;
- advocating for less carbon-intensive transportation modes such as rail, sea, or electric vehicles;
- implementing reverse logistics practices that minimize the environmental impact of product returns and end-of-life management; and
- introducing ways to measure harvesting or recycling benefits while calculating landfill usage.

Evaluating the Environmental Effects of Green Reverse Logistics

Managing returns consumes resources and has environmental implications. To fully comprehend the impact of running return operations, it is essential to understand the environmental outcomes of restocking, repairing, recycling, or disposing of a product. These outcomes can be classified into three categories: (1) **direct impacts**, (2) **indirect impacts**, and (3) **cumulative impacts.**

1. **Direct impacts** can be easily quantified and measured, such as CO^2 emissions, water consumption, electricity usage, etc. These elements often have a direct, tangible impact on the environment. They are typically expressed in units of measure that are commonly used, such as tons of CO^2 or kilowatt-hours of electricity.

   a. *Energy Consumption. The process of transporting returned goods back to the seller or a processing facility consumes energy, usually in the form of fuel for vehicles. This results in greenhouse gas emissions, contributing to global warming.*

   b. *Waste Generation. If returned items are found to be defective and cannot be repaired or recycled, they might end up in a landfill, generating waste.*

   c. *Resource Use. Repairing and repackaging returned items consumes and depletes resources like spare parts, packaging materials, etc.*

2. **Indirect impacts** are less tangible and harder to measure directly, like traffic congestion, noise pollution, **biodiversity loss**, etc. These elements have a secondary or tertiary impact on the environment and on human health and well-being, but their effects are more challenging to translate into units of measure that are readily understood.

   a. *Behavioral Impacts. If a company makes it easy for customers to return products, it could potentially encourage more returns, increasing the environmental impacts associated with the return process. This is an indirect impact because it is a behavioral change prompted by the return policy.*

   b. *Waste Management Impacts. If returned items end up in landfills, this contributes to problems like habitat destruction, soil and water pollution, and greenhouse gas emissions.*

3. **Cumulative impacts** are the combined impacts of various activities related to managing returns over time. The combined effects of waste, emissions, resource depletion, etc., from managing returns can contribute to larger-scale environmental problems like **climate change**, **air and water pollution**, and loss of biodiversity.

These categories highlight the need for a comprehensive approach to environmental-impact assessment. The immediate (direct) and broader long-term (indirect and cumulative) effects should be considered in green logistics planning. Both green logistics and reverse logistics strategies can help minimize these impacts by reducing waste, increasing efficiency, and promoting the reuse and recycling of products and materials.

Holistic Approach toward Green Logistics Management

Adopting a **holistic approach** is crucial in green logistics goals, particularly in reverse logistics. While the best strategy is undoubtedly to prevent unwanted returns, it is equally important to establish a robust plan for efficiently managing the inevitable returns in a way that minimizes environmental harm. Green logistics initiatives in reverse logistics focus on reducing the use of packaging materials, implementing effective recycling programs, refining corporate policies, and promoting the reuse and repurposing of products and materials. Moreover, addressing the underlying causes of unnecessary returns is a key part of green logistics. This involves improving product quality, refining the sales qualification process, and enhancing sales practices to significantly reduce the frequency of returns, thereby diminishing the associated environmental impact.

It is important to recognize that outright refusal of returns might not always align with environmental goals. For instance, if a customer ends up discarding a product due to a denied return, this could have a more detrimental environmental impact compared to a scenario where the company accepts the return and processes it sustainably. This underscores the importance of striking a balance between customer return policies and environmental obligations.

To manage customer returns while also lessening their environmental footprint, businesses can leverage specialized returns processing centers that are designed to maximize recycling, reuse, and other sustainable practices, ensuring that returns contribute positively to a company's sustainability objectives. This comprehensive strategy in reverse logistics not only aligns business operations with environmental sustainability but also underscores the dual importance of preventing unnecessary returns and handling inevitable returns in the most environmentally considerate manner possible.

Companies can also extend their commitment to **environmental stewardship** by offering **complimentary recycling assistance**. A notable example of such a corporate initiative is Cisco's 100 percent **takeback guarantee**. In this program, the tech giant pledges to accept returns of any Cisco-related item, bearing all associated costs. This guarantees that returned products are handled with responsibility, ensuring that items which can be spared from landfills are prepared for parts or component reuse. This aligns with green logistics principles, showcasing a proactive stance in reducing the environmental footprint of returns.

Internalization and Forced Internalization

Governments have started to initiate regulations to ensure businesses address returns ethically. They now mandate companies to accurately represent the complete costs of their goods and services, factoring in environmental expenses, in a shift termed **forced internalization**. Both individuals and enterprises are now responsible for their effects on pollution, the depletion of resources, and harm to ecosystems. The government's desired outcome is to boost market efficiency and persuade consumers to lean toward sustainable options. The government can guide company behavior by means of legislation, taxes, or rewards.

Governments around the world are increasingly recognizing the environmental- and consumer-protection benefits of products that can be repaired rather than discarded. As a result, they are implementing

Right to Repair legislation, compelling manufacturers to design their products in a way that allows them to be fixed rather than replaced. This legislation also mandates companies to provide consumers and repair shops with the necessary tools, parts, and information to effectively fix their products. By doing so, these laws aim to extend product lifecycles, reduce electronic waste, and encourage sustainable consumption.

California has been pioneering this movement in the US. Recently, the state passed Senate Bill 244, which mandates manufacturers to guarantee the availability of parts for phones for up to seven years. The legislation was met with unanimous support, passing with a 50–0 vote, and it currently awaits the governor's endorsement. If ratified, it is anticipated to be implemented in 2024.[11] This move by California comes on the heels of a similar legislation adopted by New York and Minnesota, making it the third state in the US to champion the right of consumers to repair their electronic devices. Such legislations are pivotal examples of forced internalization. Historically, several companies erected barriers to the repair of specific components in their products, nudging consumers toward buying new products rather than mending existing ones. The Right to Repair laws are now ensuring these firms bear the responsibilities and costs tied to product sustainability and waste they previously externalized.

Environmental, Sustainability, and Governance

Many companies are starting to focus on the **environmental, sustainability, and governance (ESG)** outputs of their companies. As of 2022, over 42 percent of all Fortune 500 companies have published sustainability goals with achievable targets by 2030, and there is a growing recognition of the importance of environmental consciousness in reverse logistics.[12] There is an emerging presence of Chief Sustainability Officers (CSOs) in corporate boardrooms.

Challenges of Green Logistics for Reverse

The reverse logistics industry faces several challenges in advancing toward green logistics desired outcome. One of the primary challenges is that the effects of green logistics are often subtle or indirect.[13] For instance, quantifying the impact on global temperatures when recycling products instead of sending them to landfills is challenging. Similarly, pinpointing the exact influence of reused products on new sales or the additional sales revenue garnered from product trade-ins is not straight-forward. A common counterpoint is speculating the actions that would have transpired without such a program in place. Such correlational benefits are frequently labeled as soft benefits.

While we can directly measure the use of materials and energy within returns processing centers, gauging the broader impact on global resource consumption due to, say, a free return policy, becomes elusive. Revenues from trade-in programs can be managed directly, but ascertaining the precise increase in a company's sales from adopting buy-back, leasing, or **early upgrade** programs (which incentivize returns) is complex. Unable to measure the long-term advantages of returns, many firms implement policies to deter them.

The difficulty of measuring the impact of returned items arises from the subjective nature of correlating information regarding the environmental and economic effects of these actions. Many companies struggle to justify investments in more sustainable practices when the benefits are perceived as indirect or intangible.

Another obstacle in implementing green logistics in reverse logistics lies in the relative scale and visibility of reverse logistics expenses compared to those of forward logistics and manufacturing. The expenses associated with reverse logistics are often smaller and less noticeable within the larger context of a company's operations. This lack of visibility can lead to less priority and fewer resources being allocated to optimizing and greening reverse logistics processes, even though they are crucial for a more sustainable and efficient supply chain management.

For instance, in a 2021 Adidas environmental footprint analysis, only 3.3 percent of the environmental impact was related to end-of-life treatments of products.[14] As a result, a larger push from a chief sustainability officer may be on the manufacturing, assembly, or transportation process than recycling due to the limited impact Adidas is able to report on end-of-life management.

In chapter 4, we will explore the **new-equipment product curve** and the used-equipment product curve. The high-level concept is that products that are sold will not be returned in the same volume because customers will choose to keep products and dispose of them themselves and they will dispose of products differently as time passes. It is easy to understand a company that has a 7 percent initial return rate will spend more effort managing impacts to forward logistics than reverse because most of the financial and environmental resources are consumed by making a product and distributing it to the first customer.

Green Logistics, being a relatively recent practice, often involves financial commitments that may not initially strike as appealing. For instance, transitioning from a fleet of gasoline vehicles to electric ones might be **eco-friendly**, but the upfront costs can be daunting. Similarly, choosing biodegradable packaging, though environmentally sound, might be costlier and warrants thoughtful deliberation.

Understanding the interplay between various desired outcomes as they relate to green logistics is important. Adopting practices like alternative fuels may initially increase reverse logistics costs, potentially impacting cost management, but in the circular economy, integrating reverse logistics can enhance both profitability and environmental friendliness in the long run. Moreover, a sustainable approach aligns with the preferences of a new generation of consumers ready to pay more for eco-friendly products.[15] Despite initial expenses, implementing reverse logistics is essential for achieving sales-enablement, cost prevention, and sustainability goals.

2.5 Desired Outcome 4: *Circular Economy*

Overview of the Circular Economy

The circular economy is the fourth desired outcome of reverse logistics. Instead of aiming to reduce returns, the circular economy stimulates more returns to encourage reuse and cultivate a positive outlook on returns. While many companies express a desire to be environmentally responsible, actualizing this goal proves challenging. A common hurdle is figuring out where to begin and how to develop a model that effectively integrates the financial aspects of their reverse logistics requirements.[16] Reverse logistics teams play a pivotal role in achieving the fourth desired outcome of reverse logistics. Reverse logistics involves recollecting, refurbishing, and redistributing the product to the next customer, thereby forging a **closed-loop system**, which reduces waste, extends the product's lifecycle, and potentially reveals new revenue avenues by tapping into new customer demographics.

The optimal outcome of a reverse logistics process can be thought of as the integration of returned goods back into forward logistics, thus realizing the circular economy's goals. This dynamic approach focuses on maximizing the lifespan and utility of products and materials and eliminating waste, thus aligning economic operations with environmental sustainability.

Difference between Green Logistics and Circular Economy in Reverse

The term "circularity" boasts over a hundred definitions, leading to varied interpretations across different audiences.[17] The absence of a universally recognized definition for the circular economy has seen numerous organizations striving to embrace its principles. Consequently, there's a frequent overlap or confusion between green logistics and circular economy strategies.

Though both share the overarching aim of minimizing environmental harm and endorsing sustainability, they fundamentally serve distinct purposes. While green logistics is centered on reducing environmental footprints, the circular economy's ambition lies in extending an item's lifecycle. Highlighting their individual emphases and their role in the context of ESG metrics will provide clearer guidance.

Recycling is a key aspect of green logistics, which involves the breakdown of a product into its core components, such as plastics and metals, that can then be reused to create new products by any company. Closed-loop recycling is an example of a circular economy approach that takes this process a step further by creating a circular system within a single company. This system involves recycling the components of an old product to create a new one within the same company. It is an intentional process, one that requires careful consideration during the design and manufacturing stages to meet specific aesthetic and performance standards.

For example, some materials such as rubber or plastic can be challenging to color match once they have been dyed. Thus, the design process must consider such factors. Designers might select a color shade that can be reused across multiple products or choose materials that can be effectively broken down and recycled.

In this way, closed-loop recycling allows companies to reduce waste, conserve resources, and decrease the environmental impact of their products. Reverse logistics teams, which are responsible for facilitating the movement of products from the customer back to the recycling point, ensure the smooth conduct of closed-loop operations.

Nike's Eco-Innovation: Transforming Waste into Opportunity with Nike Grind

Nike, like many large corporations, was confronted with significant challenges related to waste and sustainability, many of which were connected to both their brand image and practical manufacturing concerns. Specifically, Nike was facing two main challenges: the high volume of waste from used and discarded products, and the difficulty in replicating specific color shades in rubber components during the recycling process.[18]

The first challenge was dealing with the massive number of shoes that were discarded every year, contributing to environmental waste and negatively impacting Nike's brand image. This waste was not only harmful to the environment but also represented a lost opportunity for recycling and reutilizing valuable materials.

The second challenge was related to the color consistency of recycled materials, particularly rubber components. During the recycling process, shoes of various colors were mixed, resulting in uneven shades that were difficult to control and replicate. Rather than being seen as a flaw, however, Nike decided to embrace this as an opportunity for innovation.

Nike addressed these challenges through a closed-loop recycling operation, which resulted in the development of Nike Grind: a product made from used shoes and manufacturing waste that would otherwise be discarded.

Nike Grind takes the mixed colors and materials from recycled shoes and apparel (i.e., manufacturing scraps), then transforms them into a new product. The resulting mix of colors is seen as a feature, not a bug, and is celebrated in the new product line. Nike Grind is utilized in a variety of applications from track surfaces and carpet mats to furniture and even new sneakers.

For example, the Space Hippie and Ari Zoom SuperRep 2 shoe models utilize Nike Grind in its sole. This means that every sole has a unique mix of colors from the recycled material, making each shoe unique. This makes for not just a distinctive product, but a revenue-generating product effectively made from recycling waste material.[19]

Nike Grind

Figure 2.5. The Nike Air Zoom SuperRep 2 shoe is manufactured with at least 20 percent recycled material including Nike Grind .

This approach has resulted in several significant benefits for Nike. First, it has helped reduce manufacturing costs by reusing materials that would otherwise be discarded. Second, it has introduced new revenue streams, with Nike being able to sell products in categories one might not typically associate with a shoe company, such as carpet padding. Third, it has reduced the company's environmental impact and improved its brand image by showing a commitment to sustainability and innovation.

Nike has established a network of donation centers across the country, providing a convenient avenue for customers to responsibly dispose of their unwanted items. These centers can be easily located via the "Nike Sustainability" webpage. When customers drop off their items at these locations, the products are gathered and transported to a returns processing center via a systematic reverse logistics process. Here, the items are either transformed into products like Nike Grind, taking a new lease of life, or responsibly recycled using other environmentally friendly methods.[20]

Nike's approach to these challenges illustrates the potential of closed-loop recycling. Not only can it address significant environmental concerns, but it can also create opportunities for cost reduction, innovation, and new revenue streams. As of June 2023, over 140 million pounds of shoes have been recycled into products via the Nike Grind system since it began in 1992.[21]

The "Economics" of a Circular Economy

The circular economy is, at its core, an economic model in which resources are used, reused, and recycled in a closed loop, minimizing the use of new raw materials, and reducing waste and pollution. Manufacturers and wholesalers may choose not to participate in the secondary market because they may not have developed the necessary accounting methodologies to understand the return on investment. However, there may be other reasons why companies are hesitant to participate in the secondary market, including concerns about **cannibalization** and the desire to move toward a true circular economy.

By not participating in the secondary market, manufacturers and wholesalers are allowing it to grow despite their efforts. They are in the best position to control the secondary market but are very limited in their ability to destroy it. Therefore, the best corporate strategy for products with residual value is to be the best in the market, rather than trying to fight back the tide.

While there may be concerns about cannibalization and the desire to move toward a circular economy, there are several advantages to participating in the secondary market, including the **cash-to-cash cycle** and the intelligence that can be gained about where used products are going. By leveraging the residual value effect and using strong brands to compete in lower-tier markets, manufacturers and wholesalers can expand their customer base, grow their install base, and strengthen their market position.

Ellen MacArthur: Championing the Circular Economy and Influencing Global Sustainability Practices

New champions have emerged to advance the concept of the circular economy, with Ellen MacArthur standing out as a notable figure. MacArthur, known for setting the record as the fastest person to sail solo around the world in 2005, witnessed extensive oceanic waste during her journey.[22] This experience prompted her to establish the Ellen MacArthur Foundation in 2010, marking her transition from a record-breaking sailor to a pioneering advocate for the circular economy as she searched for a solution.[23]

By 2012, MacArthur had made significant strides in promoting this concept. She published a report for the World Economic Forum titled "Towards the Circular Economy Vol. 1: An Economic and Business Rationale for an Accelerated Transition." This publication presented case studies and concepts, arguing that a subset of the EU manufacturing sector could achieve net material cost savings worth up to US$630 billion annually by 2025.[24] The idea was that the circular economy would stimulate activities in product development, remanufacturing, and refurbishment.

In the years following the report, the Ellen MacArthur Foundation has grown to be recognized as an authoritative organization in developing circular economy programs. The foundation holds a significant influence in discussions with global government leaders and is a key participant at major conferences, including the annual World Economic Forum. The foundation advocates for expanding the technical cycle of a device to keep it in use for as long as possible, as this is far less damaging to the environment than recycling or manufacturing a new one.[25] The Ellen MacArthur Foundation's initiatives and insights have become instrumental in shaping global perspectives on sustainable economic practices.

Competition for Product in a Circular Economy

Notably, in the circular economy, customers often have the upper hand. They have the ability to list and sell products at their convenience and are likely to choose the most beneficial return point for them, regardless of corporate policies or brand protection concerns. Consequently, in a circular economy, companies must compete for product returns. For instance, Apple (a manufacturer) and Verizon (a distributor) both operate their own trade-in programs, intending to buy back a device and sell it at a higher value. Yet, these two Fortune 50 companies compete against other entities like Eco-ATM, eBay, and social media marketplaces that enable peer-to-peer selling, which offer alternative methods for customers to extract value and generate revenue by matching Product One to the next customer.

Competing for customer returns may be a novel concept for many businesses, but it is an established practice in industries like automotive. Purchasing a new car at the Lexus dealership does not mean that the customer will sell their car back to them. These industries offer not only programs to provide financial incentives for vehicle returns but also specific financing and warranty options for customers seeking used products. Highly valuable and highly durable products are ideal for a circular economy.

It is important to note that customers will only participate in reclamation programs if they offer value. If the offer to return is not greater than what the customer can get from another outlet, such as a reseller or secondary market, they will choose the highest-priced option. In other words, customers often care more about their own financial benefit when they participate in the circular economy than they do about a manufacturer's fear of cannibalization. An example in the automotive industry would be a consumer deciding to trade or sell their old car, caring more about the value they receive than who made or sold the car in the first place. This preference underscores that in the circular economy, customers prioritize their financial interests over manufacturers' concerns.

Embracing the Circular Economy: Cisco's Innovative Journey in Sustainable

Revelations of the Circular Economy

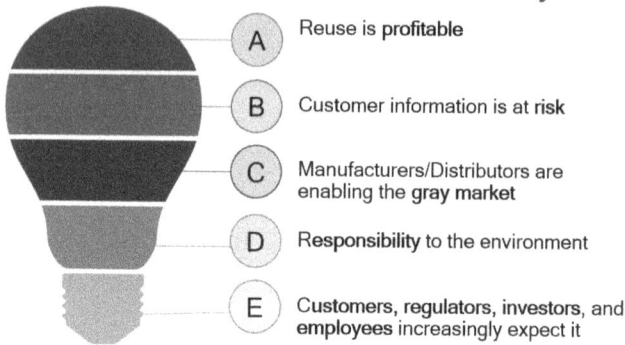

A — Reuse is profitable

B — Customer information is at risk

C — Manufacturers/Distributors are enabling the gray market

D — Responsibility to the environment

E — Customers, regulators, investors, and employees increasingly expect it

Figure 2.6. The "Lightbulb Moment" shows key moments of corporate understanding the circular economy.

The realization that promoting reuse is profitable has been a "lightbulb moment" for many manufacturers and distributors in recent years. As companies have become more aware of the environmental, financial, and reputational benefits of promoting circular economy practices, they have begun to recognize the opportunities that exist in the secondary market. The truth is that even if the company does not provide the venue for returns, customers will find value where it is available.[26]

The lightbulb moment for many manufacturers and distributors is the realization that promoting reuse and circular economy practices is not only the right thing to do, but also the financially prudent thing to do. By addressing the challenges associated with data security and working to promote reuse, companies can reap the benefits of circular economy practices and achieve their goals of reducing waste, enhancing sustainability, and maximizing profitability.

Chuck Robbins, CEO of Cisco, understood the power of the circular economy, and in 2018, he made a 100 percent product return pledge at the World Economic Forum to demonstrate his commitment to promoting sustainability and minimizing waste. Under this pledge, Cisco committed to providing its customers with an easy way to return 100 percent of their products at no charge anywhere in the world.

To execute its commitment to sustainability, Cisco has implemented initiatives that encourage the return of products by offering economic incentives and promoting the reuse of these products. When products are returned, Cisco is dedicated to implementing a closed-loop system, which involves using materials from previously used products in the manufacturing of new ones. A prime example is the development of models in Cisco's popular 8800 series IP phones, which are made using 100 percent post-consumer recycled (PCR) resin.[27] By recycling plastics from old Cisco devices, the company can repurpose these materials as part of the feedstock for new Cisco products. Additionally, Cisco has introduced the Return to A-Stock (R2A) program, which directs unused products from their reverse logistics centers back to contracted manufacturing sites for reuse. Products that are returned as "new in-box" undergo testing and, if necessary, reconfiguration. This process not only enhances the reuse of products but also meets the demand for new equipment without the need for new manufacturing. This innovative approach marks a significant milestone for Cisco and is expected to reduce the use of virgin plastic by over 3 million pounds annually, demonstrating a strong commitment to environmental sustainability and efficient resource utilization.[28]

The 100 percent Product Return Pledge by Chuck Robbins and Cisco is a great example of the positive impact that companies can have on the circular economy by making a commitment to sustainability and promoting reuse. It demonstrates the power of leadership and the important role that companies can play in driving change and accelerating the transition to a more sustainable, circular economy.

Figure 2.7. "Cisco Capital Equipment Pledge" taken from Cisco's Returns Portal for sending back no cost pick up items.

2.6 New Revenue Streams Enabled by the Circular Economy

The circular economy presents a wealth of opportunities for businesses to create new revenue streams. By redefining the life cycle of their products and services, companies can engineer solutions that prolong the utility of their goods and facilitate the handover from one consumer to another. This section delves into the diverse strategies that companies can employ, guided by the circular economy principles illustrated in the image in Figure 2.8.

These elements interlock, much like a jigsaw puzzle, to form an integrated approach that amplifies the value derived from products across successive periods of ownership, thus generating supplementary revenue and endorsing sustainable commerce.

Incremental Circular Economy Revenue Puzzle Pieces

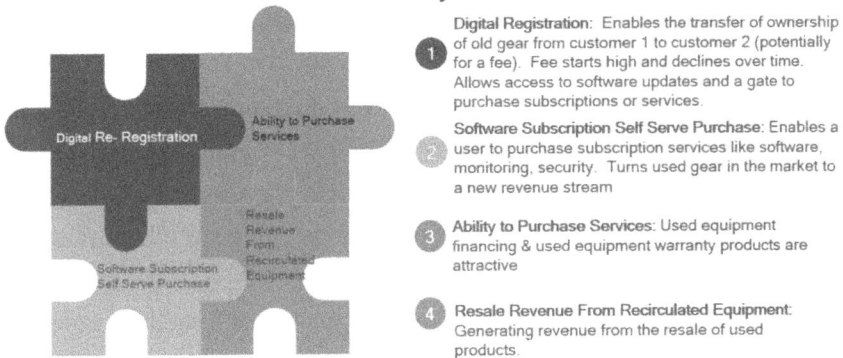

1 Digital Registration: Enables the transfer of ownership of old gear from customer 1 to customer 2 (potentially for a fee). Fee starts high and declines over time. Allows access to software updates and a gate to purchase subscriptions or services.

2 Software Subscription Self Serve Purchase: Enables a user to purchase subscription services like software, monitoring, security. Turns used gear in the market to a new revenue stream

3 Ability to Purchase Services: Used equipment financing & used equipment warranty products are attractive

4 Resale Revenue From Recirculated Equipment: Generating revenue from the resale of used products.

Figure 2.8. Four complementary revenue opportunities that exist for organizations that sell products and services in a circular economy.

The sale of used equipment in a company offering a mix of hardware and software services can be measured in four buckets, which are as follows:

1. **Digital Registration**. The transfer of ownership of the used equipment can be monetized and provides the company with information about where the used equipment is going, which can help them target products and services to potential customers.

2. Moreover, the ability to reregister used equipment enables companies to gather valuable data about their customers'

behavior and preferences. This data can be used to better understand customer needs and develop new products and services that cater to those needs, thus expanding the company's customer base.

3. The transfer of ownership and the ability to reregister used equipment are powerful tools for companies in the circular economy. This service can also be sold to customers as license to access products and services.[29] By embracing these strategies, companies can not only generate new revenue streams but also increase their customer base while building a more sustainable and loyal customer base.

4. **Software or Subscription Services**. Used equipment often comes with access to software or network subscription fees. These fees for programs, cellular service, applications, or other subscription-based services can be attractive to both new and used customers. Once a product is reregistered, purchasing other services is a smart strategy.

5. **Warranty or Financial Products**: Just like the used car industry, used equipment can be sold with abbreviated warranties that offer lower coverage or **same-unit repair** options. An extended return policy may also be acceptable, and financing for both used and new products is possible.

6. **Resale Revenue from Recirculated Equipment.** This revenue can take place in a variety of functional or cosmetic conditions and through different sales channels like certified pre-owned (all cosmetic conditions), wholesale channels, or through e-commerce.

7. Each of these four buckets represents a different strategy for selling used equipment, and companies must determine which approach works best for them. By understanding the different value propositions of each strategy, companies can maximize their revenue potential from used-equipment sales.

Assessing the Secondary Market Value

The easiest way to begin assessing the secondary market value is to analyze prior new sales in order to estimate the anticipated market size. As mentioned earlier, the success of the product's initial customer directly reflects the market for Customer Two+. Additionally, it is important to recognize that the value of a product typically diminishes over time, while services such as customer support, financing, and warranty tend to retain more stability in the long run. By combining all the tangible benefits of revenue-generating activities with Customer Two, we can complement the intangible benefits like increasing upgrade cycles or encouraging higher-value purchases, which are not as straightforward to establish a direct correlation with.

Cisco's Revenue Breakout

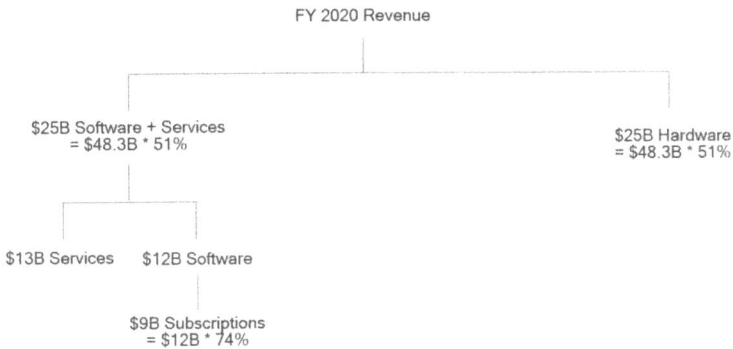

FY 2020 Revenue

$25B Software + Services
= $48.3B * 51%

$25B Hardware
= $48.3B * 51%

$13B Services $12B Software

$9B Subscriptions
= $12B * 74%

Figure 2.9. Forward-looking secondary opportunity based upon published financial results from Cisco in FY20.

In 2020, Cisco recorded approximately $50 billion in revenue, consisting of $25 billion from hardware sales, $13 billion from services and warranty, and $12 billion from software.

Regarding hardware, it is expected that the second period of used equipment (S2) would be valued at less than $25 billion, as customers typically anticipate a lower price for used products. The resale value of equipment is influenced by its condition, with fully refurbished items commanding higher prices compared to those with cosmetic or functional imperfections.

Concerning services and warranty, the cost of recirculating a used product will be higher if it requires full restoration or comes with a comprehensive warranty. However, customers might be willing to pay a reduced price for items with limited warranty or repair options, thereby lowering the cost of recirculation. Consequently, the revenue generated from the warranty for used products should be lower than that of new products.

A conservative estimate suggests that used network gear retains only 10 percent of its original value after a certain period of use or when sold in the secondary market. Hence, if the market value of new Cisco equipment was $25 billion, a conservative target for the value of used equipment would be $2.5 billion when it is no longer desired.

Consequently, businesses and organizations aiming to sell used Cisco equipment should strive to generate $2.5 billion in incremental revenue through secondary market sales. It is important to note that this estimate is conservative, and actual values may vary based on factors such as equipment age, condition, market demand, and technological advancements in the industry.

In addition to potential revenue from selling used network gear, there are opportunities to generate revenue by offering services and software to customers using the used equipment. Leveraging the used equipment to expand the installation base of active users enables businesses and organizations to increase the potential market for their services and software. For instance, customers purchasing used Cisco equipment may also be interested in acquiring software subscriptions or support services compatible with the equipment.

This represents additional potential beyond the conservative estimate of 10 percent residual value for used network gear. By leveraging the used equipment to sell services and software, businesses and organizations can potentially generate revenue that surpasses the initial estimate for used equipment sales.

2.7 The Circular Economy Struggle

The **Cannibalization Effect** refers to the belief that promoting the reuse of returned products may lead to a decrease in the sales of new products, as customers may opt to buy the used product instead. Manufacturers are hesitant to promote reuse because they fear that a used product may compete with their new product and reduce their sales. The **Resale Value Effect** is the opposite of the Cannibalization Effect. It considers the potential benefits for the manufacturer of promoting the reuse of returned products. These benefits include the ability to generate additional software or warranty revenue, leverage the residual value of the product to drive future purchases, and sell the same product to another customer.

The resistance to returns and the fear of returned devices being resold as a threat to new sales have impeded the adoption of the circular economy by many companies. Industries like the mobility industry initially believed that customers only wanted like-new warranty devices and overlooked the impact of the internet in connecting used supply with used demand. But as customers sought value and both retailers and manufacturers sought to minimize returns, customers started to sell devices to each other through online marketplaces like eBay, Craigslist, and Facebook pages.

Carriers were the first to offer trade-in services, outpacing manufacturers like Apple and Samsung. To date, Verizon is the only carrier offering the sale of devices in various conditions on their website, while others continue to sell only like-new devices through direct channels. These fears and resistance to returns have hindered the development of the circular economy and prevented companies from fully realizing the benefits of a closed-loop system.

The Struggle

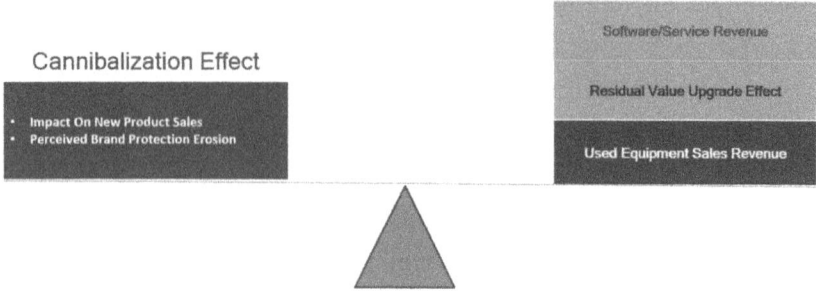

Cannibalization Effect

- **Impact On New Product Sales**
- **Perceived Brand Protection Erosion**

Software/Service Revenue

Residual Value Upgrade Effect

Used Equipment Sales Revenue

Figure 2.10. Illustration of the fear of the Cannibalization Effect versus the Resale Value Effect.

Overcoming the fear of cannibalization is a daunting task because it often relies on soft measurements. The difficulty in directly linking a customer's preference for used rather than new products, due to fragmented data across platforms, fuels cannibalization concerns. These concerns can be alleviated by leveraging the circular economy's advantage, which enhances new product sales through the residual value of used items and opens new prospects for sales teams with subsequent owners. This collaborative approach can eclipse the fear of market cannibalization.

The four elements of incremental circular revenue yield concrete data on the financial upsides of relicensing, servicing, and reselling of used products. Another benefit is the **Residual Value Upgrade Effect**, where a trade-in adds value to a customer's purchase, encouraging further investment, similar to a higher vehicle trade-in prompting the acquisition of a new model. Although correlating trade-ins with subsequent purchases can help quantify spending patterns, establishing this connection through direct customer feedback for every sale is often not practical enough to produce concrete data.

Without access to secondary market data, manufacturers and retailers may develop a confirmation bias, believing the market for used equipment is negligible or nonexistent. In chapter 6: The Secrets of the Secondary Market, we will explore how the secondary market evolves despite company hesitations.

2.8 Circular Economy Reuse Case Study One: *Verizon's Trade-In Program Launch*

Verizon's Trade-In Program Launch: Pioneers in the Mobile Circular Economy

In 2011, Verizon Wireless, a leading US mobility carrier, started phasing out its retention program, New Every Two. This program gave customers a $100 discount on their next phone in return for a new two-year agreement. At that time, phone subsidies were the norm; carriers like Verizon would buy devices from manufacturers such as Apple, Samsung, Motorola, and LG at full price, and offer them to customers at a substantial discount, making up for the cost through the monthly service revenue for voice and data services. Customers were conditioned to expect promotions like "Buy one, get four free!", and the US consumer was not accustomed to purchasing a phone—just agreeing to a service contract.

However, the 2010 launch of the iPhone 4 significantly altered the landscape.[30] The iPhone 4, with its more costly components such as the LCD screen, and a more complex assembly, was much more expensive than other smartphones, like the easily disassembled Blackberry. This cost increase led carriers like Verizon to rethink their subsidy and retention programs. As a result, Verizon started exploring new ways to incentivize customers to renew their contracts or switch from other service providers.

The iPhone's introduction had a dual effect: it placed significant financial strain on Verizon due to the high upfront cost of purchasing the device to sell it subsidized, and it also introduced a device with significant residual value. Apple's successful marketing campaigns led to customers queuing up to buy the latest model, leaving behind older but still valuable devices, often in a drawer. This scenario provided an opportunity for Verizon to utilize the residual value of the customer's old device toward their next purchase.

By the time the iPhone 4S was set to launch in the fall of 2011, Verizon was preparing to phase out the New Every Two program. The company, spread across twenty-one different US regions, began a partnership with a recycling firm in one of these regions. This program was designed to buy back customers' devices, apply the device's value to the next purchase, and receive a commission on each returned device when it was sent by the stores to their partner's centralized return center.

Although the concept of the trade-in program made sense, the idea still faced resistance within Verizon. The primary hurdles were:

- **Financial Accounting Obstacles**. The conventional belief was that returns were negative, with no accounting system or point-of-sale systems in place to manage buying back products.
- **Cannibalization Fear**. As an Apple distributor, Verizon was concerned that Apple would not approve of a program to reintroduce used devices due to the potential cannibalization of new sales.
- **Reverse Logistics**. The process involved six distinct steps, from appraising the device, providing customers with gift cards, shipping the device, inspection by their partner recycling firm, and finally, payment issuance to Verizon. The store transaction time increased by two to four minutes and introduced complexity for trade in transactions.

The success of the program was evident, stemming from the sales team's straightforward approach that asked customers, "What are you doing with your old device?" This led to customers receiving more value from their old devices, which the sales team used to promote additional products and services, growing sales and establishing a new revenue stream from the returned equipment. In a regional review later that year, the district managers from the trial areas where the trade-in program was active were ranked first and second in major sales key performance indicators. Conversely, district managers from the other thirteen districts voiced concerns about their inability to match such performance due to the lack of a similar program.

Prior to the launch of the iPhone 4S, the trial region had already implemented the trade-in program across all its locations. Being one of twenty-one, the trial region showcased a substantial increase in revenue and sales attachment rates for all devices, especially the iPhone 4S, which were presented to senior leadership during an area review. The impressive results encouraged Verizon to expand the retail trade-in program to all its retail locations.

Significantly, the Verizon trade-in program originated from a sales channel aiming to capitalize on the residual value of devices to boost sales rather than being a product of the supply chain channel typically in charge of logistics. However, the program's triumph hinged on a strong reverse logistics process, incorporating all **four desired outcomes of reverse logistics**. This highlights the dynamic interplay between sales and logistics, demonstrating how such collaborative efforts can develop programs like trade-ins and bring them to the market to generate new opportunities and revenue streams.

iPhone 4S Reuse Case

From its inception in 2011 to 2016, Verizon's retail trade-in program witnessed substantial success. As revenues linked to traded-in devices grew, Verizon saw the opportunity to insource the trade-in program, transitioning from its partnership with the aforementioned recycling firm. The new arrangement allowed Verizon to receive traded-in devices via local stores, business-to-business channels, and online platforms at their CRTC for value generation.

By 2016, Verizon's used equipment business was projected to surpass $1 billion in revenue just as Apple prepared to launch its iPhone 7. During this period, Verizon faced the dilemma of the cannibalization effect of traded-in devices on their partners' brands versus the immense value being generated from the program through the resale of equipment and corresponding up sales taking place. Each iPhone release brought enhanced features such as better durability, improved cameras, voice digital assistants, mobile pay, and higher price tags, maintaining the financial balance on Verizon's books while extending the useful lifecycle of their equipment.

Simultaneously, Verizon shifted its strategy from offering devices to customers at a subsidized discount to financing the device's purchase price via monthly installments. This model allowed customers to upgrade after a year, trading in their used device, which Verizon capitalized on due to its residual value. This method helped maintain Verizon's contractual relationships with customers while also yielding a profit. This achievement was possible due to Verizon's capacity to sell used devices in global markets, straining relations with their supplier, Apple, until the latter identified the benefits of this strategy.

In August 2016, with the world waiting in anticipation for the launch of the iPhone 7, a mobile retail provider on the tropical island of Aruba had a different plan. They took the unusual step of launching a device that was already considered "old" in some markets: the iPhone 4S.[31] This was the very device that Verizon was preparing to roll out when they first piloted their trade-in program, but five years later, that product was no longer new—it was approaching new minus 5 models (n–5).

In the US, as the allure of the iPhone 4S waned and consumers coveted newer models, the 4S was becoming one of the top traded-in devices. Nevertheless, the US market's shift toward the latest gadgets did not dim the demand for the iPhone 4S elsewhere. In other parts of the globe, and even within certain niches in the US, the iPhone 4S maintained a robust demand as a used device.

The release of the iPhone 4S in Aruba was met with overwhelming excitement. Enthusiastic customers formed a queue that wound its way out the store's doors and stretched down the block. Noticeably absent was the presence of Apple's corporate entity, as they were concentrating their efforts on the launch of their new product in fresh market territories.

- iPhone 7 Launched 1 months later
- 0% of these customers were going to buy a 7
- 100% of these customers got an iTunes account
- Catalog values for the 4s increased as demand rose
- Catalog values/ trade in rate rose
- Trade rate & value drove incremental sales

iPhone 4S Launch Aruba - Aug 2016 Case Study

Fig 2.11. Images taken from a drone during the launch of the iPhone 4S on launch day in Aruba.

The simple truth was that those standing in the enthusiastic Aruba queue had no desire to purchase the yet-to-launch iPhone 7—it was simply too pricey and not available at that time. Their hearts were set on the "new" arrival, the iPhone 4S, demonstrating the significant appeal that a well-positioned "old" device could still hold in the right market.[32]

To activate an iPhone, customers had to register their details, including credit card information, on the iTunes platform. This resulted in additional revenue for Apple from purchases made through the platform, even from regions they were not actively selling devices to. This secondary market led to competition among Verizon's customers, such as Mio Mobile, for used-equipment supply. As demand grew, the value of used iPhone 4S devices rose, enabling Verizon to increase their catalog values for these devices, leading to increased trade-in value for customers and additional revenue for Verizon.

Every year, stores like Mio Mobile migrated to the next used device in the Apple sales cycle, effectively competing with sales of competitor products like Huawei. This competition occurred not because Apple encouraged trade-ins, but because of the market's demand and Verizon's attempts to match demand with used supply.

By January 2019, Apple CEO Tim Cook had highlighted the benefits of device trade-ins in a letter to investors. According to Cook, the simplicity of trading in a phone, financing it over time, and facilitating data transfer not only benefited the environment and customer but also helped grow Apple's installed base.

Apples Action Plan to Drive Revenue

"One such initiative is making it simple to trade in a phone in our stores, finance the purchase over time, and get help transferring data from the current to the new phone. This is not only great for the environment, it is great for the customer, as their existing phone acts as a subsidy for their new phone, and it is great for developers, as it can help grow our installed base."

Letter To Investors Jan 02, 2019

Figure 2.12. Quote from Tim Cook in 2019 from his letter to investors explaining Apple's plan for Q1.

The success of the iPhone 4S and the corresponding upgrade cycle offers a valuable case study in overcoming the cannibalization effect and the incremental advantages of a circular economy. Both Apple and Verizon succeeded by making it easy for customers to digitally re-register on iTunes, generating revenue through software and application sales, modifying extended-warranty programs to account for used devices, and leveraging the residual value of old devices for profit.

Ultimately, the case of the two companies highlights the power of the circular economy in modern business. Even industries that do not have an apparent residual value, like fashion apparel, are exploring similar models. This case study is also an illustration of how an intentional strategy of building markets for Customer Two+ can help businesses grow their consumer base in nontraditional ways.

The strategy itself is deceptively simple, yet its execution is quite intricate. Here is a more comprehensive breakdown of the process explored in the case study:

1. Provide customers with a fair price for their outdated equipment. This requires an understanding of how to buy at a low cost, sell at a high price, and liquidate all acquisitions before they depreciate.

2. Motivate customers to utilize this value to upgrade from Product One to Product Two+.

3. Facilitate the **re-registration** of old equipment to the next customer (Customer Two+). Implement a self-service system, like iTunes, that customers can subscribe and pay for.

4. Repurpose that technology for Customer Two+, which expands the user base and generates subscription revenue from older equipment.

5. Establish growth desired outcome for the Customer Two+ market and ensure the sustainability of Product One.

6. Claim credit for contributing to environmental sustainability by recycling old devices.

Mobility Use Case Summary

Nearly two years later, this initiative was in full effect. Apple, in the week of October 17, 2020, introduced newer models with a higher price tags than the previous year's models. According to a report by CNN, Apple offered up to $500 off the purchase of an iPhone 12 in exchange for an old smartphone, depending on its age and condition.[33]

Apple can provide this value because they comprehend three vital aspects of the secondary market:

1. They understand the worth of older models. They have a process for buying low and selling high. While not every model fetches $500, even older models retain some value.

2. They factor potential software and service value for Customer Two+ into their offer. Apple earns 30 percent of all software revenue generated on their platform, and every customer must register with a payment method to utilize their phone.[34]

3. They are prepared to offer a certain discount to encourage a customer to upgrade their phone.

Apple combines all three benefits into a single customer-oriented offer to maximize both the perception of value and their own benefits.

Apple demonstrates their understanding of how to purchase old phones at a lower cost, potentially refurbish, and sell them at a higher price. They understand the revenue potential with the next customer and the business logic of facilitating both the customer's upgrade and the reuse of the old device by the next customer. The latter may not be able to afford a new Apple device, but they can certainly afford the older one. Apple's business model capitalizes on both, and it is proving to be successful.

Chapter 3

The Three Fundamentals of Reverse Logistics

3.1 Overview of Reverse Logistics Fundamentals

This chapter moves from discussing the varied expectations placed on reverse logistics teams to the specific logistical steps required to process products effectively, in line with current reverse logistics best practices. We explore the product journey, a concept that traces a product's route from its point of use, through reverse logistics processes, and on to its next destination.[1] We will delve into the various stages of this journey, spotlighting the crucial steps and strategies that enable efficient product transitions, all while maintaining cost-effectiveness. The journey of the product is fundamentally shaped by the decisions and actions of reverse logistics teams in moving items from one point to another to achieve their organization's desired outcomes.

Transitioning from Desired Outcomes to Logistics

The four desired outcomes of reverse logistics encapsulate the specific results a company expects to achieve through its sales-enablement programs, which serve as the cornerstone for reverse logistics operations. This chapter delves into the diverse logistical capabilities that companies can utilize to succeed.

The central components of reverse logistics operations can be streamlined into three key steps of the returns process.

1. **Asset recovery**. This involves coordinating the physical and systemic process of returning a product to a designated location.
2. **Reverse operations.** This includes processes such as packaging, transportation, **receiving**, sorting, **data erasure**, testing, grading, storage, repair, quality control, kitting, picking, and shipping.
3. **Value generation**. This involves deciding whether a product can be redeployed for value or disposed of responsibly.

Depending on where an organization exists in the supply chain, these fundamentals may require modification based on the type of return activity. For example, a manufacturer who sells to a distributor/retailer who receives large returns shipped in pallets will have different operational requirements than a retailer who receives returns in small quantities from customers. Manufacturers may need to engage in more re-kitting, repair operations, and generate value in bulk, while retailers may accumulate returns and generate value by simply returning the product to vendors. Regardless of the method, companies can also count on customers to always expect to receive maximum value from their returns.

Crafting a Framework for Efficient Reverse Logistics

Given the company's objectives of assert recovery, reverse operations, and value generation, it is imperative that each return process is meticulously structured to facilitate the seamless movement of products, establishing a sequential flow of information and goods vital for completing a transaction. To facilitate this movement, a few key considerations need to be evaluated.

Element 1: Standardizing the process. The initial phase of any returns process is to establish a standardized procedure based on the customer promise, which involves identifying the necessary information to fulfill the return according to the customer promise.

Key aspects include determining the product being returned, its value, how the customer will receive the benefit, and the expected outcomes if the customer fails to fulfill their part of the deal, such as returning the wrong product or missing the specified timeframe. Based on these expectations, a standardized data table can be constructed to facilitate the integration of **pre-inspection** and **post-inspection information**.

Element 2: Developing interface tools to facilitate returns. The second step involves developing **interface tools** that enable the completion of a return. This entails designing the methodology for fulfilling the deal, including capturing information regarding the expected benefit and how the customer can agree to the terms. Additionally, it encompasses creating the necessary shipment information if transportation is part of the customer promise. These interfaces can be either assisted by a representative or self-service, but in either case, the return process commences with data. It is crucial to build these interfaces to be user-friendly, reliable, and straightforward, offering customers convenient options for returning the product.

Element 3: Developing effective business tools and rules. The third and final step in constructing a sales-enablement program involves developing effective business tools and rules to manage the process. These rules include determining a trusted data source, establishing the value associated with the return, creating terms or contracts that clearly communicate expectations to the customer, expressing a commitment to enforce those terms (some companies may opt not to charge for unreturned products or offer no-questions-asked refunds, but accurately identifying returned items is still part of the process), and establishing a communication method for updating internal or external customers on the progress of the return.

Both sales-enablement programs and reverse logistics teams can utilize these steps to enhance their efficiency and efficacy in managing returns.

Optimizing the Return Process: Sequential Flow, Communication, and Analytics for Efficient Operations

Once the essential elements are established, a sequential flow of information can be repeatedly implemented. Let us examine each step:

Step 1: Initiating a return and creating shipment information. This step involves using the interface to initiate a return and generate shipment information. Customers agree on what they are shipping back and specify the expected benefit. The interface facilitates the creation of pre-inspection information, which can be communicated to the next point in the process. Multiple interfaces or return reasons may be utilized, but standardizing the data for the subsequent stages simplifies the overall reverse logistics operation.

Step 2: Communication of data layer to the next delivery point. In this step, the **data layer**, comprising information on the expected return items and their condition, is communicated to the next delivery point. This layer encompasses elements such as RMA numbers, serial numbers, tracking information, RFID characteristics, and customer details. This information aids the receiving operation in matching the received items to the expected order during the operational process.

Step 3: Communication of post-inspection information. The receiving party communicates post-inspection information, which identifies the actual arrival of the products and their condition.

Step 4: Information consumption logic and next steps information. **Information consumption logic** is utilized to determine the subsequent actions in the return process, such as issuing a refund, providing credit, or concluding the transaction while avoiding non-return fees. This logic can also identify any issues and communicate variances to internal or external customers. It serves as a reporting methodology for managing programmatic success. Additionally, if an order lacks return information, a reminder notification can be sent to the customer regarding the pending return. Depending on a company's sales-enablement strategy, reminders may be sent for certain returns, such as trade-ins, while customer guarantee returns may not benefit from reminder notifications if the customer initiated the return and developed an attachment to the product.

Step 5: Analytics. Returns begin and end with data. By leveraging **analytics**, companies can enhance the performance of the return process in alignment with the outcomes identified in the four desired outcomes.

Through these five steps, companies can establish an efficient and effective return process while utilizing data-driven insights to continually improve their operations.

Introducing Key Metrics: Cost to Reuse and Blended Benefit

The operation of returns programs yields a **cost to reuse (CR)**. Within every value-generation channel, there exists a **blended benefit (BB)** specific to each product. The primary goal of the reverse logistics fundamentals is to enhance the value and speed of each product while reducing the costs or achieving the desired outcomes in green logistics, as defined by the four desired outcomes.

The outcome of the comparison between BB and CR dictates the next steps: if BB surpasses CR, products are deemed suitable for reuse. Conversely, if CR exceeds BB, the product should be earmarked for responsible recycling. A more comprehensive understanding of these calculations will be provided in chapter 5 ("Financial Management of Reverse Logistics").

Utilizing Level-One Process Flow and Value-Stream Mapping

A high-level map encompassing asset recovery, operations, and value generation can be developed by aligning **returns-enablement programs**, operations, and value generation capabilities within a **Level One Process Flow** document. A Level One Process Flow document is a fundamental tool used in business process management and engineering. It provides an overarching view of a system or process, depicting the primary stages or functions without delving into detailed tasks or procedures. Each stage or process is typically represented by a box or other shape, and the flow of information or materials is shown with arrows. This allows for a bird's eye view of the entire process, making it easier to identify overarching patterns and trends. Each step within this high-level map can be dissected further to delineate costs and programs in a value stream map. This mapping can be instrumental in identifying opportunities for improvement. The benefits of such a high-level map for planning purposes include the visualization of the entire process, the ability to spot bottlenecks or inefficiencies, and the provision of a shared language to discuss and understand the process. Understanding the options that can be incorporated or removed, such as enabling new programs or value generation channels or altering how or where operations are carried out, can significantly influence both CR and BB.

By manipulating the various factors within this map, companies can proactively shape their reverse logistics strategy. For instance, they can optimize their operations or shift resources to lower the CR, or they can find new ways to increase the BB. In this way, the high-level map becomes an essential tool for strategic planning and continuous improvement in reverse logistics.

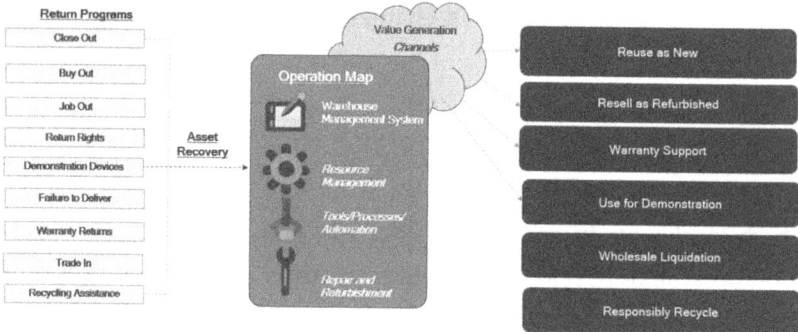

Reverse Flow to a Manufacture Examples

Reverse Logistics Moves a Product FROM Another Point

Figure 3.1. Examples of a manufacturer return process flow.

Reverse Flow from a Customer to a Retailer

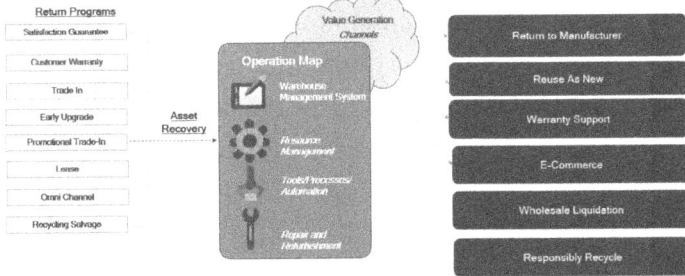

Reverse Logistics Moves a Product FROM Another Point

Figure 3.2. Example of a retail return process flow.

Navigating the Reverse Logistics Journey: From Sales-Enablement to Value Generation

In the process flow map above, you can observe all three core elements at play, starting from the initial sales-enablement programs. As discussed in chapter 2, these programs are responsible for product returns. Each return stream is associated with a specific reason for return, and there is an expected value for the customer to send back the device based on the program's guidelines. The return party must ensure that the correct device is returned in the specified condition and within the designated time frame.

3.2 Fundamental 1: *Asset Recovery*

Initiating and Managing the Returns Process in Asset Recovery

Asset recovery, within reverse logistics, refers to the systematic process of managing the movement of products from the point of return generated from the sales-enablement program to the designated returns processing location.

This process can range from a straightforward drop-off at a local Goodwill through a drop box to a more intricate procedure involving palletizing products and coordinating transportation. In modern asset recovery, the initial step involves inputting data into an interface that acknowledges a customer's intention to return a product and provides an estimated value. Asset recovery teams then monitor the movement of the assets from the collection point to the designated returns processing location. The asset recovery teams play a crucial role as the communication point between logistical operations and customer service teams, specifically in facilitating and troubleshooting returns.

Asset recovery teams also work closely with customer service teams. They provide regular updates on the status of returns, relay any customer feedback or requests, and help resolve any issues that may arise during the return process. By serving as the central communication point, they ensure that information flows smoothly between all parties involved, ultimately enhancing customer satisfaction and streamlining the return experience.

Return Material Authorization

A **return material authorization (RMA)** is a process used by businesses to authorize the return of a product or material to the manufacturer, supplier, or distributor. It is a formalized procedure that ensures the return is properly documented, tracked, and managed.

The RMA process typically involves the following steps:

1. **Request.** The customer or client contacts the supplier or manufacturer to initiate the return process. They provide details about the product, reason for return, and any supporting documentation.

2. **Authorization.** The supplier or manufacturer reviews the request and determines whether the return is eligible. They may consider factors such as warranty status, product condition, and the reason for return. If approved, they issue an RMA number and provide instructions for returning the material.

3. **RMA Number.** The RMA number serves as a unique identifier for the return. It helps in tracking and managing the return throughout the process.

4. **Packaging and Shipping.** The customer packages the material securely, following the instructions provided by the supplier or manufacturer. They may be responsible for covering the shipping costs, or the supplier may provide a prepaid shipping label.

5. **Inspection and Evaluation.** Upon receiving the returned material, the supplier or manufacturer inspects and evaluates its condition. They may check for defects, damages, or any other issues reported by the customer.

6. **Resolution.** Based on the evaluation, the supplier or manufacturer determines the appropriate resolution. This could include repair, replacement, refund, or credit toward future purchases. They communicate the decision to the customer and initiate the necessary actions.

The RMA process ensures that returns are handled efficiently, reducing confusion and streamlining the resolution for both the customer and the supplier or manufacturer. It helps in maintaining customer satisfaction, managing inventory, and identifying potential product issues.

Difference between a Return Material Authorization and Return to Vendor

As with many acronyms used in supply chain processes, the terms return material authorization and **return to vendor (RTV)** are occasionally grouped together despite representing distinct aspects of the overall process.

An RMA acts as an inflow from the purchaser to the originating supplier or vendor. This triggers an inbound order that is then directed toward a return collection center. In the context of an RMA, the customer expects some form of value such as a refund, exchange, or credit from the organization responsible for processing the return.

By contrast, an RTV describes an event where a returned product is transferred from a distributor back to their supplier. This is an action that generates value for the distributor or retailer, as they anticipate receiving a refund, credit, or replacement from the supplier or vendor from whom they originally purchased the product. In this sense, the RTV represents an outflow from the return processing center.

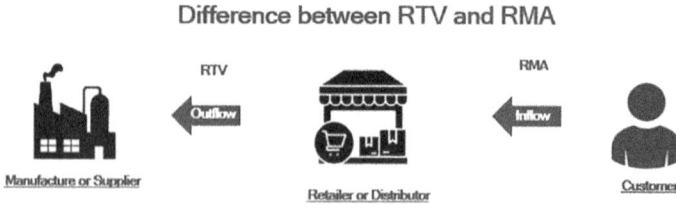

Figure 3.3. RMA is a return source to a collection point, and RTV is an outflow source from a collection point.

Both RMA and RTV relate to return processes within a supply chain, but RMA is an inflow with the customer expecting value from the organization while an RTV is an outflow with the organization expecting value from the original supplier or vendor. We will discuss elements of how an RTV process occurs in Section 3.3, Value Generation.

Managing Disagreements and Communication

A customer, distributor, and manufacturer may disagree on various aspects of a return, leading to friction in the reverse supply chain as opposed to a sales relationship, where promotions and programs are aligned with each other.

- **Condition of the Product.** A customer may claim that the product was defective or damaged, but the distributor or manufacturer may dispute this, leading to a disagreement on the condition of the product being returned.
- **Value of the Product.** The customer, distributor, and manufacturer may have different opinions on the value of the product being returned, leading to disputes over the amount of compensation or refund.

- **Timely Response.** The customer may expect a prompt response to their return request, but the distributor or manufacturer may take longer to process the return, leading to frustration and dissatisfaction on the part of the customer.

These disagreements can result in a breakdown in communication and trust between the parties involved in the reverse supply chain. This is to be expected because interests are not as harmoniously aligned as they are in a sales relationship.

Reverse logistics teams often find themselves answering questions about failed processes, as they are the last group to handle the product, making it a game of logistics hot potato. To ensure that the process works as intended, it is crucial to have a comprehensive understanding of the entire process from start to finish.

Expected and Unexpected Returns

When a customer initiates a return, the goal is to match the returned item to the corresponding order so that the customer's desired outcome can be fulfilled, such as receiving a credit, repair, or replacement. When the returned item can be successfully matched to the order, it is called an expected or identified order. However, when the returned item cannot be matched to an order, it is called an unexpected or unidentified order.

It is a common occurrence when what a customer intends to return does not match the expected order. Consider an example where a customer buys a Samsung LCD monitor from Amazon and desires to return it. A return order is created, and the customer is expected to send the product back in the mail for credit. In this case, the customer is provided a tracking number, a return order, and the serial number of the product ordered is captured electronically.

When the product arrives back to the return center, a floor operator must be able to successfully match the item received to that order. Order accuracy is a specific task that is repeated over and over in these types of processing operations. Variations can exist from operator to operator, and statistical process controls can help identify deviations that lead to inefficiencies.

Dealing with unexpected returns can be costly and time-consuming for businesses. Customers may be seeking a benefit that cannot be provided, leading to dissatisfaction and potentially negative reviews or word of mouth. In addition, businesses must spend more time and resources to resolve issues related to unexpected returns.

To identify orders and prevent unexpected returns, businesses can capture **pre-inspection information** in the return interface. This information may include common fields such as order number, expected benefit, shipment tracking number, serial number, customer name, and customer address.

Businesses can also leverage the shipping label for a return to include customer information and order number, making identification of the returned item easier from the outside of the package. Including a return slip inside the box with the same information can provide redundancy in identifying the order if the shipping label becomes damaged or the customer uses their own shipping label.

While it is important to ensure that the product received matches the customer's order, it is also important not to overengineer the return process and make it too complicated for customers to complete their returns. Customers expect returns to be simple, dependable, and have easy options to complete. Therefore, businesses should aim to strike a balance between identifying orders and making the return process user-friendly for customers.

Happy Path Returns

A **happy path return** refers to a smooth and successful return process where the received product matches the original order and meets the expected condition. It signifies that both the reverse logistics operational center and the customer are satisfied with the transaction. In the happy path scenario, the return is processed without any discrepancies or issues, allowing the transaction to be closed. This outcome benefits both the business and the customer, since the product is returned as intended, ensuring customer satisfaction and facilitating the smooth operation of the reverse logistics process.

Discrepant Returns

A **discrepant return** refers to a situation where a product received through the return process does not match the expected product or meet certain conditions. This can include receiving the wrong item, a product in the wrong condition, or a return that exceeds the agreed-upon return window. In reverse logistics, the primary desired outcome is to accurately identify and record what actually has arrived. Each company may have its own policies and procedures for handling these discrepancies.

In addressing discrepant returns, serial-number validation emerges as an important tool in fraud prevention. By verifying the serial number, companies can determine if the returned product matches the one that was initially sold. This is vital for identifying cases where the discrepancy may be due to fraudulent activities, such as returning a different item or an illegitimate product. Effective use of serial number validation can be a key factor in resolving the reasons behind discrepant returns.

Communication methods for handling these situations can vary. Some strategies might involve adjusting the refund amount, rejecting the return and sending it back to the customer, accepting the return as-is and absorbing the loss, or finding alternative solutions based on the specific circumstances. The ultimate goal is to resolve the discrepancy efficiently while considering the impact on customer satisfaction and minimizing friction in the return process.

Best Practices for Managing Multiple Shipments for an RMA

While managing RMA processes, it is common to encounter a significant time gap between the approval of a return material authorization and the actual shipping back of the product. This gap can lead to scenarios where an RMA, initially requested by a customer, is no longer needed. For instance, a retailer or distributor might request an RMA for a stock rotation, aiming to return products that are not selling. However, if they manage to sell these products before initiating the return, the RMA is no longer required, thus avoiding unnecessary returns—a favorable outcome for all parties involved. These situations illustrate how the delay between RMA approval and product return can result in expected return orders being initiated but not received, impacting inventory forecasting and return process management.

When an RMA is created to authorize the return of a product, or a specific quantity of a product, tracking the products linked to that RMA can be challenging, particularly if they are returned across multiple shipments with different tracking numbers. To correctly match the product with its corresponding RMA and ensure the condition and quantity align, individual tracking numbers should be linked to the RMA, alongside detailed information about the shipment's contents.

In essence, an RMA outlines what is approved to be received, whereas an **advanced shipping notice (ASN)** or a **transfer order** is necessary to match the contents of the shipment to a return processing center. For example, if an RMA is approved for 500 items and the customer arranges shipping back, splitting the order into two packages (each containing 250 items with different tracking numbers), identifying any errors or missing items can be difficult if contents and details are not communicated from the customer to the receiving point. If the return processing center is not informed of the exact quantities in each shipment, pinpointing where a mistake occurred becomes a challenge because one RMA may be comprised of multiple transfer orders to be completed.

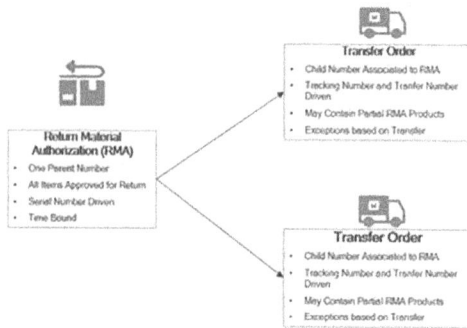

One RMA May have Multiple Transfer Orders Shipped at Different Times

Figure 3.4. Illustration describes the parent-child relationship between approved RMAs and transfer orders.

Implementing systems that use an RMA as a primary identification point and allow for multiple ASNs or tracking numbers can streamline the return process and minimize errors if customers decide to keep products. These systems would require the returning party to clearly specify the contents of each shipment.

Distributors are generally averse to terms stating that a large quantity of items will be purchased and shipped in random increments at unpredictable times without clear communication of the details of incoming shipments. Such practices invite confusion, errors, and make troubleshooting issues harder. Return centers can create a similar level of advanced planning notice with ASN or transfer order capabilities.

Constructing systems that facilitate the use of multiple tracking numbers for each RMA, alongside providing the expected contents for each shipment through an ASN or transfer order, can significantly improve operational efficiency. This allows teams to accurately match the contents of a return with the right sender.

An RMA serves as an agreement allowing a customer to return specific products within a given timeframe. Simultaneously, an ASN provides detailed accounting of how and what products are returned, enabling the creation of expected orders for receipt, thereby fostering a more streamlined and precise receiving process. Creating an ASN or transfer order is a best practice that allows the return processing center to resource plan for inbound orders.

Advanced return systems can perform cost-benefit analyses prior to product receipt, potentially directing products straight to recycling centers instead of return processing centers. This preassessment of value and destination can help avoid wasteful practices, such as receiving a product at one location only to have to ship it to another. This is particularly useful, as customers generally are not concerned about where they send their product as long as they receive their expected benefit.

3.3 **Fundamental 2:** *Reverse Logistics Operations*

Integrating Operational and Refurbishment Strategies in Return Processing

In Fundamental 2, we explore the operational and refurbishment elements of reverse logistics. These include the movement of products and the enhancement of their condition through repair or refurbishment. Reverse operational activities are centered around establishing and managing the necessary infrastructure for reverse logistics, such as systems, transportation, and resource management. Physical activities, meanwhile, focus on specific tasks involved in handling and processing returned products, including receiving, sorting, inspecting, testing, repairing, storing, **packing**, picking, and shipping.

Despite the high costs involved—sometimes up to 70 percent of the original item's cost—the primary goal of reverse logistics remains the effective management of returns.[2] This is achieved by breaking down the process into smaller, more manageable tasks, not only to streamline operations and reduce costs but also to identify the root causes of returns, thus benefiting all parties.

Reverse Logistics Operational Activities

- **Systems** refers to the development and implementation of the necessary software systems to track and manage returned products, including inventory management, customer service, and data analysis tools.
- **Transportation** in reverse logistics involves coordinating the movement of returned products from the point of return to their respective destinations, such as repair facilities, refurbishment centers, or disposal sites. It also involves selecting the appropriate transportation methods, carriers, and optimizing routes.
- **Resource Management** encompasses efficiently managing the resources required for reverse logistics operations. It includes planning and allocating staff, equipment, facilities, and other essential resources to ensure smooth operations.

Reverse Logistics Physical Activities

- **Receiving** involves accepting the returned products into the reverse logistics system. It includes verifying the returned items against the RMA or transfer documentation, checking for initial damages, and initiating the warehouse tracking process.

- **Sortation,** the act of sorting returned products, is crucial, as it involves categorizing them based on various parameters like product type, reason for return, condition, or subsequent process steps. This classification aids in directing items to their appropriate destinations. At this stage, a product analysis is conducted to decide whether the product should progress further in the process or be responsibly recycled. If a product does not pass specific conditions, such as falling short in cosmetic or functional assessments that decrease the anticipated blended benefit, it can be extracted from operations and shipped for recycling at any following step in the process.

- **Inspection** of returned products involves assessing their condition and identifying any defects or faults. This stage is pivotal in determining the appropriate next step for each item, whether it is repair, refurbishment, recycling, or disposal. During this phase, a **cosmetic grade** can be assigned to the product, which can be leveraged for value improvement or value generation. Cosmetic grading scales may range from A+ to F, denoting conditions from "new" to "damaged" in descending order. The specific nomenclature for cosmetic grading varies across companies and is often formulated within the organization. The desired outcome is to differentiate between new, best, better, good, and failed conditions.

- **Testing** is conducted to evaluate the functionality and performance of returned products, helping to determine whether items can be repaired or should be discarded. Some companies may opt to test before inspection, and the sequence between steps three and four may be interchanged depending on the product and the results of **value-stream mapping** exercises.

However, both inspection and testing are carried out prior to any repair work. After these steps, post-inspection data can be compiled, and the RMA can be closed. By this stage, an accurate item description, reflecting the correct cosmetic condition and functional characteristics, should be completed. In instances where a revenue share process is in place, the post-assessment data may be finalized after value-generating activities occur.

- **Restoration Refurbishing/Repairing** stages represent uniform value improvement activities aimed at enhancing a product's aesthetics and functionality through cleaning, re-kitting, or replacing parts. These processes address issues identified during inspection and testing, utilizing skilled technicians to return products to a functional state. While some businesses maintain separate departments or locations for repair work due to its complexity, the operational activities remain consistent, regardless of whether the product undergoes value improvement. Any repair effort on an item in perfect condition is economically unwise; therefore, receiving, inspection, and testing activities must precede repair. Following these value improvement stages, storage and shipping operations are required to conclude the operational cycle, thus incorporating the intricate process of repair operations that we will discuss in detail in the next section.

- **Storage/Warehousing** of returned products is a crucial step until further action is determined. This can include arranging the items in a specific area, ensuring suitable storage conditions, and tracking inventory. Items may be stored based on SKU description, serial number, or license plate numbers (unique identifiers that can serialize items lacking serial numbers, thereby assigning the appropriate cosmetic and functional attributes). Some companies might opt for storing miscellaneous items in a Gaylord, a pallet with walls to hold multiple loose items, classifying them by category and weight.

- **Packing** involves preparing the products for their next stage, such as reshipment, refurbishment, or recycling. This includes packaging the items securely, adding necessary documentation, and labeling.

- **Picking** refers to retrieving the required products from storage based on specific orders or demands, which could involve selecting items for value generation, repair, refurbishment, or recycling based on predetermined criteria.

- **Shipping** involves sending the products to their designated destinations after all necessary activities are completed. This includes organizing transportation, preparing shipping documentation, and ensuring prompt delivery. The shipment of a product characterizes a forward logistics process as it advances a product to another point. One of the rare instances in which a product continues moving backward in a reverse logistics process is a return-to-vendor (RTV) scenario, in which the directional flow retraces the original forward sale.

- The operational process identifies a product's name, its functional and cosmetic condition, and its location. The state of a product remains the same until there is a change in its condition—meaning it is restored, refurbished, repaired, moved, or subject to rule changes that alter the current state of the product. For instance, a B-graded product or package cannot be upgraded to an A-grade item until it has been reconditioned to meet the communicated A-grade standards as promised to the customer. Likewise, a product that is defective upon assessment should remain in a defective condition until it undergoes repair.

The upcoming section explores specific challenges and nuances associated with processing returns in varying conditions—whether they are in their original packaging or opened—and how these factors influence their processing through reverse logistics operations.

Packaged versus Open-Item Returns: Inspection and Refurbishment Practices

One important distinction between managing forward logistics versus reverse lies in the chaotic nature inherent to the reverse logistics process.

In the case of new products, they are neatly assembled and dispatched, following a specific protocol with consistent labels and sizes. However, returned products may not be in their original packaging, and the items contained within a package may not correspond to the markings on the box exterior. For instance, if a customer buys two products, uses both, but chooses to return one, they might not place the correct product back in the correct box. Throughout the reverse logistics process, disorganized merchandise from various sources are meticulously inspected, categorized, and sorted into manageable lots, all with the aim of preparing for value generation.

Given that a product may either be returned in its original packaging or removed from it, with box markings potentially missing, companies may choose to set grading and inspection standards differently for each scenario.

Scenario 1: Products in their original packaging. The primary goal is to verify the integrity of the product and its packaging. Inspectors need to check if the product has been tampered with, damaged, or if there are any visible signs that the product's factory condition has been compromised. They might also need to check for missing elements like instruction manuals or accessories. In terms of refurbishment for products that have not been used or tampered with, the process will generally be minimal. Resealing the packaging or replacing missing manuals or accessories may be all that is needed. This minimal intervention maintains the product's "new" status, which can help retain its value for resale.

Scenario 2: Open Items. The inspection for these items is more complex. Inspectors must thoroughly assess both the physical and functional conditions of the product. This involves checking for cosmetic damage, missing parts, and operational defects. It is also necessary to verify that the product complies with all safety and regulatory standards. For refurbishment, these items may require extensive repair or reconditioning to restore them to a resaleable condition. This could involve cleaning, repairing, or replacing damaged parts and repackaging the item. In some cases, the product might be disassembled and reassembled to ensure it functions as intended. Each refurbished item should undergo a final quality check to ensure it meets the company's standards before being marked for resale.

Restoration/Refurbishment/Repair Operations

Repair, refurbishment, and restoration operations are organizations focused on enhancing product value. Their core purpose lies in augmenting a product's existing condition to outshine its previous state. Repair organizations can evolve into intricate supply chains akin to manufacturing entities.

These teams might need to access spare parts, tools, software development, and kitting, which are readily obtainable in bulk during initial manufacturing. However, as the product progresses through its lifecycle, procuring these materials may prove more challenging and potentially more costly. Certain parts of a product may be designed for easy repair, while others could be practically impossible to mend. Predicting the failure of specific components over time as the product ages can be an arduous task.

In this section, we will explore the various stages of product enhancement. The three most prevalent components of value improvement for products or packages include:

1. **Restoration.** Restoration of products entails the removal of dirt or soiling, thereby facilitating their reuse or enabling a more thorough inspection.

2. **Refurbishment.** The refurbishment process employs proactive measures beyond mere cleaning, targeting the enhancement of a product or package's cosmetic grade from its current state to improve its overall aesthetic appeal.

3. **Repair.** The repair process entails replacing parts of a product to regain functionality, with repair operations aiming to revive nonfunctional products or enhance their performance rate, all while adhering to strict quality control protocols to ensure optimal performance.

Restoration

Products often get soiled during general usage, trials, transportation, and handling throughout their lifecycle, requiring thorough cleaning before they can be reintroduced to consumers. Much like a clean vehicle having greater appeal than a dirty one on a dealership lot, the value of many products can increase substantially when they are properly cleaned. Restoration, particularly of returned products that need cleaning, is a critical process to boost the product's value. This process involves diligent inspection, precise cleaning techniques, and meticulous quality control.

The initial stage of restoration involves a thorough inspection of the returned product to ascertain the level of cleaning required and to detect any potential damage. This could include spotting stains, odors, or dust that may have accumulated during a brief period of use or trial under the customer guarantee.

The next step is to apply appropriate cleaning techniques suited to the product's material and the degree of usage. The cleaning process might involve the use of professional-grade cleaning solutions, steam cleaning, or dry cleaning with a preference for gentle and eco-friendly products that uphold the integrity of the item while ensuring cleanliness.

Post-cleaning is vital to reinspect and regrade the product. It may not always be possible to fully restore the product to its original condition through cleaning alone, but significant improvements can be made from a sanitization standpoint. The product's condition post-restoration should match the customer promise for its next sale.

In businesses like tuxedo rental companies or fashion rental platforms like Rent the Runway, items are regularly reused. Similarly, the hospitality industry offers amenities such as sheets, beds, and bathrooms that require frequent restoration. Modern consumers expect these items to be sanitized and safe for reuse. For such recirculated products, terms like "refurbished" or "reconditioned" often come with the assurance of thorough sanitization. An attractive product generally leads to better sales, which reinforces the point that quality control is a critical part of the restoration process.

Some companies are harnessing new technologies to enhance their green logistics ambitions, seeking to minimize chemical reliance and boost operational quality. A recent innovation from a company called Cold Jet exemplifies this trend. This pioneering cleaning technology employs dry ice and compressed air to freeze and then blast away imperfections. The effectiveness of this method has earned it a place in industries such as automotive, consumer electronics, and food and beverage, where high standards of cleanliness and hygiene are paramount.[3] By utilizing CO^2 from the air instead of chemicals like alcohol, this process further diminishes the environmental impact associated with restoration processes.

Refurbishment

A more extensive effort than restoration, refurbishment incorporates not just cleaning but also substantial enhancements to a product's cosmetic appeal *without* impacting its functionality. The process may involve re-kitting to replace damaged packaging incurred during use or transit, switching out worn tags, applying fresh shrink wrap, replacing outdated or damaged cardboard packaging due to changing marketing strategies, and replacing worn cosmetic parts. In general, refurbishment might involve more aggressive measures like polishing to rejuvenate the product's exterior. While these alterations do not modify the product's functionality, they majorly improve its aesthetic appeal. In **advanced exchange** warranty operations, refurbished products should present like-new or A+ cosmetic condition, indicating the requirement to upgrade from the lowest to the highest cosmetic grade.

In the context of a circular economy, in which products are repeatedly reused, the collective benefits of refurbishment must surpass the reuse costs. The product's cosmetic grade should exhibit significant improvement post-refurbishment.

Repair

The topic of repair in reverse logistics is a complex one. This process has a significant bearing on a company's brand, customer satisfaction, operational costs, sustainability efforts, and overall business success. Repair extends the product's lifecycle, reduces waste, and enables a company to recover value from returned products. However, as products progress through their lifecycle and are superseded by newer models, access to necessary parts can become a challenge.

Different companies, especially manufacturers, approach this issue in various ways depending on their position in the value chain. Some might prioritize brand protection and worry about potential threats such as cannibalization or the fear that repaired products may not live up to their quality standards. In all cases, the level of repair should align with the customer promise made when a customer purchases a product.

Common Approaches to Repair in Reverse Logistics

There are five common approaches to repair in reverse logistics, each serving a different purpose and requiring different levels of resources.

1. **Advanced exchange** involves sending a replacement device to a customer who reports a defect, and the customer is expected to return their faulty device. It is labor-intensive and costly, primarily due to the requirement of both functional and cosmetic repairs on the returned devices. In addition, a stock of refurbished devices must be maintained for rapid replacement. Despite the cost, it often ensures the highest level of customer satisfaction due to minimal disruption to the customer's use of the product.

2. **Same-unit repair** means that only the nonfunctioning part of the product is repaired. It requires secure access to replacement parts but reduces the need for a full stock of replacement products. Cosmetic repairs are not typically included unless the product is damaged during the repair process. However, this strategy may leave the customer without their product until the repair is complete, but the situation can be mitigated by some companies offering loaner devices.

3. **Assisted self-repair** involves shipping a replacement part to the customer, along with instructions for them to repair

the device themselves. It removes the labor component from the repair process but still requires stocking and shipping replacement parts. Furthermore, technical assistance may need to be available for customers who encounter difficulties during the repair process. This method has the advantage of reducing repair time and costs, but it may not be suitable for complex products or customers without technical aptitude.

4. **Repair for resale** aims to improve the functionality of devices to raise their resale value. It could involve replacing parts to extend the life of the device or upgrading components to make the device more appealing in the secondary market. Some companies facilitate this by providing customers with replacement parts and instructions, allowing them to carry out the repair themselves.

5. **Harvesting** involves dismantling a product into individual parts, which can either be used for future repair operations or sold for their residual value. This strategy can prevent fully intact units from entering the secondary market, reducing the risk of cannibalization. Compared to recycling components into raw materials, harvesting usually offers better benefits in terms of cost-effectiveness and resource conservation.

The choice of approach and whether to use used, reclaimed, refurbished, or aftermarket parts depends on the company's policies and sometimes on government regulations. There is no one-size-fits-all strategy for repair in reverse logistics. Different approaches are suited to different products, market conditions, and company policies. However, they all share a common goal: to maximize the product's useful life, recover value, fulfill the customer promise, and minimize environmental impact.

Best Practices for Cost Management in Repair and Refurbishment

There are many strategies to control the costs associated with repair and refurbishment in reverse logistics, and these can vary by industry and the specific point in the distribution model. Considering the nuance and detail involved in this aspect of the supply chain, it is not surprising that many companies have not deeply analyzed it. However, as customer expectations evolve, optimizing repair operations becomes increasingly important for managing recirculation costs. There are five best practices for controlling these costs.

1. **Ship from a centralized warehouse.** Some organizations keep replacement parts stocked in local outlets, but this practice can lead to higher inventory costs due to the need for larger stock volumes across multiple locations. Centralizing these parts in one warehouse can lower costs by reducing the total inventory required.

2. **Offer like-for-like or like-for-better alternatives.** Maintaining stock for older products can be challenging and costly. To address this, some companies offer support for a specified period, after which they might replace an older unit with a newer or higher-quality one. Customers are often pleased to receive an upgraded device, and the cost of replacing it with a newer unit may be lower than maintaining a large catalog of aging parts. This can be used for a model or a cosmetic grade. If a used device in good condition is sold, then replacing that device with a **"like-new" or "excellent-condition" product** may not be needed to fulfill a customer promise.

3. **Leverage harvested parts instead of new parts.** This strategy involves using parts from returned products to repair other devices. As long as the quality of the product matches customer expectations and meets any legal or contractual requirements, this approach can extend the product's useful life, minimize waste, and reduce costs.

4. **Offer money-back warranty options.** This approach involves offering extended money-back guarantees. Customers are given a refund that they can put toward the purchase of their next product, rather than the company bearing the cost of maintaining a large parts supply. This strategy can be particularly effective in the used market where sellers may offer extended warranties in

exchange for a higher price. The offers can be designed to require the customer to spend the credit at the place of purchase and limit the number of exchanges to prevent abuse.

5. **Offer self-service or remote diagnostics.** Many issues with electronic items are not hardware-related but can be resolved by adjusting settings or updating software. Companies can deploy application diagnostics or self-service tools to prevent products from being returned when there's no identifiable hardware failure. These tools can also provide valuable data that can inform improvements in product quality, instructions, and future product design to promote sustainability.

By carefully considering these strategies, companies can find ways to meet their customers' expectations, fulfill their brand promise, and manage the costs of repair and refurbishment in reverse logistics.

3.4 Fundamental 3: *Disposition and Value Generation*

Value Generation Overview

Just like how every return incurs an operational cost, every return has the potential to generate value, and the speed at which this value is realized is called **velocity**. Value generation activities can propel logistics operations from cost centers to profit generators by selling returned goods or offsetting costs. Moreover, revenue from associated services or software, like finance or warranties, may be realized if a suitable product and condition is enabled to flow from one customer to the next.

Value generation primarily aims for waste reduction, minimal revenue loss from products, or, in the best scenarios, realization of benefits that surpass the product's original acquisition or production costs. The ways a company elects to route products to subsequent consumers encapsulate these value-generating activities. Integral to the concept of a circular economy, astute businesses have methodologies set for what might be referred to as Customer Two+. This denotes strategies to prolong a product's life cycle by targeting its next potential user.

It is worth noting that companies have showcased ingenuity in deriving value from unwanted returns for many years. A case in point is Hallmark cards. During the early to mid-1990s, representatives from Hallmark would gather out-of-season merchandise only for these items to be destroyed, yielding no value recuperation. Fast forward to 2001, and Hallmark transitioned to a more resourceful approach. The company collaborated with a third-party firm that would accumulate excess seasonal stock, subsequently repackaging these items for reintroduction into secondary markets.[4]

In this section, we will explore various **outflow methods** and best practices that manufacturers or retailers/distributors can choose to engage in. These methods can be mapped out on a Level One Process Flow for each chosen method. Also known as **dispositions**, these methods denote how a company handles its returned goods. Disposition, in this context, refers to the way returned goods are moved out of the return operation. This could include resale, refurbishment, recycling, donation, disposal, or any other means through which the product is transitioned from its returned state to its next lifecycle phase.

The intended disposition of a product and expected value drive the operational activities in order to prepare a device for its next use. To correctly prepare a device for its next stage in the **reverse value chain** from a return center, it is essential to identify the item, assess its cosmetic condition, and determine its **functional status** based on operational processes. A precise evaluation of the product allows for maximization of realized value.

In certain dispositions, such as selling as "new," offering "**certified refurbished**," or using a **warranty replacement**, a promise is made to the customer that the reused product is a specific item, in a particular condition, with a confirmed level of functionality. Understanding a product's grading and functionality is a key factor in establishing dispositions for value generation and ensuring that the right product reaches the appropriate customer, in the expected condition, at the right time.

Rules of Engagement

Value generation teams in reverse logistics can face restrictions on how, where, and under what conditions products are resold when reintroduced into the market. Some companies may opt to sell solely via certified like-new channels that they control, maintaining rigorous quality standards. Others might guide product flows into or out of specific markets with the intention to manipulate market prices. These restrictions function as gatekeeping mechanisms, controlling the flow of products to minimize the risk (or the perception of risk) of cannibalizing their primary markets.

For instance, during the rollout of their 4G network and the corresponding launch of the first iPhone, Verizon implemented a strategy that involved phasing out their 3G operation. The remaining 3G devices entailed higher operating costs compared to 4G devices. To avert the resale of these devices in the US and to reduce the pressure on their network infrastructure upgrade, Verizon implemented promotional initiatives to eliminate legacy devices. They strategically collaborated with third-party vendors with proficiency in overseas markets where the 3G network was still popular.

Strategies in which a company seeks to control the geographical markets for its used products, determine the channels for value generation, or set the conditions for product sales are commonly guided by established **business rules**. These rules, typically set by sales, marketing, and brand protection departments can limit a company's ability to extract value from returned products or influence the speed at which products move through the return and resale process.

While it is relatively straightforward to find listed prices for products on secondary markets, it is more challenging to ascertain if a product actually sells for the listed price, and how many units are sold at that price. Data obtained through price scraping might lack accuracy due to this uncertainty, leading some companies to prioritize protection against market cannibalization over resale value.

When companies abstain from engaging in buyback programs or facilitating the journey of used products to their next owners, they may inadvertently bolster the secondary market. This is particularly true for products that have a high intrinsic value and durability. In such cases, the demand for these products in secondary markets can grow as customers seek ways to acquire them at lower prices or in used conditions.

Therefore, it is crucial for reverse logistics teams to understand and influence these rules of engagement. Such understanding enables them to optimize the benefits drawn from the four key desired outcomes of managing returns: sales-enablement, cost management, green logistics, and circular economy. By grasping these business rules of engagement, reverse logistics teams can not only add value but also boost the speed at which products circulate through the reverse logistics process.

Value Generation Options

The presence and types of value generation activities can vary depending on an organization's role in the supply chain. Manufacturers that sell in bulk and produce their own products may operate with different rules of engagement than their distribution or retail partners. These discrepancies often occur because distributors might have to manage sunk costs if manufacturers do not offer returns programs.

Accordingly, it is advantageous to precisely define the allowable value generation activities within a company's rules of engagement using a Level One Process Flow map, as demonstrated in Figures 3.1 and 3.2. This approach offers a clear visual depiction, not only of their existing operational processes but also of potential avenues for value generation. Such a representation fosters enhanced transparency and facilitates the exploration of alternative options. Here are some best practices of value generation activities.

- **Reuse as New.** If a returned product is in a condition that can be ethically and legally restored to a "new" state (e.g., re-kitting damaged packaging during transit), it may be reintroduced to the forward distribution channels for resale. The product and packaging must meet customer promise requirements. The advantage of this practice is it prevents unnecessary resource expenditure in remanufacturing products.

- **Resell as Refurbished.** Various cosmetic conditions can be marketed to customers, from "certified like-new" to "good," "better," and "best" conditions. In order to resell as refurbished, companies must provide customers with a clear understanding of the product's functionality, warranty, and cosmetic condition. Selling refurbished products usually generates a lower price point than new products, barring unusual supply constraints like the COVID-19 supply chain crunch.

- **Warranty Support.** Many companies offer "like-new" condition warranty replacements, allowing them to recondition returned products or extract parts for use in their warranty chain. This reduces the need to manufacture a new product for warranty claims.

- **Use for Demonstration Devices.** If a company allows customers to try out products before purchase, returned equipment that has been cleaned and sanitized (including data sanitization) can be reused multiple times rather than breaking the seal on new products.

- **Use for Leasing or Rental.** Companies may repeatedly lease or rent out the same product for short durations, under the agreement that customers will pay for its usage and then return it. In such situations, customers are often prepared to receive a pre-used device that is circulated until the end of its useful lifecycle.

- **Wholesale Liquidation.** Companies may choose to sell products in bulk to the secondary market, generating revenue while transferring the responsibility of distributing high quantities of products to other partners.

- **E-Commerce.** Some companies might choose to sell products directly under their brand or sub-brand, thereby maximizing value. This approach requires more customer support than wholesale but can generate higher value.

- **Re-Commerce.** Also known as reverse commerce, **re-commerce** refers to the process of selling previously owned or used products, often through online platforms. It emphasizes the resale of items, giving them a second life and promoting sustainability by reducing waste and the need for new production. Popular examples of re-commerce include platforms like eBay, Poshmark, and ThredUP, where users can buy and sell pre-owned goods.

- **Harvest or Recycle.** Companies can break down a product to its usable parts or reduce the product to raw materials for closed-loop consumption in their own supply chain. They can also offer these materials to the market for others to use.
- **Donation.** Donating products offers an opportunity for the dual benefit of supporting charitable causes and promoting sustainability. By directing a product toward a preferred charity, donors not only potentially secure a tax credit but also gain the assurance that their item is poised for reuse by another recipient. This not only extends the product's lifecycle but also reinforces the ethos of reducing waste and fostering community well-being.
- **Idle Inventory.** If a product is unsold and aging, its net benefit is zero, and the cost to reuse it increases. Understanding the aging of products is crucial in managing resources and maintaining efficiency.

Strategic Seed-Stock Management: Upholding the Certified Like-New Promise

Seed stock refers to products procured in a brand-new condition specifically to support a warranty loop, particularly when a company promises customers a certified like-new replacement. At the onset of a product's launch, the absence of returned stock means that new items are the sole available resources to fulfill such warranty commitments. Consequently, planners and inventory managers will secure new-conditioned items to ensure they can uphold the "like-new" guarantee. An optimal practice in **seed-stock management** involves the gradual replacement of these new products with returned items that have been refurbished to match the original promise. This strategy harnesses the residual value embedded in returned goods and sidesteps the potential devaluation of brand-new products, ensuring that these new items can be redirected to sales channels, thereby maintaining their value and the integrity of the "like-new" pledge to customers.

Value Generation Blind Spots

It is important to distinguish between business rules of engagement—and legislation. While the former involves a company's internal guidelines dictating its operations, the latter refers to laws imposed by government or regulatory bodies. Companies might choose not to engage in certain markets or refrain from dealing in a range of functional or cosmetic dispositions of product sales. However, if there is demand for these products, businesses and customers will find a way to connect. Simply ignoring a market does not lead to its disappearance.

Manufacturers or distributors should ponder this question: if eliminating the secondary market is not feasible, should they aim to be the best at participating in it to maintain control? Many companies operate under the mistaken belief that they can eliminate the secondary market by abstaining from participation or resorting to product destruction. However, in an era marked by significant advancements in technology, customers have become adept at seeking value: they will seek out and find avenues to purchase products at conditions and prices that suit their preferences.

Instead of steering clear of secondary markets, companies may find it advantageous to participate in them actively and constructively. By doing so, businesses can exert a level of control, safeguard their brand, and potentially create additional revenue streams, all while meeting customer needs. Overlooking the secondary market does not prevent customers from utilizing it to their advantage.

3.5 Importance of Data Erasure in Reverse Logistics

With the rise of connected devices and the growing storage capabilities of modern products, the protection of customer data has become a critical concern for businesses engaged in reverse logistics. As such, managing **consumer information (CI)** and responsibly removing it during the returns process is one of the most important aspects of effective reverse logistics.

Data erasure is especially important in the hardware and consumer electronics industries where returned products contain valuable and potentially harmful information. The R2 V3.0 standard for data is defined as "the private, personally identifiable, confidential, licensed, or proprietary information contained on an electronic device or memory component that requires secured management and sanitization under this standard."[5] R2 does permit general information to remain on products. General information is publicly available information such as the device's operating system.[6] Customer information in the mobile-device market refers to any data that is stored on a device that can be used to identify the previous owner of the device, such as personal contacts, messages, emails, photos, call history, and financial information.

Risk Assessment and Threats to Consumer Data

In the context of returned products containing data, an asset or actor is an entity with the motivation to exploit the exposed data, either for personal gain or theft-related reasons. This vulnerability exists from the moment the product is removed from use until the data is erased. While the theft of a device during transit or by a warehouse worker may result in the loss of value from reusing or reselling the device, the real risk to all parties concerned is the theft of the information stored on the device.

This is similar to how cars are broken into more frequently in places like Silicon Valley to steal electronics. It is not necessarily that laptops are worth more in California, but rather the value of the intelligence on the laptops that makes the risk of leaving electronics in a vehicle greater. In reverse logistics, theft of information is one of the most significant risks that exists, and businesses must take proactive steps to manage this risk and protect **consumer data**.

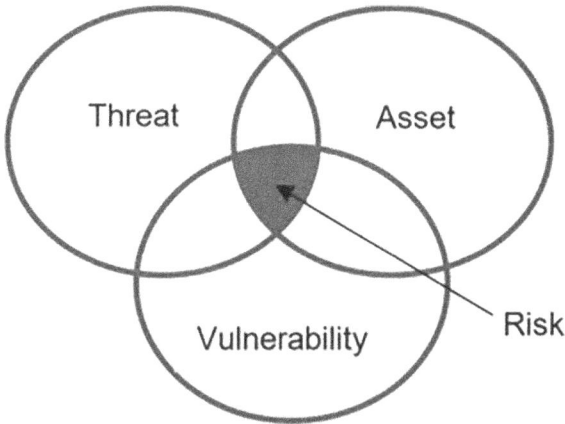

Figure 3.5. The *Risk Assessment Venn diagram* is a framework used to understand and manage risk. It consists of three interrelated components: the threat, the asset, and the vulnerability.

Levels of Data Clearing

Data erasure is the process of securely removing sensitive information from electronic devices, such as computers and smartphones, before they are disposed of, recycled, or repurposed. The National Institute of Standards and Technology (NIST) provides guidelines for **data clearing** in NIST SP 800-88 r1, "Guidelines for Media Sanitization," one of the most common industry guidelines providing direction for data clearing today.[7]

According to NIST, there are three levels of data clearing:

1. **Clear.** Data clearing at the clear level means that all data on the device is made inaccessible and unrecoverable through normal means. This level may be appropriate for devices that will be resold or repurposed as determined by the company's rules of engagement. Clearing information from devices using manufacturer tools may not erase the data but will eliminate the pathway to access the data.[8]

2. **Purge.** Data clearing at the purge level means that all data on the device is made inaccessible and unrecoverable through

normal means, and the information on the product removed in such a way that makes it difficult to recover data. This level is appropriate for devices that contain highly sensitive information. Purging information can include overwriting information on storage sectors.[9]

3. **Destroy.** Data clearing at the destroy level means that the device is physically destroyed to the point that it cannot be used again and all data on the device is made inaccessible and unrecoverable. This level is appropriate for devices that contain highly sensitive information. Destruction is the easiest method to eliminate data but is also the most wasteful.[10]

Published in 2014, NIST 800-88 rl may not sufficiently address the rapid advancements in data-storage technology. Experts have noted that the technology landscape, especially concerning data storage, shifts approximately every eighteen months.[11] With an increasing reliance on solid-state technology in mobile devices and hard drives, traditional methods of data erasure, such as three-pass or seven-pass overwrites that were suitable for hard disk drives, may not be as effective with solid-state hard drives. In fact, sectors in these new devices tend to be retired rather than overwritten, leaving a potential risk.

Recognizing the evolving nature of storage technology, new standards have emerged. For instance, the Institute of Electrical and Electronics Engineers (IEEE) introduced publication P2283, which offers updated guidance. However, this standard has not achieved the same widespread adoption as NIST 800-88 r1.[12] One point of contention in NIST 800-88 r1 is its allowance for users to execute an erasure command from a preinstalled manufacturer tool and simply document its completion without ensuring the erasure was effective. Consequently, numerous companies have taken the initiative to develop their own erasure tools or incorporate third-party software to ascertain that devices are genuinely restored to their factory settings. Verification often involves comparing the memory usage of the wiped device to a new unit and ensuring a return to default settings.

Although methods such as erasure and purge commands play an important role in securely removing data from storage devices, concerns over data breaches have led many organizations to prefer physical destruction methods, resulting in over 90 percent of hard drives being shredded, which contributes significantly to electronic waste.[13] This not only raises environmental concerns but also misses out on the economic benefits of reusing intact hardware.

Electronic validation tools offer a solution by providing records that data has been cleared from a device and sometimes even confirming that the device has been restored to its original memory configuration and boot screen. This process protects end-user privacy and ensures sensitive information is securely handled while aiding compliance with data privacy regulations like the **General Data Protection Regulation (GDPR)** and California Consumer Privacy Act.

When an electronic data erasure is performed, it captures essential details such as user, date, device specifications, storage capacity, and serial number for documentation and shipping. If a device's electronic record matches a previous data clearing record, it can verify that the software configuration and memory utilization remain unchanged.

The Role of Standards and Certifications

Standards and certifications in the returns industry can help ensure that companies can handle returns, data sanitization, and waste in a responsible and sustainable manner. There are three widely recognized standards and certifications:

1. **R2** is a globally recognized standard for responsible recycling. It provides a framework for the responsible handling of electronics waste, including the reuse, refurbishment, and recycling of electronics products.

2. **ISO 14001** is an international standard for environmental-management systems. It provides a framework for companies to develop and implement an environmental management system that helps them minimize their environmental impact, reduce waste, and comply with environmental regulations.

3. **e-Stewards** is a globally recognized standard for responsible electronics recycling and data destruction. It is managed by the Basel Action Network, a nonprofit organization focused on combating toxic trade, and requires certified organizations to adhere to strict environmental and social responsibility criteria, including the responsible management of hazardous materials, a prohibition on exporting electronic waste to developing countries, and safeguarding sensitive data throughout the recycling process.

These standards and certifications help to ensure that companies handle returns and waste in a responsible and sustainable manner, reducing their impact on the environment and improving their environmental performance. They also provide consumers and stakeholders with a level of assurance that the company is reliable and operating with environmental impacts in mind.

3.6 Resource Management in Reverse Logistics

Resource management refers to the actual physical movement and positioning of resources, such as people, equipment, and facilities, to support the reverse logistics process. This might include, for example, setting up a dedicated warehouse or facility for handling returned goods, or positioning a team of employees to manage the collecting and processing of returns.

In terms of personnel, determining whether to directly staff a reverse logistics operation or to use a **third-party logistics (3PL)** provider is an important aspect of resource allocation in reverse logistics. This decision will depend on factors such as the volume and complexity of returns, the resources and capabilities of the organization, and the costs and benefits of each option.

Staffing Options

In the case of **insourced reverse logistics**, the company handles the entire process internally using its own resources. This may include dedicated personnel, facilities, and equipment to manage activities such as product collection, sorting, refurbishment, or recycling. Insourcing provides the company with direct control over the entire reverse logistics process but requires significant investments in infrastructure and expertise.

Outsourcing reverse logistics to a **third-party service provider (3PSP)** involves hiring an external company to handle specific aspects of the reverse logistics process. The 3PSP provider assumes responsibility for tasks like product collection, transportation, sorting, and disposal or resale.[14] This approach allows the company to leverage the expertise and resources of the 3PSP provider while reducing the need for internal investments. However, it may result in less control over the process and reliance on the capabilities of the 3PSP provider.

A fourth-party logistics (4PL) provider takes a more comprehensive role in managing reverse logistics. A 4PL provider acts as a strategic partner, overseeing the entire reverse logistics process on behalf of the company. They coordinate various third-party logistics (3PL) providers, manage information flows, optimize processes, and provide strategic guidance. This approach offers a higher level of coordination, visibility, and efficiency but requires a strong partnership and clear communication between the company and the 4PL provider.

A hybrid approach to resource management in reverse logistics combines elements of insourcing and outsourcing. Companies may choose to handle some aspects of reverse logistics internally while outsourcing others to specialized service providers. This allows the company to retain control over critical functions while leveraging external expertise and resources where needed. It provides flexibility in tailoring the reverse logistics process to specific requirements, optimizing efficiency, and cost-effectiveness.

3.7 Technology in Reverse Logistics

The 1999 publication *Going Backwards* brought to light a significant gap: the intricate world of returns management had no robust systems dedicated to reverse logistics.[15] One main reason was the allocation of

IT resources to projects deemed more pivotal, sidelining the development of comprehensive reverse logistics systems.[16] Even after a span of twenty-five years, the market has not witnessed a definitive leader in return technology that has a comprehensive system capable of evaluating the functionality, aesthetic value, worth, and salability of used products across diverse categories. One company, however, does exhibit promising leadership in the field and warrants closer examination. The next section 3.8 will look into the reuse case of goTRG.

Despite the slowness of logistics to adapt, advancements in technology cannot be overlooked. Key practices from 1998, like electronic data exchanges, barcodes, and return rationale codes, remain relevant but are now supercharged by the abundance of interconnected devices. The push to minimize returns that are less favorable and amplify those that are desirable is growing, buoyed by the enhancements brought about by artificial intelligence and machine learning in the realm of supply chains. In light of these changes, businesses are diligently crafting tools that weave together various data strands, creating integrated systems for seamless daily business procedures.

Understanding the historical patterns of rapid industrial change is crucial in comprehending the current and future impact of technology on reverse logistics. There have been four industrial revolutions, with the fourth one potentially having the most significant influence. Let us briefly take a look at these revolutions.

- **The First Industrial Revolution** (late 1700s to mid-1800s) introduced mechanization, such as steam power and textile manufacturing, shifting production from manual labor to machine-based processes, which significantly boosted productivity.
- **The Second Industrial Revolution** (late 1800s to early 1900s) witnessed the emergence of mass production and electrification. Innovations like the assembly line, interchangeable parts, and widespread electricity usage brought further advancements in manufacturing, transportation, and communication.
- **The Third Industrial Revolution** (late 1900s), also known as the Digital Revolution, saw the rise of electronics, computers,

and automation. Semiconductors, microprocessors, and the internet revolutionized communication and information sharing, which ushered in the era of digital technology.

- **The Fourth Industrial Revolution** (present), also known as **Industry 4.0**, involves advancements in how data can be leveraged through **augmented reality (AR)**, artificial intelligence, machine learning, applications, and the internet.

The concept of the Fourth Industrial Revolution evolved from a project in the high-tech strategy of the German government that promoted the computerization of manufacturing.[17] While Henrik von Scheel is recognized for his pioneering work in 2008, the concept of Industry 4.0 gained widespread attention after Klaus Schwab's mention at the World Economic Forum (WEF) in 2015.[18]

Industry 4.0 will profoundly shape the future of reverse logistics, which relies on data-driven processes. While manual approaches can handle reverse operations for products arriving from unknown sources or in unknown quantities, leveraging data is the most effective way to achieve positive outcomes in four key desired outcomes of reverse logistics: enabling sales programs, reducing returns or costs, optimizing transportation routes to minimize environmental impact, and facilitating the circular economy. Artificial intelligence and machine learning can play a vital role in revolutionizing how data can be captured, manipulated, analyzed, and presented, transforming the logistics and supply chain industry as a whole.

The success of technology can be measured by the adoption rate of users. Tools that are accurate and make life easy get used. At a 2023 Reverse Logistics Association event, Thomas Maher from Dell Technologies presented a graph showcasing the time it took various technologies to reach 100 million users. The mobile industry took sixteen years, the internet took seven years, Facebook took four and a half years, while an AI engine called ChatGPT achieved the same milestone in just three months. This highlights how data-driven technologies are revolutionizing the logistics and supply chain industry.[19]

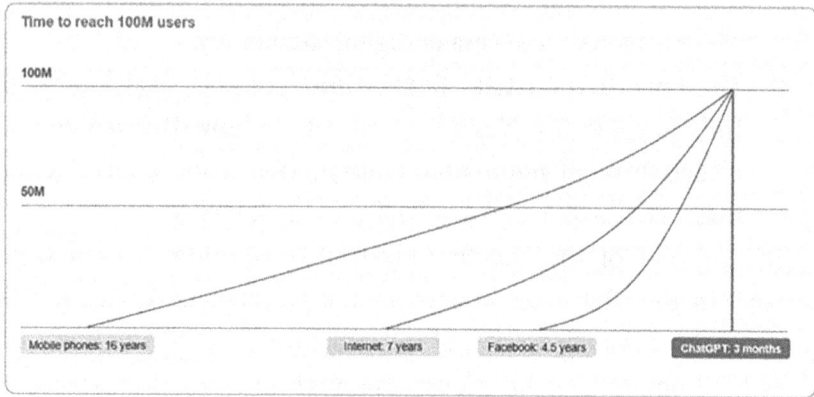

Figure 3.6. Slide shared by Thomas Maher from Dell Technologies at the June 2023 Reverse Logistics Association Show in the Netherlands.

As governments strive to understand the benefits and challenges of AI and ML, various industries, including the entertainment sector, are experiencing labor concerns.[20] There is a union strike involving writers and actors that fear AI could replace them by generating scripts or creating replicas of individuals.[21] The ethical, labor, and legal struggles surrounding AI and ML adoption will be vetted out similarly to the adoption of previous transformative technologies like computers, calculators, the internet, and smartphones. It is not a question of *if* AI and ML will be used but rather *how* they will be utilized. AI can be used to generate work instructions, write job descriptions, and analyze data for better decision making, among other applications.

Investment Status in Artificial Intelligence and Machine Learning in the 2022 Supply Chain

Percentage of respondents

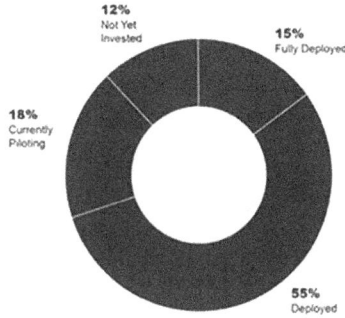

12%
Not Yet
Invested

15%
Fully Deployed

18%
Currently
Piloting

55%
Deployed

Figure 3.7. A 2022 Gartner study surveyed thirty-three professionals specializing in supply chain planning and inventory management. They were asked to indicate the investment status of their supply chain organizations in various technologies. (Participants who were unsure or found the question irrelevant were excluded.)

A Pareto chart from a 2022 Gartner study, shared by Thomas Maher, indicated the adoption status of AI and ML investments in the supply chain. At that time, 15 percent claimed to have fully deployed AI and ML, 55 percent had deployed it in some form, and the remaining 30 percent were in the early stages of implementation. Nonetheless, the information age is rapidly expanding the capabilities of competitors, customers, and potentially malicious actors, necessitating their consideration as reverse logistics continues to evolve. With the availability of smart data, the reverse supply chain can make smarter decisions on how the fundamentals of asset recovery, operations, and value generation can be conducted, improving a company's ability to compete, reducing unwanted return rates and costs, minimizing environmental impact, and supercharging the circular economy.

By streamlining work instructions, simplifying request for proposal requirements and responses, and adopting a score-based approach, these firms can achieve superior outcomes through various systems that facilitate the reverse logistics process. In this section, we will explore some of the essential systems utilized in reverse logistics operations and the tools designed to empower the three fundamental aspects of reverse logistics.

Information Systems in Reverse Logistics: Enabling Efficiency and Value with CRM, TPS, DSS, WMS, EIS, and ERP

One of the critical factors that influences the effectiveness of reverse logistics are the systems that collect information and assist in the planning and transportation of products to meet organizational goals. Currently, the industry heavily relies on common tools that revolve around the management of inventory movement for both forward and reverse logistics processes. These tools are vital in streamlining operations and optimizing the entire supply chain. Each individual element in a transaction is called a task, and transaction process systems (TPS) can combine multiple tasks together to complete a transaction.[22]

A diverse array of systems can be optimized to execute reverse logistics successfully:

- **Transaction processing systems (TPS)** are instrumental in enabling smooth returns processing, ensuring that products can be efficiently sent back when necessary.

- **Point-of-sales (POS) systems** record the sale of goods or services to a customer, handling the financial transaction and often updating inventory levels in real time. This immediate processing of information is characteristic of TPS, which are designed to handle and record routine transactions efficiently. In addition to handling sales transactions, many POS systems integrate with other functionalities like **customer relationship management (CRM)**, inventory management, and employee scheduling, making them multifunctional TPS tools in the retail environment. POS systems facilitate product returns as well.

- **Customer relationship management (CRM) software** helps identify trends that drive desired sales behavior while also providing valuable insights into return behavior. By analyzing customer interactions and preferences, businesses can better understand the reasons behind product returns, leading to improved decision-making and customer satisfaction.

- **Warehouse management systems (WMS)** are designed to assist operational staff in handling product movements upon arrival. These systems enhance inventory accuracy and enable efficient tracking of goods throughout the reverse logistics process, optimizing warehouse operations.

- **Decision support systems (DSS)** are designed to enhance productivity and reduce costs by leveraging data sets to automatically determine the optimal path for managing returns. This aids in making informed decisions in the reverse logistics context, leading to cost savings and improved efficiency.

- **Enterprise resource planning (ERP)** tools play a crucial role in combining various systems into a centralized location to support the entire corporate operation. From finance and human resources to planning, sales, and procurement, ERP systems foster better collaboration and streamlined processes across the organization.

- **Executive information systems (EIS)** provide a simplified high-level accounting of the activities taking place, enabling performance management and impact measurement. Executives can use these systems to make strategic decisions based on real-time insights.

The ability to harness AI and ML technologies will set one company apart from another, as these innovations revolutionize the efficiency, effectiveness, and responsiveness of reverse logistics processes. Effective data control will help companies modify their products, advertisements, and policies to make their customers purchase a good experience while maintaining profitability. There is no doubt that tools like CRM, TPS, DSS, WMS, ERP, and EIS systems are more important now than ever. In this section, we will explore how reverse logistics teams are harnessing the potential of each of these systems.

Transaction Processing Systems (TPS)

TPS are integral components in both the forward and reverse supply chains, ensuring smooth sales- and returns-initiation processes. In the forward supply chain, TPS are employed to complete sales transactions between different parts of the supply chain, involving customer agreement to purchase a good or service in exchange for payment. These systems initiate the logistical process, ensuring that the right product is available at the right place and time, in accordance with the customer promise.

TPS are employed to facilitate both sales and returns. The data collected during a sale can be used to populate information in the event of a return. Sales and returns, although distinct transactions, can be processed seamlessly in a TPS. By leveraging information from the initial sale during the return process, we can validate whether the return adheres to the customer promise (such as return windows), ensure the item returned matches the purchased item, and identify payment methods for appropriate refunds.

Warehouse Management Systems (WMS)

A specialized software application focused on optimizing the operations of a warehouse or distribution center is known as a **warehouse management system (WMS)**. In the context of reverse logistics, a WMS plays a crucial role in managing the complexity and variability of returned items. The system aids in efficiently processing these returns, assessing their condition, and determining the most value-generating path forward for each item. Some key elements of a WMS in reverse logistics are:

- **Ingesting Return Information.** The WMS starts by capturing data about returned items. This includes reasons for return, condition of the product, customer information, and return authorization. Integration with customer service or ERP systems is often essential to ensure this data is accurate and complete.

- **Receiving and Sorting Products by Condition.** Once returns arrive at the warehouse, the WMS facilitates their sorting. Products are categorized based on their condition—whether they are damaged, defective, in good condition, or have been returned for other reasons. This sorting is crucial for deciding the subsequent steps for each product.

- **Routing through Testing, Repair, or Refurbishment.** Based on the condition, returned items may need to be assessed, repaired, or refurbished. The WMS manages the workflow of these processes, tracking each item's progress and ensuring that resources are allocated efficiently for these tasks.

- **Inventory Control.** The WMS updates inventory levels in real-time as returns are processed. This includes items that are ready to be resold, those in the process of repair or refurbishment, and those marked for disposal or recycling. Accurate inventory control is vital for efficient warehouse operation and for providing reliable data for decision-making.

- **Preparation for Final Disposition.** Once the returned items are processed, the WMS helps in preparing them for their final disposition. This could be reselling, recycling, returning to the vendor, or disposing of them. The system ensures that items are properly packaged and labeled for their respective destinations.

- **Configuring Items for Shipment.** The WMS organizes the final shipment of processed items, whether they are to be shipped individually or in bulk (like on pallets). This includes determining the most cost-effective and efficient shipping methods and ensuring compliance with shipping regulations.

- **Value Generation.** Throughout this process, the primary goal of the WMS in reverse logistics is to maximize the value recovered from returned goods. This could mean refurbishing products for resale, recycling materials, or efficiently disposing of goods to minimize losses.

- **Data Analytics and Reporting.** Advanced WMS solutions offer analytics and reporting features that help in understanding patterns in returns, identifying areas for improvement in product quality or logistics, and optimizing the entire reverse logistics process.

As illustrated, a WMS is an integral part of reverse logistics, turning potential losses from returns into opportunities for value recovery and enhancing overall supply chain efficiency.

Enterprise Resource Planning (ERP) Systems

ERP systems are comprehensive software platforms designed to integrate and manage all the major functions of a business. These systems consolidate various business processes, including finance, HR, manufacturing, supply chain, services, procurement, and others into a single, unified system. This integration facilitates streamlined operations, improved data accuracy, and enhanced decision-making capabilities. In the context of reverse logistics or proper disposal, ERP systems play many critical roles.

- **Integrated Data Management.** ERP systems enable a unified view of all aspects of reverse logistics. This includes integrating sales data, customer interactions, warehousing information, and financial records related to returned products. Such integration ensures efficient tracking and processing of returns.

- **Inventory Management.** Effective management of returned products is crucial. ERP systems aid in real-time tracking of these products, whether they are to be refurbished, resold, or disposed of. Thus, they maintain accurate inventory levels and prevent issues like overstocking or stock shortages.

- **Contract Management.** ERPs maintain detailed records of contracts related to purchases and returns. This includes information on return policies, vendor agreements, and expiration dates, which is vital for managing the return process effectively.

- **Financial Implications.** Returns can have a noticeable impact on a company's finances. ERP systems automate the accounting for refunds and the costs associated with processing returns, thus maintaining accurate financial records.

- **Customer Service Enhancement.** By providing real-time data on product returns, ERPs enable customer service teams to offer immediate updates to customers about their return status, refunds, or replacement queries.
- **Performance Analysis.** ERPs offer analytics on return rates and reasons, which helps businesses identify product defects, service issues, or market trends. This information can guide improvements in product design, quality control, or customer service protocols.
- **Supplier Interactions.** When frequent returns are due to manufacturing defects, this data, managed by the ERP, can be communicated back to suppliers for quality improvement. This helps in enhancing quality across the entire supply chain.
- **Environmental and Regulatory Compliance.** For businesses dealing with recyclable or hazardous materials, ERP systems assist in ensuring compliance with environmental regulations. This includes tracking and reporting on how returned goods are processed.

By uniting diverse company information under one comprehensive system, ERP systems play a pivotal role in streamlining reverse logistics, enhancing efficiency, and driving value generation.

Executive Information Systems (EIS)

Leaders need information that is both succinct and clear. To cater to this requirement, EIS are tailored to communicate key activities, trends, and performance metrics effectively. Recognizing that raw information is not inherently valuable, successful businesses depend on reliable and relevant data for their strategic decisions. EIS are instrumental in this regard, as they gather extensive data and reformat it into reports that are both actionable and easy to comprehend. Executive information systems stand out by distilling this data into summaries that enable senior leaders to quickly understand their company's performance, thus supporting efficient and well-informed decision-making processes.[23]

Product Identification Best Practices

Returns management challenges arise when the item's exterior packaging does not match its contents. When a product is returned, it might not be in its original packaging, and even if it is, the item inside could differ from the label. For instance, a customer might buy Product One, decide to return it, and inadvertently or intentionally place it in the box of another product. This mismatch can cause confusion especially with products that are not serialized, such as books, clothing, and accessories, which can vary in functional and cosmetic conditions.

WMS rely heavily on identification methods to efficiently manage inventory, track movement, and optimize the entire supply chain. To minimize discrepancies and guarantee precise tracking, businesses utilize a range of identification systems. An SKU and a UPC serve as distinct yet complementary identifiers that are frequently transformed into barcodes, which facilitate easier tracking and management of products in various retail and warehouse settings. Here is how they operate and their relevance in the context of warehouse management and commitments to customers:

1. **Product Identification**. While UPCs are universal identifiers standardized across various platforms and stores, SKUs are specific identifiers assigned by individual retailers or manufacturers. These unique identifiers can encapsulate various attributes of a product such as color, size, and condition ("like new," "used," etc.), assisting in detailed inventory management.

2. **Use in WMS**. SKUs play a crucial role in WMS by helping track inventory levels, order points, and sales in a detailed manner since they are assigned by individual retailers based on specific categorizations. Conversely, UPCs serve as standardized barcodes used ubiquitously for retail items across different stores and platforms, aiding in a more universal product-identification and tracking system.

3. **Receiving and Tracking.** When products arrive at a warehouse, their SKUs or UPCs are scanned as part of the entry log in the WMS. This crucial step ensures that the items are correctly registered in the inventory system, with accurate tracking of their location and availability at any given point. As products maneuver through the warehouse or are shipped out, their journey status is consistently updated through repeated scans of these codes, maintaining an accurate record of product flow.

4. **Pricing and Customer Commitments.** Having different UPCs for products facilitates differentiated pricing strategies and enables retailers to uphold distinct customer promises based on the product condition. Moreover, it aids in enhancing the customer experience by offering clear insights into product status and facilitating appropriate product returns and warranty management.

5. **Barcode Characteristics.** Barcodes representing SKUs and UPCs must be visibly accessible for scanning and remain static, meaning they cannot be altered once generated.

6. **Customer Experience.** Differentiating products based on their conditions through varied UPCs allows customers to make informed decisions based on their preferences, ensuring they receive the product in the condition they expect, thereby fulfilling the right customer promise.

Together, SKUs and UPCs work synergistically to bolster the efficiency and accuracy of product management systems, ensuring streamlined operations and fostering positive customer experiences through transparent and accountable product tracking and management.

Quick response (QR) codes are another modern tool. Unlike barcodes, QR codes can contain multiple data fields that can be updated, reflecting any changes in product condition. Their versatility and adaptability can be seen in their swift adoption in both WMSs and receiving and tracking.

-   **Use in WMS.** QR codes can store detailed information such as product details, origin, expiry date, and more. They can also be linked to databases, allowing dynamic updating of information.

- **Receiving and Tracking**. Upon receipt in the warehouse, QR codes are scanned, which then updates the WMS with the item's details. As products move, QR codes can be rescanned to adjust inventory levels, track product location, or update item specifics such as changes to grading or cosmetic condition if needed.

Radio frequency identification (RFID) offers a more advanced solution. While it is pricier, its advantages can justify the cost. Unlike barcodes and QR codes, RFID tags can be detected from any direction, eliminating the need for a direct line of sight. They can store multiple data fields on a single label, which can be rewritten as needed, and allow bulk reading—features that barcodes lack.

- **Use in WMS**. RFID tags are embedded with a small amount of data, which can be read wirelessly. This technology supports real-time inventory management, enabling more accurate and efficient stock handling.
- **Receiving and Tracking**. As products with RFID tags enter or move within a warehouse, RFID readers automatically detect and update their status in the WMS. This eliminates manual scanning and reduces human error. Its ability to read multiple tags simultaneously also speeds up bulk processing. Some industries are embedding RFID in forward orders where the product is expected to be returned to aid the receiving process.

A rising trend within reverse logistics is the use of **license plate numbers (LPN)** as the primary means of tracking, particularly over serial numbers. This is crucial for products that lack serial numbers, as assigning a unique **license plate identification** essentially serializes such products. In reverse, one product may have different functional and cosmetic attributes. License plates allow facilities to identify how many products they have and what condition they are in. Additionally, since a product might circulate through a facility multiple times (e.g., a returned product that is then resold or reused for warranty replacements), using a unique license plate avoids confusion. This approach ensures that

WMSs and ERP systems can accurately track each product's journey, accounting for its age and the specific movements associated with its current state.

- **Use in WMS.** Instead of using product-specific serial numbers, LPN assigns a unique code (like a license plate) to every product, pallet, or batch. This is particularly useful for products without serial numbers or those returning to the warehouse multiple times.

- **Receiving and Tracking.** Products with LPNs are scanned upon entry, and their specific details—origin, condition, previous movements, etc.—are logged in the WMS. This method provides a comprehensive history and status of each item, ensuring accurate tracking and handling throughout its journey in the warehouse.

These identification methods serve as the eyes and ears of a WMS, enabling it to oversee vast inventories and complex logistics with precision and efficiency.

Industry 4.0 Applications in Reverse Logistics

In the realm of manufacturing, the concept of "smart factories" has emerged, signaling industries' embrace of smart technology. Some digital manufacturing technologies being employed to tackle challenges in manufacturing, forward logistics, and reverse logistics include augmented reality, **edge computing**, **big data**, **cloud-based systems**, mobile applications, AI and smart systems, and the **Internet of Things (IoT)**.[24]

Augmented Reality (AR)

AR superimposes digital information onto the physical environment. In reverse logistics, AR aids workers with tasks such as identification, step-by-step guidance for testing, repair, grading, navigating warehouses, and cleaning. This technology enables customers to self-repair devices at their location by creating a digital twin of a product. It also allows a technician to guide or assess a product remotely before making an on-site visit or the product is physically returned. Today, devices employ object recognition to identify returned objects using stored images. These images help detect cosmetic damage by comparing them with undamaged references. The level of damage on a device can be assessed against preset conditions to categorize its cosmetic state—such as "good," "better," or "best"—using image results.

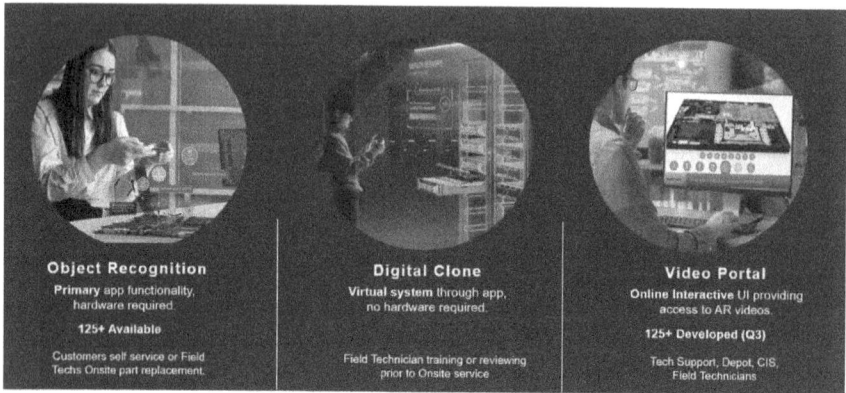

Figure 3.8. *Augmented Reality* slide presented by Thomas Maher from Dell Technologies at the RLA European Summit in June 2023.

Edge Computing

Edge computing processes data near its source, like on an operation floor, instead of a remote cloud-based system. This proximity decreases latency and expedites real-time decision-making in reverse logistics settings.

Big Data

With multiple types of devices and sensors generating extensive data, big data analytics is invaluable for drawing insights, enhancing operations, and predicting trends. In reverse logistics, products traverse multiple stages. Information like image capturing, data erasures, testing, and grading can seamlessly move from one stage to the next, allowing each stage to apply its grading criteria based on client requirements. Once a credible data entry is captured, there is no need to repeat the process at subsequent stages.

Cloud Systems

These platforms provide expandable storage and computational capabilities. Those in reverse operations can access cloud services as needed, promoting enhanced collaboration, data exchange, and analysis.

Mobile Applications

Mobile apps facilitate real-time oversight and control, spanning tasks from shipment tracking to machinery operation. These apps offer workers and managers immediate data access via handheld devices or AR tools like glasses. They can scan, print barcodes, labels, plates, input grades, assist with diagnostics, and more.

AI and Smart Systems

AI can anticipate product maintenance needs, streamline supply routes, project demand, and engage customers for return prevention. Intelligent systems process incoming data to optimize operations dynamically. For instance, Dell Technologies employs proactive monitoring with its Support Assist program. Here, computers notify Dell about their status, allowing Dell to address potential issues even before the customer recognizes and reports them.

Internet of Things (IoT)

IoT encompasses devices and systems that communicate and share data. Within reverse logistics, this could be sensors monitoring machine operations or automated devices moving products. In broader logistics, trackers on shipments offer real-time location insights.

Automated Grading

Image-capture technology is increasingly being employed to identify and immediately relist returned items, streamlining inventory-management processes. Modern systems, equipped with advanced cameras, can swiftly recognize received items, associate them with their respective SKU, capture their image, and list them for sale. A notable beneficiary of this technology is Goodwill, which handles a high volume of donations globally. Through the integration of conveyor and camera technology, they efficiently determine the market value of donated clothing and decide which items can be monetized. This innovation has markedly decreased operational expenses while boosting value generation.

An illustrative example of this technology in action is the HAMMOQ conveyor system. Products are placed on the conveyor, passed under a camera, and subsequently identified using post-image capture. In a 2023 article by the *Washington Post*, HAMMOQ's CEO highlighted the technology's efficiency, suggesting that items could potentially be processed for as nominal a cost as US$1.00.[25]

Furthermore, image-capture technology has expanded its scope to the domain of cosmetic grading. Using high-definition cameras, it is now possible to scan an item in detail and measure imperfections to the minutiae, such as their length, width, depth, or elevation. After visual inspection, this data can be utilized to define common damage profiles and assign appropriate cosmetic grades. A significant step toward standardizing this grading was taken in 2018 when CTIA introduced the Wireless Device Grading Scales Criteria. This publication laid out clear definitions for damage characteristics and criteria by surface.[26] Such detailed data, stipulating the thresholds for imperfections, can be fed into image-capture systems to automate cosmetic grading.

3.8 Circular Economy Reuse Case Study Two: goTRG, Pioneers in Reverse Logistics and Software Solutions

goTRG Overview

One company that specializes in enabling brands or retailers to deliver on their customer promise for returns by enhancing the post-purchase experience is goTRG. They provide dedicated returns SaaS that leads to cost-efficient and **eco-friendly logistics** throughout the product's reverse lifecycle, bringing returned items back to life by applying value-add services such as refurbishment. They provide a re-commerce platform as well, with connected liquidation, wholesale, and B2C-retail resale channels to promote a circular economy and help their clients achieve higher recoveries for their returns. When considering the leading returned product categories worldwide—apparel, home goods, and consumer electronics ranking as the top three—goTRG plays a pivotal role in the management of these diverse product categories. goTRG estimates a 60 percent recovery on returned products' acquired value.[26]

To solve the problem of returns, retailers and brands need to address every part of the post-purchase process from the time a return is initiated all the way through to its next life. goTRG strives to handle the entire process through its core services, which include:

1. **SaaS**
   a. *R1 Enterprise Returns Management*
      i. point-of-sale and e-commerce disposition and shopper experience
      ii. policies and contracts
      iii. intelligent pricing and disposition
      iv. reverse warehouse management systems (RWMS)
      v. re-commerce integration
      vi. external integrations
      vii. flexible returns, exchanges, and "keep it" options
      viii. trusted customer setup
      ix. drop-off location integration
   b. *ReturnPro Small-to-Medium Returns Management*
      i. marketplace integration and shopper experience
      ii. trusted customers and instant refunds
      iii. flexible returns, exchanges, and "keep it" options
      iv. drop-off location integration
      v. integration of supply-chain service provider
      vi. Re-commerce resale marketplace integration
      vii. messaging and notifications center

2. **Reverse Supply Chain Services**
   a. *receiving*
   b. *sorting*
   c. *return-to-vendor*
   d. *inspecting*
   e. *repairing*
   f. *sanitizing*
   g. *refurbishing*
   h. *data wiping*
   i. *repackaging*
   j. *fulfillment*

3. **Re-Commerce Services**
   a. *catalog management*
   b. *pricing management*
   c. *listing management*
   d. *marketplace management*
   e. *velocity management*
   f. *returns management*
   g. *customer support*
   h. *brand protection*

Category	Software As a Service		Logistics	Value Generation
Core Services	R1 Enterprise Returns Management	ReturnPro Small to Medium Returns Management	Reverse Supply Chain Services	ReCommerce Services
Service Offerings	Point-Of-Sale & eCommerce disposition and shopper experience	Marketplace integration & shopper experience	Receiving	Catalog management
	Policies and Contracts	Trusted customers & instant refunds	Sorting	Pricing management
	Intelligent Pricing and Disposition	Flexible returns, exchanges and "keep it" options	Return to vendor	Listing management
	RWMS (Reverse Warehouse Management Systems)	Drop-off location integration	Inspecting	Marketplace management
	ReCommerce integration	Supply chain service provider integration	Repairing	Velocity management
	External integrations	ReCommerce resale marketplace integration	Sanitizing	Returns management
	Flexible returns, exchanges and "keep it" options	Messaging & notifications center	Refurbishing	Customer support
	Trusted Customer setup		Data wiping	Brand protection
	Drop off location integration		Repackaging	
			Fulfillment	

Figure 3.9. goTRG core products offerings by category.

Managing the complexity and volume of product returns is a daunting task for many retailers, including the largest ones. These businesses often find themselves ill-equipped to handle the nuances and sheer scale of returns management.[27] Building the necessary teams, tools, and software system to manage complex returns effectively would not just be a substantial financial undertaking for these retailers, it would divert their focus and resources away from their core business activities as well. This is where specialized firms like goTRG come into play, offering expertise and dedicated resources to efficiently handle returns, allowing retailers to maintain their focus on primary business operations. These unique solutions and services they offer enable retailers and brands to navigate the challenges of returns management without burdening them with the additional expenses and complexities.

goTRG maintains an extensive catalog of over 100 million UPCs across their customer base and are skilled at processing high volumes of products, with over 40 million units flowing through their network of return centers each year.[28] They developed cutting-edge solutions that address the inherent complexities of reverse logistics. Their commitment to streamlining and improving these processes is evident in the innovative approaches and technologies they employ. goTRG helps enterprise businesses, brands, and small- to medium-size sellers across industries solve their returns challenges by getting as close to the point of return as possible and providing upstream, supply chain and re-commerce returns services and solutions that enhance the post-purchase experience, optimize the product returns journey, increase recoveries, and reduce costs.

In an interview conducted with Sender Shamiss, CEO of goTRG, he describes the company's value-added services into three pivotal categories:

1. **Software as a Service (SaaS)**
2. **Supply Chain Solutions**
3. **Re-Commerce**[29]

In this reuse case, we will revisit the best practices and concepts discussed in the first three chapters, demonstrating their real-world application in modern reverse logistics. This will showcase how these practices effectively manage a product's journey to achieve the four desired outcomes of reverse logistics. We'll delve into each of these offerings in detail, highlighting how goTRG adeptly realizes these outcomes through their innovative return solutions and services. Specifically, we will explore how goTRG helps navigate the product's journey across the three fundamentals of reverse logistics: (1) asset recovery, (2) operations, and (3) value generation.

"As a child of the 90's I remember the slogan reduce, reuse, recycle (in that order). The concept of reduce is not realistic in today's consumerist society, but "reuse" is a driving force for how we have modeled our company and values. We don't want to touch just one part of an inefficient returns ecosystem. We want to solve the entire problem at every step along the way first by reusing, and then, as a last resort, recycling."

– Sender Shamiss, CEO and cofounder

Figure 3.10. In the 2021 annual sustainability report of goTRG, CEO and co-founder Sender Shamiss reflects on the core principles that inspired the formation of the company.

Offering One: Software and Systems

Optimizing Return Processes through Advanced Data Management

Recognizing the pivotal role of data in optimizing reverse logistics, goTRG's expertise not only spans automation and data management but also includes the adept handling of multi-channel returns.[30X] Central to this expertise is their expansive data lake comprising over 100 million UPCs, forming the backbone of database, and allowing them to make intelligent disposition recommendations on an ever-expanding assortment of products.[31] For every UPC in their system, goTRG meticulously captures a minimum of seven core attributes such as size, weight, country of origin, photographs, and detailed item descriptions. These attributes are essential for maintaining data consistency at an individual unit level and enable the engine to identify the most profitable disposition path for each item.

goTRG's robust enterprise, the returns-management platform, was originally tailored for large retailers, designed to handle scaled volumes of returns with efficiency. Recognizing the diverse needs across the retail spectrum, propelled by e-commerce growth, goTRG has also distilled the best features of this enterprise software into a more accessible platform, ReturnPro.[32] ReturnPro is specifically crafted for small- and medium-sized brands, enabling them to effectively manage their returns on major marketplaces like Shopify, Amazon, and Walmart. This strategic segmentation of their technology offerings underlines goTRG's commitment to providing scalable and versatile solutions, catering to the varied demands of the retail industry.

Revolutionizing Reverse Logistics: goTRG's Integration of AI and ML in Disposition Intelligence and Value Generation

At the heart of goTRG's platform is their AI-powered disposition intelligence engine—a cutting-edge DSS crafted to adeptly steer the journey of products the moment a return is initiated through to its next life. This advanced tool plays a pivotal role in optimizing the lifecycle of returned items by directing them to the most lucrative path, thus significantly refining the return process and enhancing its efficiency.[33]

The engine operates by analyzing real-time market data alongside historical sales velocity metrics. Through this advanced AI-driven analysis, it ensures that each item is channeled to the most economically or environmentally friendly sales avenue or disposal method, thereby maximizing its potential value and streamlining its journey through the supply chain. In addition to this, their technology plays a vital role in the real-time listing, modification, and repricing of items.

This technology enables them to minimize manual handling (or "touches") of products, thereby enhancing efficiency and reducing cost. Whether it is determining if a product should be restocked, refurbished, liquidated, recycled, donated, or disposed of, AI and ML provide goTRG with the capability to make these decisions quickly and accurately.

The result is a highly efficient reverse logistics process that maximizes the return on the product's value with fewer touches. This not only benefits goTRG and its clients but also contributes to the broader goals of sustainability through reducing unnecessary shipping and waste.

The integration of their disposition intelligence engine across the company's SaaS, supply chain, and re-commerce operations facilitates the effective routing of products for value generation, whether it involves value improvement, individual packaging, or preparation for bulk shipping. The AI-powered disposition engine within goTRG's extensive contract management system is crucial in determining the optimal routing for each product, further streamlining their reverse logistics operations.

Complex Contract Management and Uncovering Value within the RTV Process

As discussed above, companies like goTRG are progressively utilizing automation and AI-supported item disposition to enhance efficiency and reduce the processing costs associated with reverse logistics. By implementing this intelligent disposition capability as far upstream as possible (meaning as close to the point of return-initiation as feasible), these systems can make more accurate and timely decisions that benefit the retailer's resources and business.

Before a disposition can be made, however, the system needs to check against the policy set forth by the retailer and their vendor partner to see if there are any contractual requirements for the returns merchandise authorization (RMA) process, or handling of the item being returned. The problem is that policy management software does not typically take into account returns management and mostly focuses on forward logistics related to the purchase of product. Most retailers have thousands of vendor policies to keep track of and as new SKUs or generations get introduced, they need to continuously update and manage those policies. Most often these policies are stored in legacy systems or on spreadsheets and rely on internal knowledge to understand the nuances of these policies. They also do not automatically sync or communicate with other areas of the retailers' and vendors' ecosystem like their website, **point-of-sale (POS) systems,** or accounting systems. As a result, they are often full of data errors, outdated information, and other inconsistencies that lead to conflicts, miscommunication, processing delays, and wasted dollars.

Within these contracts, there is an even more overlooked component, which is how the retailer and vendor should treat returns and what the allotment is for the retailer to send back to the vendor and claim credit for. Because retailers and vendors do not track their RTV returns systematically, they often play guessing games as to how many units were received and arrive at a compromised number without any tracking, data, or evidence. goTRG estimates that currently only 70–80 percent of return authorization (RA) allotments are being exercised because of the existing inefficiencies within the process. Often, retailers cannot even push disposition recommendations further upstream to reduce processing costs because their agreements (merchant, vendor, accounting, legal, etc.) live in disparate locations. Handling over two hundred thousand vendor contracts, the goTRG returns SaaS capacity is evident; its impressive track record includes managing over twenty thousand vendor contracts for a single client. This extensive management led to the filing of an additional $1.8 billion in vendor credits in just one year, showcasing its significant financial opportunity impact within the RTV process.

To address the challenges around the RMA and RTV processes, the company built a contract management module as one of the core components to their software offering.[34] This module serves as a shared workspace for retailers and vendors to upload and manage all of their returns contracts in a single location and gives them the power to instantly update disposition rules, manage RTV policies, returns authorizations, automate notifications, credits, and shipments as well as file credit approval requests. The software ensures that their data is clean, unified, current, and can be dynamically updated and maintained in a centralized database, which is essential for the effective management of reverse logistics operations, and ensures a robust foundation that provides pertinent, actionable insights exactly when needed.[35]

goTRG's Data-Driven Approach to Sales-Enablement and the Customer Journey

The backbone of goTRG's approach to handling multi channel returns lies in their advanced returns-management solution, designed to optimize the post-purchase experience for retailers. This system goes beyond mere data management; it actively contributes to reducing returns, optimizing costs, and cultivating customer loyalty.[36] Central to this is a consistent returns experience, whether online or in-store. The platform can be integrated into any in-store POS system or online e-commerce platform to enable retailers to configure specific reason codes for each item. Customers can provide detailed feedback on their return reasons as well. This feature is complemented by convenient return options, including instant exchanges and flexible drop-offs at a network of over ten thousand points, even offering box-less returns for added convenience. Further enhancing the customer experience, the system is equipped to mitigate fraud effectively. Retailers can set criteria to identify trusted customers and offer them additional flexible return options like "keep it" services or partial refunds. This tailored approach to returns not only reduces losses but also strengthens customer trust and loyalty.

goTRG's returns platform helps retailers and brands facilitate flexible, direct communication with customers through various channels, including SMS, email, and WhatsApp.[37] This versatility ensures that customers are reached in the most convenient and effective manner, further enhancing their overall experience and satisfaction. By focusing on these aspects, goTRG's solution ensures a smooth, efficient, and customer-centric returns process, key to driving long-term success for retailers.

goTRG's system adeptly associates return-reason codes such as "product defective" from the TPS, with corresponding testing results uploaded after a product has been received and triaged at one of their dedicated returns centers. This association is instrumental in providing constructive feedback to manufacturers, leading to improvements in product quality and pinpointing specific causes for increased returns, whether they stem from product issues or fraudulent activities. Such detailed analysis is key in identifying and addressing the underlying reasons for returns, enhancing the overall efficiency of the return process.

Offering 2: Supply Chain and Same Unit Value Improvement Services

goTRG offers a suite of third-party logistics services, designed to simplify the complexities of (reverse) supply chain management for manufacturers and retailers. These services are delivered through a global network of returns centers, which are crucial in managing the lifecycle of returned products. To ensure the highest quality, compliance, and consistency in these centers, goTRG adheres to a rigorous framework of formal standard operating procedures. In total, over four hundred standard operating procedures govern every activity within their warehouses. These are further supported by an extensive library of over five hundred training documents, encompassing user guides, ads sheets, videos, and more.[38] Each returns center is staffed with specialized labor, proficiently trained in utilizing goTRG's software platforms. This meticulous approach ensures efficient and standardized processing and management of returns, reflecting goTRG's commitment to operational excellence and reliability in its 3PL services.

The software platforms they developed are critical in providing the infrastructure needed for tracking, diagnosing, and deciding the fate of each returned item. By integrating these systems with their logistics services, goTRG ensures a seamless transition for products from the point of return to their next destination—be it restocking, recycling, or refurbishment. The sophistication of the software coupled with the skilled labor at these centers allows for a nuanced approach to handling returns, which can be a significant pain point for retailers and manufacturers alike.

Reverse Warehouse Management Systems (RWMS)

Traditional warehouse management systems excel at managing new inventory. WMS can accurately document stock statuses, manage storage, move items around facilities, and arrange transportation. They offer visibility into a business's entire stock while overseeing fulfillment from distribution to store shelf. goTRG built its own custom reverse warehouse management system (RWMS) to optimize the reverse flow of products in a warehouse environment and make data-driven decisions every time a warehouse worker touches the product from the minute returns pallets are offloaded into the facility.[39]

Their reverse warehouse management systems, with all the standard WMS and enterprise resource management (ERP) functionality, consists of everything needed for intelligent retailers to maximize returns recovery. goTRG's RWMS can implement large-scale operational changes fast and inexpensively with a drag-and-drop, no-code workflow creator. The RWMS is integrated with their intelligent disposition engine to ensure inventory is always moving down the path that maximizes recovery. And beyond normal warehouse activities like check-in, inspection, and sortation, goTRG's RWMS offers specialized modules like a repair workstation to handle nuanced tasks such as refurbishment and repair. Throughout the process, the software guarantees the best possible business decisions for maximum recovery. This includes assessing the value of on-hand inventory and updating disposition recommendations based on its stage, from receiving and refurbishing to palletization.

Ultimately, RWMS provides goTRG's clients with the benefits of higher recoveries and faster velocity by continuously moving products through their reverse lifecycle, increased revenue with disposition intelligence, and warehouse efficiency that minimizes costly touches.

Automated Sortation: The Walmart Return Example

Consider the reverse logistics needed to support the retail behemoth Walmart. With vast brand product assortment—from apparel and home goods to electronics, health, beauty, toys, and automotive—Walmart's returns from all over the United States are directed to centralized returns centers and eventually make their way to goTRG.

Figure 3.11. This is an example of one box received at a goTRG facility containing multiple products. This image was featured in a 2022 CNN article on the expense of returns.

The sorting process of these returned items can be labor-intensive given their sheer volume and diversity of brands. goTRG takes up this challenge by employing an **automated sortation** tool when packages arrive at one of their dedicated returns centers. This system utilizes return information from an RMA or a transfer order and matches it with the expected contents, or manifest, of the return order. When a shipment arrives, it is unloaded and placed on a conveyor belt, which transports it past an image-capturing system. The image-capturing system photographs all sides of the box, records tracking information, and matches it to the expected order. The images serve as verification of whether the package incurs damage, or if the item is not packaged, what condition it might be in to make a determination on the resale strategy.

Figure 3.12. Image of goTRG's automated receiving system, featured in a 2022 CNN article called "Just Keep It."

The tracking information, captured via a barcode on the shipment label, feeds into a decision support system, which matches the tracking information to the order and the order to the contents. This information enables the automated sortation system to direct the box to the appropriate chute in a logical order. For instance, home goods might go down one chute, while electronics follow a different path, and apparel is sent to another. Complex returns with multiple category types can be routed to more experienced operators. Boxes with unmatchable tracking numbers are segregated and immediately sent to a troubleshooting team specialized in handling exceptions. After this process is completed, products are categorized and moved to the optimal processing stations that can triage the expected contents of the shipment.

This automation reduces the need for manual sorting and directs products to appropriate stations for grading and testing. Given the wide range of product categories from clients like Walmart, automated sortation can significantly impact labor cost and productivity in return locations.

The image of goTRG's automated sortation system in Figure 3.12 depicts an efficient returns processing center. It features a conveyor belt system that feeds packages to different output lanes, programmed for daily receipts in advance of the products' arrival. This planning allows for labor optimization during receiving, improving the speed at which orders can be processed, thus enhancing customer experience.

The image shows nineteen different receiving chutes, each receiving boxes of varying contents. This part represents the intake process. Toward the top-left, organized racks display shrink-wrapped, similar products prepared to be shipped to the next stage in the reverse logistics process. The image does not capture the in-between operational processes. However, the contrast between the variety of boxes in shapes and sizes on the conveyor belt system and the organized approach of outbound products perfectly represents the essence of reverse logistics. It shows how advanced companies like goTRG are leveraging technologies to maximize the value and speed of their products in support of their customers.

License Plating and Item Routing

Once goTRG has automatically sorted a package into the most efficient processing lane, the next phase is **product identification**, condition evaluation, and outlet selection for value generation. The operator determines the identity of the item by scanning its UPC or looking it up in a database. A license plate identification is then attached to the item, verifying that the received item corresponds with the one noted in the return merchandise authorization or transfer order and individually identifying that item for the product journey. goTRG has branded their LPN a serialized license plate (SLP), which serves the same function—being a unique identifier.[40] This method not only streamlines the return process but also plays a vital role in fraud prevention by ensuring the authenticity and correct categorization of returned items.

After identifying the condition and potential of each returned item, goTRG's AI-powered disposition engine systemically determines the most suitable value-generation outlet, in accordance with the partner's predefined conditions.[41] The most lucrative strategy involves reselling the item as new. The AI-powered disposition engine is able to reintegrate a returned product back into the retailer's supply chain to be sold again and generate retail sale revenue for the partner. This approach is applicable when the product is confirmed to be unused or in saleable condition.

For items that do not qualify for "resale as new," alternative value-generation routes are employed. These include either returning the product to the vendor or value-added touches such as refurbishing, testing, data wipe, sanitization, or leveraging a diverse range of over twenty different platforms to realize its value. Each strategy is meticulously evaluated to align with the item's condition and market potential.

Once the value-generation strategy is established, goTRG's robust warehouse management system takes over, orchestrating the efficient movement of the product. The RWMS ensures that each item is correctly packaged and prepared for its subsequent journey, whether it is returning to the retail cycle, being sent back to the vendor, value-added touches, or moving through various resale platforms.

Offering 3: Re-Commerce Solutions

One of the most common challenges faced by brands and resellers is managing a single pool of inventory across multiple resale channels or third-party marketplaces. Each marketplace—Walmart, eBay, Amazon, Shopify, Back Market, Rebello, and others—has its own distinct grading description, condition, and information requirements for each product.[42] This diversity necessitates brands to manually update each third-party marketplace account, which can be a resource-intensive and time-consuming process.

goTRG's re-commerce system addresses this challenge by offering a marketplace-channel management approach, particularly for returned items. Their automated decision engine not only analyzes online marketplaces to determine the current resale value of items but also automates the listing process and pricing strategy. This includes considering key factors like marketing, repricing, and brand protection strategies to ensure the highest recovery path for each individual item.

The system effectively aligns the condition of the product entered into their RWMS system with the marketplace grade suitable for each platform (or specified by the client for whom they are managing the return), thereby simplifying the process of managing inventory across various channels.

By automating these processes, goTRG's solution significantly reduces the burden on brands and resellers, allowing them to efficiently manage their inventory across multiple marketplaces without the need for manual intervention. This streamlined approach not only saves time and resources but also optimizes the resale value of each item, ensuring a better return on investment for businesses.

Ultimately, a decision is made on the most suitable sales avenue, whether it is direct to consumers, wholesalers, or businesses. The system also handles listing items on the appropriate channels and fulfills the forward logistics process upon order submission. In some cases, it may involve exporting the goods.

Their AI-powered disposition engine manages real-time listing, modification, and repricing of items. This dynamic feature allows for immediate adjustments in the marketplace, ensuring that each item is presented and priced in a manner that reflects current market conditions and demands. By automating these processes, goTRG's technology enhances the efficiency and responsiveness of product management, facilitating a more agile and effective retail strategy. As goTRG harnesses the power of AI to optimize their re-commerce solutions, offering precise product valuation and effective online-marketplace management, they extend this innovative approach to their other B2B and B2C wholesale, liquidation, and retail platforms.

To enable retailers and vendors to protect their brand, reduce costs, and achieve maximum recoveries for their returns, goTRG recognizes that it is imperative to offer the ability to sell both finished-refurbished and overstock inventory as well as as-is pallets. This requires diverse sales channels and the ability to manage those channels. These include:

- direct-to-consumer through the original sales channel for re-furbished and overstock inventory;

- direct-to-consumer, third-party marketplace sales for refurbished and overstock inventory (Walmart.com, eBay, Amazon, etc.);
- direct-to-consumer through a proprietary dedicated marketplace specializing in sales of returned and overstock inventory (vipoutlet.com);
- business-to-business marketplace for refurbished and overstock inventory (goWholesale.com); and
- business-to-business marketplace for **"as-is"** untouched customer returns and overstock by the pallet or truck load (directliquidation.com).

goWholesale

A re-commerce application designed to address the challenge of reselling refurbished, new, and over-box returned products as well as overstock and shelf pulls, goWholesale is unlike traditional resale methods where items are typically sold individually. goWholesale introduces a novel approach by grouping these items into larger lots for bulk resale. Accessible via both a web-based interface suitable for desktop computers and laptops as well as an adapted version for mobile devices like smartphones and tablets, it offers flexibility for its users.

At the core of the goWholesale platform lies a dynamic ask/offer system tailored specifically for the wholesale goods market. This innovative approach allows registered users to not only create custom pallets or truckloads of products but also to engage in online negotiations. This approach ensures a transparent and dynamic pricing mechanism, tailored to the real-time demand and preferences of the users. Alongside this, the application provides users with the capability to view historical data and ongoing trends related to price and demand, aiding them in making informed purchasing decisions. Every product on the platform has a predetermined "ask price," which acts as an initial point of reference. From here, users can submit their offers, which may be above or below this asking price, depending on their assessment of the lot's value and the prevailing market demand.

To ensure the integrity and reliability of the transactions on goWholesale, there is a rigorous user registration and approval process in place. This process ensures that only verified and genuine buyers gain access to bid on the platform. Additionally, to maintain a trustworthy relationship with the suppliers, the platform allows them to set specific guidelines or "rules of engagement" for how their returned products are to be liquidated. Guidelines can include directives like minimum pricing, specific buyer qualifications, or other pertinent stipulations. goWholesale meticulously ensures that all these rules are adhered to during transactions, thus upholding supplier trust and ensuring compliance.

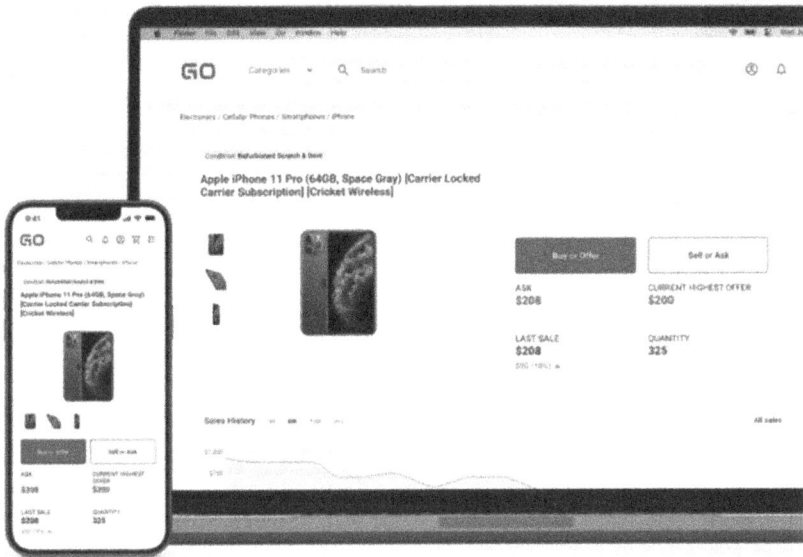

Figure 3.13. Image of goWholesale's liquidation platform for overstock or returned goods in computer and mobile format.

Direct Liquidation

Direct Liquidation.com partners with major retailers, manufacturers, and suppliers to sell as-is untouched customer returns and overstock by the pallet or truck load. This allows buyers to access affordable customer returns and overstock from a reputable source while handling the entire sales process for the sellers. The site offers a wide range of product categories such as apparel, home goods, consumer electronics, furniture, and more.

Direct Liquidation.com employs both auction-style listings and fixed-price sales. This means that buyers can participate in competitive bidding for pallets or lots of inventory or choose to purchase products immediately at a "buy now" price. Many listings on DirectLiquidation. com provide detailed manifests that help buyers make informed decisions when placing bids or making purchases.[43]

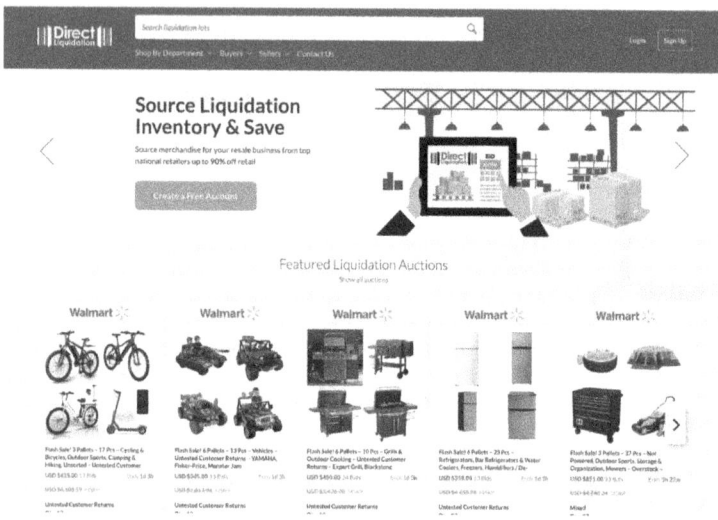

Figure 3.14. Screenshot of the Direct Liquidation.com homepage taken November 13, 2023.

Direct to Consumer (D2C)

goTRG boasts extensive integrations with major third-party market-places. In addition to leveraging these popular channels, goTRG has also established its own direct-to-consumer site, VIP Outlet.[44] By listing and selling through popular platforms, goTRG is able to help their partners find the best value as fast as possible.

Maximizing the speed of product movement directly to the next customer through goTRG's own direct-to-consumer (D2C) channels saves on the fees typically charged by third-party marketplaces. In addition to the monetary advantage, this approach also grants goTRG greater control over the customer journey.

VIP Outlet

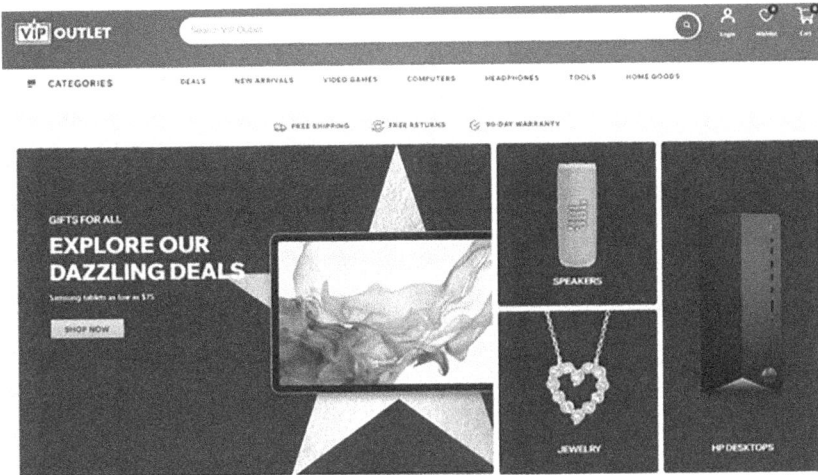

Figure 3.15. Screen shot of the VIP homepage taken November 13, 2023.

VIP Outlet serves as goTRG's primary resale channel, catering to the needs of the nation's largest retailers and manufacturers. It offers a diverse range of new and refurbished products, including apparel, home goods, electronics, and more. In contrast to other competitive marketplaces that often undervalue goods for rapid sales, goTRG adopts a more strategic approach: they focus on targeted marketing and rigorous quality control not only to uphold the brand reputation but also to ensure the maximum value recovery from every product. This dual strategy of broad marketplace integration and a unique direct-to-consumer outlet gives goTRG an edge over competing providers.

To help retailers achieve maximum recovery for their returns, goTRG recognizes that it is imperative to offer diversified sales channels, including 3P, D2C, direct D2C to the client's marketplace, their own D2C, direct B2B for finished goods, and as-is pallets. This strategy allows goTRG's intelligent disposition engine to select the most strategic resale channel for every item and deliver an extensive sales solution for their clients.

goTRG's Results

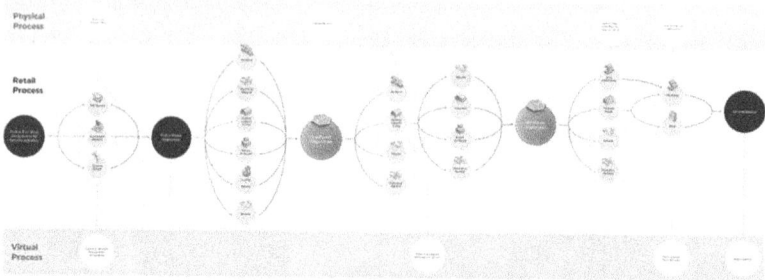

Figure 3.16. The image depicts goTRG's circular process for managing returns, indicating a sustainable and systematic approach to handling consumer returns, distressed inventory, and fixed assets.

goTRG has made significant strides in the field of retail returns and refurbishment, as evinced by their notable achievements. Their innovative software and warehouse solutions, combined with effective re-commerce strategies, have enabled retailers to recover almost 60 percent more profits from costly returns. This approach also contributes an additional 2–4 percent to retailers' bottom lines, marking a substantial financial impact.[45] Since 2015, goTRG has played a crucial role in environmental sustainability by diverting over 20 million pounds of waste from landfills, with the company itself landfilling less than 1 percent of the items it handles.[46]

Furthermore, their processes have made it possible for approximately 20 percent more returned products to be repurposed as new and sold at full price, demonstrating their efficiency in resource utilization and contribution to the circular economy.[47]

goTRG's innovative approach in handling retail returns and refurbishment not only demonstrates their capability in recovering substantial profits from returns and adding to retailers' bottom lines but also highlights their commitment to environmental sustainability by diverting millions of pounds from landfills. Their success in reprocessing and maximizing value from returns showcases the efficiency and effectiveness of their reverse logistics operations. This case illustrates an optimal modern implementation of reverse logistics principles, setting a high standard in the industry for achieving financial, operational, environmental, and customer satisfaction goals.

Chapter 4

Understanding Purchasing and Return Behavior

4.1 Navigating Returns and Consumer Behavior in the Circular Economy

When a company offers a customer guarantee or return policy, it is not a matter of *if* a return will happen but rather *when, how,* and in *what* condition. While forecasting the specifics of product returns is challenging, this unpredictability does not exempt reverse logistics teams from striving for excellence. If a company commits to customer-oriented returns programs, it must also ensure the infrastructure is in place to handle these commitments. Reverse logistics professionals must grasp the nuances of different customer segments and craft programs that resonate with their distinct needs.

The market largely consists of two customer types: those inclined toward new products (Customer One) and those opting for used products due to cost or availability (Customer Two+). Each customer type can be broken down further and analyzed for marketing strategies. An effective circular economy strategy addresses the needs of both segments and thereby tap into the benefits of a more complete business model. As product prices soar, fewer customers may be willing to pay normal prices, ushering in new market competitors of the digital age like peer-to-peer used-product marketplaces. Manufacturers that only prioritize new sales might overlook the potential of the Customer Two+ in this environment.

This chapter delves deeper into the intricate dynamics of Customer One's and Customer Two+'s buying and return behaviors. Each segment has different buying preferences according to cost and availability as well as different preferences for the "highest bidder" to which they will return their goods. Understanding their behavior will help predict the conditions of returns, build the right return services and incentives for the different customer segments, and maximize the financial investment of operating a company's return centers. Here are some other benefits of customer behavior insights:

- upholding sales promises to customers
- managing financial and human resources effectively
- ensuring adequate warranty provisions
- guiding behavior in the desired direction
- encouraging behaviors supporting green logistics

There is a new supply curve focusing on returned products that has pricing behavior that responds to the laws of supply and demand. This chapter serves as a guide to understanding this emerging market.

Customer One's Characteristics

Customer One is recognized for their distinctive purchasing and return patterns for new items, highlighting the necessity for a strategic marketing plan that not only boosts product consumption, customer expenditure, and buying frequency but also involves creating efficient return policies. This approach is crucial to comprehend their preference for new products, anticipate sales trends, and understand return motivations, thereby enabling the development of suitable tools and resources to address the underlying reasons for their product returns.

With the correct incentives in place, companies can generate value and amass the resources from Customer One required to engage their next target—Customer Two+. For Customer Two+, the main source of supply comes from Customer One's returns. Drawing from the

Diffusion of Innovation Theory, the purchasing behaviors of new customers can be categorized into three distinct groups:[1]

1. **Early Adopters (NN).** These customers are the first to embrace new products and are often seen as trendsetters. They are willing to pay a premium price and are not as concerned with cost or availability, since they are motivated by a desire to be the first to own the latest technology. Consider the launch of the new 2023 Dodge Ram. **Early adopters** will quickly upgrade to the 2024 model as soon as it is launched. Another example of this type of behavior can be seen in iPhone users who eagerly wait in line to upgrade to the next model, such as the iPhone 15, even if their current model works perfectly.

   Early adopters are known for their willingness to buy new products during the first sales period (S1), which typically results in the highest volume and value of sales for a product. The price paid for the new product is at its highest point during S1. This customer segment is crucial for companies as their early adoption helps to establish the product in the market and generate positive buzz, which can encourage other customers to make a purchase.

   During the initial sales phase of a model, returns from early adopters may be limited due to their interest in novelty and acceptance of minor flaws. However, their tendency for frequent upgrades means they often trade in or sell their old products when buying new ones. This introduces used items into the marketplace during the second sales period (S2), coinciding with the release of a new model and their transition away from the older version.

2. **Early Pragmatists (Nu).** This customer segment tends to purchase a new product during its first sales period (S1) but is not motivated to upgrade immediately with the launch of each new model. Instead, **early pragmatists** will use their product until it no longer meets their needs before considering any upgrades. They are opinion leaders, and their feedback and

return patterns can provide valuable insights for both marketing and logistics teams.

Returning to the 2023 Dodge Ram example, we can see that early pragmatists may purchase the vehicle in the first sales period but drive it until it no longer suits their needs. Many factors can lead to this behavior, such as the mileage threshold being reached, the vehicle going out of warranty, or mechanical failure. Unlike early adopters, early pragmatists tend to upgrade at a slower rate, which means that the supply of their products will become available later and be returned at a slower rate during the S2 period.

3. **Value Seekers (ON).** These customers are the most price-sensitive and will only buy a new product when it becomes more affordable. They are unlikely to be early adopters of the first sales period. Instead, they may wait until the product is widely available and the price has fallen as the next model drops—but they will still only purchase a product in new condition.

A value seeker will not buy the new 2023 Dodge Ram when it is launched as a new vehicle. When the 2024 model comes out, they expect that dealers will attempt to liquidate their remaining stock of the 2023 model, and they will purchase it at a lower price point then when it first launched, and the prices changes from the price point when the product was launched (P1) to the second price point when the new model is released (P2).

Value seekers will buy new but only when the next model or models are launched. Return rates for this group may be lower for this product when they own it because they have the benefit from others' feedback and experience incorporated into the manufacturing and support process. Their used products will become available last because their main motivation to upgrade is based on price, not the desire for the latest products.

Marketing and sales teams need to understand these customer profiles to tailor their strategies to each group's motivations. For example, early adopters may be enticed with exclusive launch events and special offers, while value seekers may be incentivized with discounts and promotions. Likewise, reverse logistics teams that understand these behaviors will be better able to predict the respective return trends.

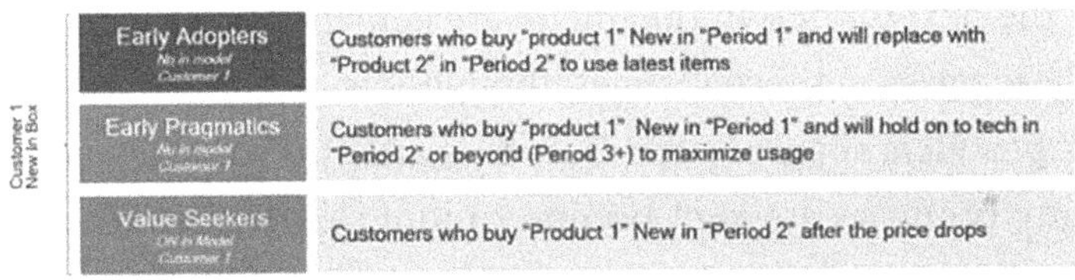

Figure 4.1. *Customer One Characteristics* provides an overview of the three primary customer characteristics. Understanding these profiles can guide marketing and sales strategies to cater to each group's unique needs and motivations.

Upholding Customer One Promises

It is no surprise that customer promises made to Customer One occupy the most attention of the marketing and sales teams. The visibility of these commitments is unmistakable, encompassing elements such as well-defined return windows, extended warranty options, and flexible options for **omni-channel returns**.

This suite of promises is far from being just a superficial marketing tactic. The marketing and sales teams are deeply committed to these promises, dedicating significant resources to ensure that their customers are not only aware of these commitments but also have confidence in the brand's ability to fulfill them. However, the responsibility for upholding these promises extends beyond these teams. Reverse logistics teams have a critical role in actualizing these promises. Their vigilance and understanding of customer adoption rates and return behaviors are essential for effective planning and smooth operational execution.

The logistics surrounding new product returns are relatively uncomplicated when a new model is introduced into the market, also known as the N phase, where parts and packaging are plentiful. The complexity increases as products move to the N-1 phase and beyond, where the next models in the lineup are launched. Handling returns in this phase poses more challenges, though it is certainly manageable.

As products age and parts become harder to source, ensuring that warranty promises are kept becomes more challenging. The company needs to be strategic in planning for these eventualities, ensuring that they can continue to support their products effectively, even as they transition through different phases of their lifecycle. This strategic planning is crucial not only for maintaining customer trust and satisfaction but also for sustaining the brand's competitive advantage in a market where Customer One is highly sought after.

4.2 New Equipment Product Curve Model

When a product enters the market (M), it is typically met with soaring demand, resulting in substantial sales at P1. In this debut sales phase, the product's production and pricing peak from the sales of early adopters and pragmatists. This high-demand phase signifies the curve's zenith in product value. As the firm gears up for the next iteration, the existing product's production slackens, causing its market value to slide.

Then as the next product version is rolled out, the product enters its next status, or N-1, because it is one model older than the latest version. Consequently, the previous version's demand dips, causing a shift in production focus to the newer model. The preceding version is typically priced lower than the fresh model to streamline sales and prevent stockpile issues. This price recalibration to P2 aligns with the market entry of value seekers. As demand for the older version recedes, a point is reached where it is phased out—depicting the curve's trough.

Notation	Definition
N	The debut product during its launch phase, like a 2023 model preceding the 2024 version.
N-1	The product one iteration behind the latest, post its successor's launch, such as the discounted 2023 model after the 2024 debut.
N-2	The product two iterations older than the current, post N-1's introduction.
N-"X"	Products 'X' iterations older than the latest, post the N-X-1 version's debut.

Figure 4.2. *Equipment Lifecycle Stages* table defines the notations used to describe the lifecycle stages of a product, particularly for models that are updated frequently.

Figure 4.3., the New Equipment Product Curve, illustrates the standard lifecycle of a product as it is produced and updated over time. This model sheds light on the product's market entry and the evolution of its pricing strategies, sales volume, and product value.

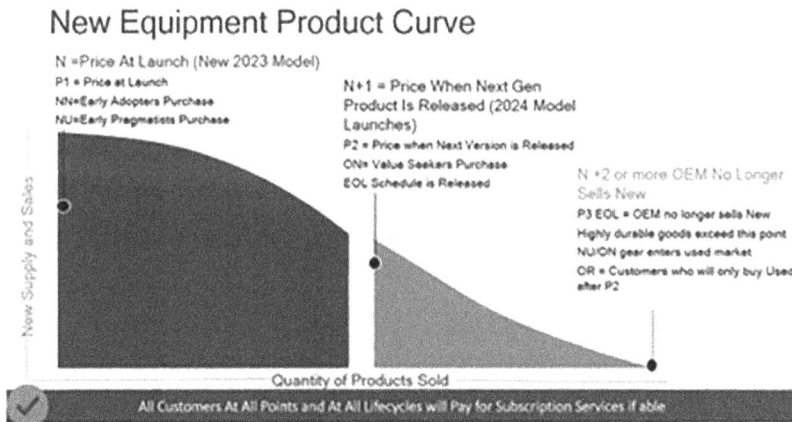

New Equipment Product Curve

N =Price At Launch (New 2023 Model)
P1 = Price at Launch
NN=Early Adopters Purchase
NU=Early Pragmatists Purchase

N+1 = Price When Next Gen Product Is Released (2024 Model Launches)
P2 = Price when Next Version is Released
ON= Value Seekers Purchase
EOL Schedule is Released

N +2 or more OEM No Longer Sells New
P3 EOL = OEM no longer sells New
Highly durable goods exceed this point
NU/ON gear enters used market
OR = Customers who will only buy Used after P2

New Supply and Sales

Quantity of Products Sold

All Customers At All Points and At All Lifecycles will Pay for Subscription Services if able

Figure 4.3. The "New Equipment Product Curve" represents the standard manufacturing supply cycle of a product introduced to the market. This visual representation contrasts new supply and sales against the product's behavior over time.

In essence, the New Equipment Product Curve offers a visual depiction of a product's lifecycle. As newer models surface, their older counterparts see reduced production, causing volume and value to drop. Use this curve to decode volume and value changes, inform your production teams, write your marketing blueprints, and ensure that products are phased out sustainably.

Marketers aim to accelerate customers' transition to the latest model. With this visual tool, marketers can use insights on demand and change product values to optimize revenue at each juncture. Pairing this curve with tailored marketing approaches for different consumer segments offers sharper targeting. The interplay of early adopters, pragmatists, and value seekers demands distinct strategies that cater to unique desires and priorities. This intel informs production, pricing, and sustainable end-of-life strategies amongst these three groups.

End of life (EOL) is a critical term in product lifecycle management, referring to the point when a manufacturer decides to completely cease the production or active support of a particular product. Whether or not a product is considered EOL is influenced by various factors, including technological advancements, reduced consumer demand, or the introduction of newer models. Once a product reaches its EOL, any remaining inventory is typically liquidated over a specified period. It is important to note that a product might go through multiple releases or iterations before being discontinued. These versions can have varied lifespans, but once a product line or series is determined to be EOL, it signifies a full cessation of its production and primary support by the manufacturer.

End of support (EOS) comes into play even after a product stops being physically produced. Manufacturers may continue to support the product through customer support, warranty services, or software updates until it no longer makes economic sense to do so. The EOS date is typically set after the product has ceased production. This ongoing support is a commitment to ensuring that the product continues to function as advertised, in line with the customer promise made at the time of sale.

The EOS phase is fundamental for maintaining the product's utility and customer satisfaction. During this period, the residual value of the product may change, reflecting the diminishing manufacturer support. However, this phase also opens opportunities for third-party companies or aftermarket services to provide support solutions, especially if there is still demand for the product.

Once a product reaches its EOS, the dynamics surrounding it change significantly. The shift from manufacturer support to third-party or aftermarket solutions marks an important transition in the product's lifecycle, emphasizing the evolving nature of product support and customer service even beyond the manufacturer's direct involvement.

The New Equipment Product Curve is a valuable tool for shaping sales strategies over a product's lifecycle, and it plays a role in developing returns programs and customer promises, particularly for reverse logistics teams. This curve is particularly relevant in sectors like automotive, technology, fashion, and home goods, where durability, value, and regular product upgrades are key.

Some fashion retailers adeptly offer extended return windows during a product launch, strategically reducing this period as the season's new lineup draws closer. The approach is particularly effective when demand for unused products decreases due to seasonal changes, such as shifts in weather. By offering a longer return window initially, customers are encouraged to become early adopters, feeling more confident in their purchases with the flexibility of a generous return policy. It also helps reverse logistics teams plan resources needed to account for variable volumes.

Such a nuanced approach not only addresses the immediate sales objectives but also considers the broader implications of customer satisfaction and brand loyalty. It demonstrates a deep understanding of consumer behavior and market trends, which is essential for maintaining a competitive edge in the market.

4.3 Customer Two+: *The Value-Driven Consumer*

There is a customer-marketing segmentation for those who are interested in purchasing pre-owned products, as there is a growing demand for these products.[2] These customers (Customer Two, Customer Three, Customer X . . .) prefer a device that is in good working condition and are willing to pay less for a device with cosmetic defects. The numbers two and three refer to the passing on of the product from one user to the next, with Customer X representing iterations beyond the initial three customers. This sequence of ownership is especially common in industries such as real estate, where assets have a long lifespan, and multiple users take turns using a singular item.

The widespread success of Customer One's returns programs has established a robust precedent of standards and practices for processing Customer Two+'s returns. Yet, a one-size-fits-all approach is not always appropriate. Customer Two+ may have distinct needs and expectations, and while the precedent offers a robust starting point, a certain level of adaptability is needed to cater to different clientele.

These customers have one thing in common: a certain degree of tolerance for imperfections. They might be willing to compromise on both the aesthetic and functional aspects of a product based on its final price. Offering them like-new products with corresponding warranties may only appeal to a subset of this group. If a product is refurbished to the extent that its price escalates, it could deter these price-sensitive buyers. Targeted product portfolios and marketing strategies can be crafted to maximize the potential of each customer segment.

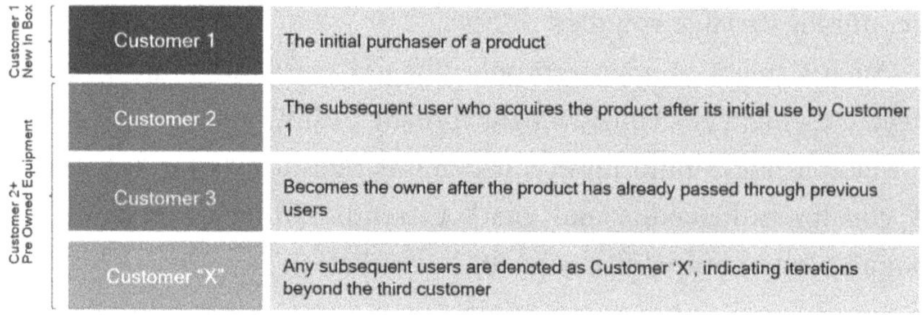

Figure 4.4. Customer Market Profiles illustrates the progression of product ownership as it transitions from one owner to the next.

Not all products acquired by Customer One will make it to the resale market; some may break or be disposed of. Therefore, the supply of used products will rarely exceed the supply of new products. When we aggregate the market sizes of Customer Two, Customer Three, and subsequent customers as newer models are introduced and older ones shift to N-1, N-2, or further N-X statuses, the collective volume of these used products in circulation could very well surpass the new customer base of a products lifecycle. In other words, it is difficult to ignore the lucrative growth opportunities within the Customer Two+ segment.

Grading the Second Life: Understanding Used Product Categories

The world of used products is as diverse as its customer base, much like the auto industry. The famous Kelly Blue Book (KBB) approach is one where vehicles are appraised based on factors like appearance, mileage, and overall health. But this KBB approach is not just for cars; it is applicable to high-value and long-lasting items ranging from electronics to jewelry and elite sporting gear. Every e-commerce platform has its unique way of categorizing used products. While names might vary, the fundamental cosmetic grades often boil down to "like-new," "best," "better," and "good." These grades broadly capture where the bulk of customer transactions fall.

The key, however, is precise **product description**. It lays the foundation for customer satisfaction. If customers know exactly what they are getting, they can gauge the value proposition effectively.

Understanding the Market Dynamics

- **Like-New Offerings.** Like-new products are almost indistinguishable from their brand-new counterparts. These might come with warranties mirroring new goods; however, only a specific segment might gravitate toward these, and over-refurbishing can hike up the price, potentially distancing the price-sensitive audience.
- **Grading and Pricing.** The charm of "certified pre-owned" is undeniable. Customers may select grades such as "like-new,"

"best," "better," or "good," particularly if they are attractively priced. The grading standards can vary, with some regions having stricter definitions of what each grade entails.

- **Warranty Considerations.** A straightforward thirty-day return policy can be enticing for those buying nearly new items, sidestepping intricate warranty procedures. For those seeking added assurance, extended warranties at an additional price can fill the gap.

Understanding the Grades

- **Like-New.** These products have the sheen of fresh-off-the-line items but are priced slightly lower. They are top-tier refurbished goods, often inheriting the warranty typically assigned to new items.
- **Best.** Products that might be elevated from a lesser grade or sold as they are are considered "best." Warranties can be flexible, perhaps offering extension options at an extra fee.
- **Better.** These are often functional items with more visible cosmetic flaws. Customers that prioritize price over perfection may opt for these products that show wear but perform without a hitch.
- **Good.** For "good" products, functionality is king. The products work but come with considerable cosmetic imperfections. Customers that shop these products are driven by value, desiring the maximum bang for their buck, even if it means embracing items with evident wear.

It is important to accurately describe the condition of the product to ensure that the customer is satisfied with their purchase. The labels help sellers tailor their offerings to best match the expectations and budgets of their target customer segment.

Re-Registration or Re-Licensing for Customer Two+

In Chapter 2, we highlighted re-registration as a significant revenue stream and explored the range of product categories it can potentially unlock. Forward-thinking companies formulate strategies to capitalize on each customer segment as a product moves through its lifecycle. When a used product retains value, consumers seek ways to unlock that value. A potent strategy for capitalizing on service options is to enable customers to re-register their equipment, either freely or for a fee. For example, Apple mandates all users to set up an iTunes account upon activating a device. This approach grants Apple real-time insights on product location and facilitates revenue generation for every purchase made on the platform.

However, not all businesses may be inclined to offer unbridled access to warranties or tools, and this paves the way for relicensing opportunities. If an original owner no longer wishes to use a product and cannot secure a satisfactory refund, the item might transition to a subsequent user. Software or support enterprises can capitalize on this by facilitating straightforward equipment registration. Whenever a customer re-registers their product to access legitimate software or services, companies have an opportunity to update their customer relationship management systems with the new owner's details. This enables them to offer additional products tailored to the interests of the next owner. The concept of relicensing as a secondary market strategy was explored comprehensively in a 2012 publication by Oraiopoulos, Toktay, and Ferguson.[3]

To strike a balance between curtailing the cannibalization of new product sales and harnessing revenue opportunities via customer support, software sales, or services, companies can offer **tiered re-registration fees**. During a product's initial sales period, a higher fee (H1) can be levied. As the product transitions to N-1 following the release of a newer version, the fee could be reduced to H2. With each subsequent release, this fee could diminish further, symbolized as HX, until it becomes nominal or nonexistent. When production of a specific model ceases, businesses might consider free re-registration or relicensing, enticing the Customer Two+ segments to invest in tools or support. Since these solutions would have already been developed, they present opportunities for additional revenue with minimal added labor costs. For instance, if software updates are mandated to ensure compatibility with Customer One products, relicensing could empower users to either access the latest software versions without charge or purchase them.

Upholding Customer Two+ Promises

Customer Two+, generally speaking, seeks value and is more understanding and amenable to receiving a product bearing signs of wear. This characteristic is essential to understanding this customer segment. Not every consumer expects a previously owned item to emulate the pristine quality of a brand-new product, especially if the item has aged. While a segment desiring near-mint-condition products indeed exists within this segment, they are certainly not the majority. Let us not forget that competitors possess the capability to process, grade, and directly sell to customers with varied cosmetic preferences. Over-refurbishing to achieve mint condition may not always be necessary, as there is a notable demand for products in various cosmetic states. Instead of focusing solely on expensive refurbishments, companies should consider creating tailored strategies to meet the needs of Customer Two+.

For example, a Customer Two+-focused initiative could include offering a thirty-day money-back guarantee instead of a full warranty, along with options for extended warranty coverage. This approach caters to customers who are willing to pay extra for services such as relicensing or customer support. As tools and practices evolve, they continue to add value beyond the initial sales cycle, offering monetization opportunities during the product's subsequent lifecycles. A strategy where businesses commit to replacing a product with a similar or better model, without refurbishing, can be more cost-effective for both the business and the consumer. Leveraging existing stock for warranty purposes, rather than maintaining a separate warranty inventory, enhances efficiency. Additionally, some companies acquire surplus used products to serve as seed stock for warranty support, mirroring their strategy for new products.

Customer Two+'s expectations evolve as product availabilities change. Understanding this flexibility can help companies adjust their strategy.

4.4 Returned Equipment Product Curve

The **Returned Equipment Product Curve** illustrates the availability of returned or used products within the circular economy over time, showing an inverse relationship to the New Supply Product Curve. Essentially, as the total supply of new products in the market increases, the potential supply of returned or used products also escalates.

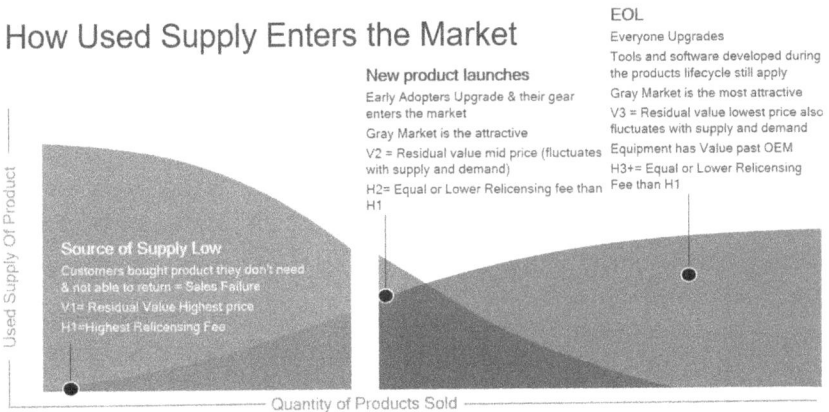

How Used Supply Enters the Market

EOL
Everyone Upgrades
Tools and software developed during
the products lifecycle still apply

New product launches

Early Adopters Upgrade & their gear enters the market
Gray Market is the attractive
V2 = Residual value mid price (fluctuates with supply and demand)
H2= Equal or Lower Relicensing fee than H1

Gray Market is the most attractive
V3 = Residual value lowest price also fluctuates with supply and demand
Equipment has Value past OEM
H3+= Equal or Lower Relicensing Fee than H1

Used Supply Of Product

Source of Supply Low
Customers bought product they don't need & not able to return = Sales Failure
V1= Residual Value Highest price
H1=Highest Relicensing Fee

Quantity of Products Sold

Figure 4.5. The Used Equipment Product Curve illustrates the influx of equipment into the market once its initial owner no longer desires it. This graph provides a comparative view between the supply curve of new equipment and the availability of used equipment throughout its lifecycle.

During the initial product launch, the quantity of returned products remains low. This is primarily due to reasons such as buyer's remorse, overstocking, or DOA failures being the only source of used products to enter the market. To minimize their losses, companies with return policies might resell these products either to third-party wholesalers or directly to consumers but at discounted prices.

In subsequent phase N-1, early product adopters begin to shift to newer versions. This transition, coupled with continuous, routine returns, leads to a surge in the supply of used products. Trade-in initiatives can be introduced by businesses to offer consumers a residual value for their used items, thus promoting the adoption of newer models. However, if these programs fail to provide a market-competitive value, it could drive customers toward the secondary market.

Just because a company discontinues the production of a product does not imply that customer demand for it ceases. In fact, if a popular model is phased out, the demand for used versions of that product may actually increase. The supply of returned goods will never equate to the original supply of brand-new products. Factors attributing to this imbalance include product failures, discarding of items, and the efforts a consumer must invest in reselling a product. Significantly, products with a higher durability and value quotient are more likely to find resonance in the secondary market.

In today's marketplace, we can see an uptick in peer-to-peer sales platforms for items ranging from consumer electronics to clothing and home goods. The Returned Equipment Product Curve gauges the flow of returned goods over a timeline and identifies the forces steering it.

We can observe the price dynamics of a returned product within this framework. As a new product transitions in its pricing from P1 to P2 with the launch of a successive model, there is a corresponding shift from V1 (initial resale value) to V2 (resale value post a new model's introduction). The term **residual value** encapsulates both cosmetic and functional assessment criteria, influencing the potential value of the product. Supply and demand principles remain foundational in determining used-equipment prices. An abundance drives down prices, while scarcity inflates them.

Typically, used products are priced lower than their new counterparts, a reflection of their diminished value. But exceptions exist. For instance, during crises like Texas's 2021 power outage when new products were scarce, used generators fetched premium prices due to heightened demand. A similar trend was evident during the COVID-19 pandemic, when manufacturing constraints inflated used car prices as new cars became rare.[4] This phenomenon is not uncommon, especially during the launch of popular gaming consoles or fashion releases that cannot meet the soaring demand.

This model sheds light on the significance of relicensing fees in the pricing equation. Initially, a steeper relicensing fee might be strategic to deter peer-to-peer reselling and curtail cannibalization, especially during phases of recouping research and development expenses. However, as newer iterations emerge, tapping into the secondary market becomes more feasible, making it viable for businesses to reap benefits from the sustained revenues of used equipment.

Financial Management of Reverse Logistics

5.1 Rethinking the Financial Best Practices of Return Management

In chapter 1, we highlighted the pivotal function reverse logistics leaders play in forging and sustaining vital relationships with core internal sectors, such as sales, marketing, manufacturing, and forward logistics. This intricate network of interactions underlines the harmony and cooperation crucial to the diverse tasks within the organization. As we transition to this chapter, we pivot our attention to a matter of utmost importance: the nuanced relationship between reverse logistics and finance, particularly regarding returns management and the circular economy. This relationship is so important that it deserves its own chapter on how to set up good financial practices to modernize the current landscape of return management and support circular programs and build strong business arguments.

When rushing a product to market, companies often prioritize establishing sales infrastructure while deferring the development of returns programs. The delay creates a mirage of safety, as returns naturally follow sales, leading to misplaced confidence that there is ample time to develop return strategies later. In their quest for efficiency, companies might implement solutions that might not be financially tenable in the long run. Moreover, once policies are established, they are difficult to change. This oversight can lead to issues: companies may end up with warehouses full of items without a clear understanding of their actual worth, and customers may turn to other sellers for better deals on used items. A comprehensive approach is necessary from the outset, balancing the urgency of market entry with foresight to manage returns and financial implications effectively.

Chapter 2 detailed the dynamics among four key objectives in reverse logistics. It examined how these objectives can either synergistically cooperate or lead to interdepartmental conflicts. Just as these objectives can either collaborate or conflict across departments, it is equally important to align financial methodologies to effectively influence and guide behavior. Finance teams often have to validate where to put resources when these areas overlap. For those in reverse logistics, it is vital to know how these areas relate and impact the company's finances.

One way to engage stakeholders in the benefits of a circular economy is to appeal to their environmental consciousness, but real commitment emerges when they recognize the economic incentives. Financial teams play a decisive role in this persuasion, as they are tasked with vetting the outcomes, identifying potential financial risks, and pinpointing areas where the company's bottom line may be affected. It is the presentation of solid numbers and clear data metrics that ultimately convinces stakeholders to support such a significant shift.

Linear Finance: An Obstacle to the Circular Economy

Linear supply chains combined with traditional return models have unintentionally given birth to **linear finance models**.[1] These financial structures push for the sale of products and discourage their return, which is in line with the linear return thought process that all product returns are harmful. Based on the going backward mindset, these models create big challenges in promoting and rewarding desired product return streams brought on by the circular economy.

Many companies boast advanced financial systems for handling revenue and inventory accounting linked to product sales. Nonetheless, there is a noticeable lack of knowledge and tools accounting for returns programs. This is because many companies lack historical data on market values and established buyback prices, making it challenging to initiate these programs as only a few organizations possess financial teams experienced in return financial areas. Some examples of differences in linear and circular financial methodologies are:

1. **Cost of Products**
   - *Linear.* The cost of products is direct. It encompasses costs from production or purchasing, typically documented through an invoice or purchase order and then categorized as a balance sheet item, expense, or capitalized inventory. Over time, the value of inventory may be allocated across its useful life using conventional **depreciation** methods in financial accounting. Upon product returns, revenue is adjusted to reflect the reversal, and the returned asset is not revalued, thus holding a book value of zero.
   - *Circular.* Accounting for returns in a circular model may be more intricate. Products are sourced from the point of consumption rather than from the point of purchase. Instead of being acquired through a traditional purchase order, they are acquired directly from the product's owner. Considerations such as market depreciation, wear and tear, refurbishment needs, and the potential resale value of these items become vital. Companies may establish distinct accounts for such returned goods and related expenses. An inventory could be valued at its current market price and decrease as the product's market value diminishes over time.

2. **Transactional Management**
   - *Linear.* The emphasis is on the sale of the product. The financial value is mainly realized at the point of sale, and any returns are viewed negatively with revenue reversals.

· *Circular.* The emphasis shifts from merely selling to also repurchasing and repurposing. Financial structures should be adapted to acknowledge and incentivize this cyclical flow of goods. Circular returns involve buying back an asset and enabling its value to offset the customer's subsequent purchase when feasible. Current point-of-sale systems and conventional financial frameworks often overlook the subtleties inherent in the circular economy. To truly embrace and thrive in a circular economy, there is a pressing need for systems that can facilitate buyback programs.

3. **Benefit Accounting**

   · *Linear.* Benefits are usually gauged by sales revenue minus the **cost of goods sold (COGS)** and other associated costs.

   · *Circular.* Benefits might include the resale value of refurbished goods, reduced waste management costs, potential tax incentives, improved brand image due to sustainability efforts, and the potential for customer loyalty. To account for these, companies might set up revenue accounts for refurbished goods sales and potentially track indirect benefits like cost savings.

5.2 Financial Accounting

Navigating Procurement, Sales Forecasting, and the Complexities of Returns

A significant role in a company's performance evaluation includes navigating procurement, sales forecasting, and the complexities of returns in inventory accounting, particularly in determining the cost of goods sold. COGS includes the direct expenses related to the production of the company's sold goods, which are deducted from revenues to compute gross profit.

When launching new products, the procurement team handles the direct purchase of products or materials needed for production, guided by a fixed budget based on sales forecasts. It is vital to balance this budget: overbuying leads to excess inventory and additional holding costs, while underbuying can result in missed sales opportunities.

Planning for parts in a new product launch is relatively easier, as there is a fixed number of parts needed to meet a build plan. By contrast, purchasing parts to support warranty programs is more challenging. Companies cannot predict which part will break, when it will break, and how often it will fail. This unpredictability adds complexity to the reverse procurement process.

The procurement process for direct acquisitions from endpoints in circular economy programs necessitates specialized planning and pricing teams, especially given the unpredictable nature of the return supply curve. Unlike new product sales, which follow a more predictable new supply curve, forecasting returns is more complex as it is difficult to anticipate the condition and timing of returned products. This uncertainty calls for an integrated approach that considers both forward and reverse inventory movements for effective management of these nontraditional inventory additions.

Adding to this complexity, the skillset and tools required for purchasing new parts, with an understanding of commodity pricing, differ from those needed for acquiring used products at market prices to build circular returns programs. The distinction is meaningful in scenarios such as trade-in programs or when determining the COGS and residual value in creating leasing or product-as-a-service models. Professionals in this area must be adept at gauging market prices to encourage customers to sell back their old products, a task that requires a deep understanding of market dynamics and residual value estimation.

There is a need for diverse expertise within procurement teams, not only in traditional procurement methods but also in innovative approaches aligned with circular economy principles. Such expertise is essential to ensure efficient and profitable inventory management, balance the acquisition of new parts with the strategic purchase of used products, and maintain a comprehensive view of both the supply and return aspects of the product lifecycle.

Balancing Customer Rewards with Financial Complexity

When a company provides value to customers such as credits or payments for product returns, the core challenge lies in determining how these transactions should be reflected in the company's financial reporting in a way that respects compliance and transparency.

Challenges in Transitioning to a Circular Approach

Accounting for residual value and creating pricing catalogs for returned products were not essential skills in the linear economy. In the absence of established methods for valuing returned or used equipment, companies must develop their own valuation practices. Relatively more mature circular economy programs, such as real estate and automotive, reveal highly developed accounting methods for handling returns, buybacks, and leasing models. In the coming years, these practices should be analyzed and adapted to meet the needs of circular finance.

Despite growing interest among many traditionally linear businesses in adopting a circular model, there is still a noticeable gap between intention and implementation. This state is largely attributable to:

- **Lack of Experience**. Circular models are relatively new, and many companies do not have the expertise in-house to manage them.
- **Resource Constraints**. Transitioning to a new business model requires investment, both in terms of time and money.
- **Limited Tools**. The existing accounting and management tools might not be equipped to handle the nuances of a circular model.

Trends in Revenue Reversal for Returns

Another challenge is determining where these new revenue streams and associated costs fit into the profit and loss (P&L) statement and deciding which department within the company is responsible for them. P&L of reverse logistics within the circular economy must consider multiple avenues for returns, such as early lease renewals, trade-ins, PaaS, or bulk donations.

These practices differ from standard returns, such as those driven by buyer dissatisfaction or product defects. With the available data, enterprises can choose from several inventory accounting methodologies:

1. **Zero-Value Returns.** This method views returns as total losses, nullifying the related revenue and costs. Therefore, the returned items hold no financial value on the balance sheet. One drawback is the potential undervaluing of returned stock, as losses have already been accounted for. This can reduce the incentive to promptly manage these items, potentially eroding any residual value.

2. **Profit Reversal and Asset Write Up.** Several companies opt to reduce their sales revenue when a product is returned and account for the returned item as an asset. This asset is then assigned either a full or partial value, reflecting its potential worth. Products capable of being resold in new condition may be assigned their full original value at their original acquisition cost.

3. **Market Value Accounting.** This approach appraises returned items according to their present market value, considering factors such as cosmetic condition, functionality, and the supply-demand dynamics in the market for used goods.

4. **Acquisition Value.** This approach—particularly suitable for lease, trade-in, or buyback programs—involves tracking each item individually, possibly through an LPN or serial number, to accurately determine its specific acquisition cost.

5. **Blended Acquisition Value.** In buyback returns, lease, or PaaS, where products vary in condition, a graded valuation system can be implemented. For example, a product initially valued at $100 for buyback might be categorized as "best," "better," or "good" with corresponding values of $120, $100, or $80, respectively. These valuations depend on the product's condition and the grading criteria applied during that specific period.

For the sake of simplifying procedures, some firms leveraging linear financial models will fully write down an item in reverse logistics inventory accounting. Though convenient for forecasting, this method might neglect real-time fluctuations in product values. Capturing these nuanced value shifts can introduce unpredictability in inventory valuation.

Inventory accounting, especially in the evolving landscape of circular business models, is complex but critical. For companies looking to innovate and transition to newer, more sustainable models like the circular approach, it is crucial to invest in expertise, tools, and processes that can handle these intricacies efficiently.

Transforming Trade-In Transactions: Verizon's Journey from Linear to Circular Finance

Revisiting the Verizon trade-in reuse case from Chapter 2, we can see that a key challenge was integrating customer rewards into existing POS systems. Initially, internal skepticism was prevalent, with some viewing Verizon as more focused on selling than buying phones. Finance leaders were hesitant to assign value to older devices despite guaranteed buyers and evident market benefits. Simultaneously, marketing efforts were directed at promoting smart accessories, such as speakers, fitness trackers, and headsets. Remarkably, by 2018, revenue from selling used handsets surpassed that from all accessories across all channels.

The central issue was devising a method to reward customers for trade-ins. Assigning value to preowned phones without overhauling the current system was complex. Verizon, cautious about investing in POS system upgrades without proven pilot results, initially resisted methods like offering direct discounts on new purchases or issuing bill credits due to their potential negative impact on financial KPIs. The interim solution was issuing gift cards, akin to dual payment methods used in the car industry.

In Verizon's case, if a new device cost $400 and the trade-in value was $50, the trade-in amount was initially applied as a form of payment through a gift card. The purchase involved two transactions: $350 in cash/credit, and the $50 gift card. After the pilot program proved successful, Verizon upgraded their POS system to directly subtract the trade-in value from the new device's purchase price, streamlining the process and removing the necessity for gift cards while adding the devices as an asset to inventory.

5.3 Residual Value Overview

Decoding the Financial Metrics of Reverse Value Chain: Cost to Reuse and Blended Benefit

The cost to reuse and blended benefit are important metrics that companies use to assess the financial viability of their reverse value chain operations. The CR represents the cost of refurbishing and reselling a returned product, while the BB represents the total economic benefit gained from the reverse value chain activities, which includes the CR, the residual value of the returned product, and any other benefits such as reduced waste and improved sustainability.

The calculation of CR and BB can vary greatly between companies in the same industry. For example, a company that has extensive in-house repair and refurbishment capabilities may have a lower CR compared to another company that relies on third-party partners or liquidators. The willingness to engage in reverse value chain activities and the level of investment in these operations can also greatly impact the CR and BB calculations.

The cultural and operational differences between companies, as well as the pressure to meet corporate sustainability goals and comply with government regulations, can also play a role in determining the CR and BB calculations. Companies that prioritize sustainability and place a high value on reducing waste and minimizing their environmental impact may have a higher BB compared to companies that are less focused on these issues.

Ultimately, determining the CR and BB is crucial for companies to understand the potential benefits and costs of reverse value chain activities and to make informed decisions about how to best monetize their returned products.

Cost to Reuse

The expenses associated with the reverse logistics process of taking a product back from a customer, repairing or refurbishing it if necessary, and then putting it back into circulation for resale is known as the cost to reuse. This can include the following:

- **Labor.** The cost related to staffing oversight, handling, inspection, and repair of returned products.
- **Infrastructure.** The cost of the facilities and equipment needed to manage the reverse logistics process, such as warehouses, repair facilities, and technology systems.
- **Technology.** The cost of the technology systems used to manage the reverse logistics process, such as order management systems, repair tracking systems, and warehouse management systems.
- **Complexity.** The cost of managing the complexity of the reverse logistics process, including dealing with returns from multiple channels, managing multiple product lines, and managing the flow of products and information.
- **Transportation.** The cost of shipping the product back to the warehouse or repair facility, as well as the cost of shipping it back to the customer after it has been repaired or refurbished.
- **Parts.** The cost of any parts that may need to be replaced in order to repair the product.
- **Storage.** The cost of storing the product while it is being repaired or waiting to be repaired.
- **Time.** The cost of the time involved in the reverse logistics process, including the time it takes to repair or refurbish the product and the time it takes to get the product back into circulation. This can also include the cost of lost sales due to the product being unavailable during the recirculation process.
- **Cost of Capital.** The opportunity cost of tying up capital in the reverse logistics process. When funds are invested in handling

returns, they are not available for other potentially profitable ventures. This cost is associated with the money that is tied up in inventory, equipment, and facilities specific to reverse logistics. Additionally, there may be borrowing costs if a company can secure external financing to support its reverse logistics operations.

The above costs can add up quickly and can impact the overall profitability of a business, so it is important for companies to carefully manage their reverse logistics processes and minimize these costs as much as possible.

Blended Benefit

A measure of the net value generated by the movement of inventory over a given period as defined by their inventory accounting practices is known as blended benefit. BB is calculated by multiplying the value of inventory (Va) by the velocity or speed in which the inventory moves (Ve). The basic idea behind BB is that the faster the inventory moves, the more value it generates for the company.

When inventory is not being used, it is considered **idle inventory**, and the net benefit is zero. In fact, when inventory is idle, the cost to reuse continues to increase due to storage fees. Therefore, it is essential for companies to keep their inventory moving as quickly as possible to maximize the value generated by it. However, there is also a negative impact associated with blended benefit due to the erosion of value as the product ages. This means that the longer the inventory is held, the less valuable it becomes, which can ultimately lead to a negative impact on the company's bottom line.

To make the best financial decisions, companies must be able to measure the erosion of residual value over time. If monetizing equipment for current market value permits purchasing a replacement at a later point, understanding which path mathematically makes sense is key. In some cases, companies may opt to hold on to the product to avoid having to repurchase a replacement. However, if the value of the equipment erodes to zero while it is being held and that value eroded is greater than the replacement cost, then the company has made a poor financial decision. Companies must understand the relationship between Va, Ve, and BB to make informed decisions about their reverse logistics processes.

5.4 Value

Value Examples

When a returned product is refurbished or repaired and then resold, the company can generate additional revenue from selling the product a second time. This revenue can offset some of the costs associated with the reverse logistics process, such as the cost of labor, transportation, parts, storage, and time. Additionally, using a returned product a second time can also result in cost savings. For example, it can save the cost of producing a new product, and it can reduce the environmental impact of disposing of a used product and manufacturing a new one.

The residual value (V1 to V2, or V2 to V3) in reverse logistics refers to the total impact of these revenue gains and cost savings and represents the net financial benefit of using a returned product a second time. By maximizing the blended benefit, companies can optimize their reverse logistics processes and improve their overall financial performance.

In Chapter 3.3, we explored various **value generation methods** in reverse logistics: **reuse as new**, return to vendor, resell as refurbished, warranty support, demonstration devices, lease or rental, **wholesale liquidation**, and e-commerce. An important connection exists between the value generation from these methods and the tangible benefits of product reuse in financial statements. Here are some ways reverse logistics and finance can harmoniously align to reap these benefits:

- **Reusing a product as new**. Let us take a tool for an example. When a hammer is returned and can be resold as new, its value corresponds to the cost saved from not having to manufacture or purchase a new one. If a hammer is produced at a cost of $5 and sold for $10, discarding it upon return would require an additional $5 to manufacture or acquire a replacement. Consequently, the store effectively spends $10 in total to make a single $10 sale, essentially breaking even because two hammers were needed to complete one net sale. On the other hand, if the hammer is resold as new, the store circumvents the additional production or procurement cost. This results in a cost-saving of $5 while also generating $10 in revenue from the resale. Reusing and reselling, particularly for in-demand products, stands as a highly beneficial strategy for managing unwanted returns, as it allows for maximized revenue and minimized unnecessary expenditure on production or procurement.

- **Returning to vendor.** If the hammer is unsold or returned and eligible for return to its original vendor, the cost of goods associated with it might be recouped. For instance, if a tool is returned and the brand permits its return to the original vendor, the initial $5 cost of goods for that product could potentially be recovered. This recovery of the cost can be a significant aspect of managing returns efficiently, especially in cases where the returned products remain in a condition that allows them to be reused or resold by the vendor.

- **Selling as refurbished.** Many companies participate in the sale of certified preowned products. The revenue from these refurbished product sales is recognized as income, against which the COGS is accounted for.

- **Reusing for a warranty claim.** If a company provides a warranty program where new products are manufactured to fulfill warranty claims, the benefit of reusing a returned product can be quantified as the cost savings from not having to acquire a new item, minus any refurbishment costs. Additionally, when companies offer extended warranty services, these can also be factored into the equation. However, the same principles regarding the time elapsed between the original purchase and the reuse of the product apply because the company may not need to purchase new items for warranty replacements and can leverage a refurbished device that has already been devalued instead.

- **Demonstration devices.** Opting to use a product for

demonstration without significant refurbishing (barring data erasure or cosmetic enhancements) can be more cost-effective than acquiring a brand-new device and then having its value depreciate once it is no longer new. Leveraging a used device may be accounted for as cost avoidance by some firms.

- **Selling as-is.** Some companies will take their returned product and sell it in bulk to save whatever they can by selling products into the secondary market. A hardware store may have a returned tool in an open package they can then sell to a company for a dollar as opposed to just discarding it. This value may be recognized as revenue by some organizations.

- **Harvesting/scrap value.** When products are no longer functional or sellable in their current state, businesses can still extract value by dismantling them and reusing the individual components or recycling the raw materials. This benefit may be accounted for as cost avoidance or as revenue depending upon the companies' accounting rules.

- **Donation value.** When businesses choose to donate returned or unsold items to charitable organizations or individuals in need, the primary benefit is not directly monetary. Instead, it is a combination of positive brand image, potential tax deductions, and the satisfaction of corporate social responsibility. If the hardware store donates the hammer, they might not recover any of the original $5 acquisition cost.

- **Idle inventory.** Inventory that is sitting on a shelf has a net benefit of zero dollars. The amount of time the product is idle should be measured. Idle inventory incurs additional cost to reuse, as the product is audited and stored, not to mention its being subject to general depreciation.

5.5 Velocity

The blended benefit in reverse logistics not only includes the financial impact of using a returned product a second time, but also takes into account the velocity—the speed at which the product is returned and resold—and the impact of the depreciation of the real value of an asset over time. By quickly finding suitable outlets for the value of returned products, companies can minimize their storage time, leading to reduced carrying costs. This strategy can accelerate the return on investment. However, the real value of an asset will inevitably decrease over time due to factors such as wear and tear, obsolescence, and market trends. As a result, the value of the returned product tends to decrease over time, which can impact the potential revenue that can be generated from reselling it.

Cash-to-Cash Cycle

The concept of velocity is also referred to as the cash-to-cash cycle. The goal of the auction purchase is to generate a 10 percent return on every auction we participate in. Another way to look at that is if we spent $1.00 on an item, can we turn it into $1.10 and how fast can we turn it into $1.10? If it takes one year to generate a 10¢ return, the cost to hold that item for the year is added to the recirculation cost, and the net benefit is reduced. When the value and velocity are compounded, the true benefit can be revealed.

- **1 year at 10 percent = $1.10**

Turning the product over at 5 percent profit every three months yields a 21.5 percent return = $1.21.

- **$1 × 1.05 = $1.05 in 3 months**
- **$1.05 × 1.05 = $1.10 by month 6**
- **$1.10 × 1.05 = $1.16 by month 9**
- **$1.16 × 1.05 = $1.21 by month 12**

The product represents not just a returned item, but a dollar in value. The objective is to reuse this dollar to its maximum potential in the shortest possible time. It is important to note not only the value generated by recirculating a product but also the frequency of its turnover. Often, companies focus on maximizing the return from their returned products and end up overlooking the losses incurred due to products languishing on the shelf.

Value Generation Optimization

When a company has multiple avenues for generating value, the most profitable channel might not always have the capacity to handle the full product inventory. For companies with diverse value generation channels, strategically utilizing those outlets can maximize product consumption, but it requires a detailed analysis of the anticipated supply and demand dynamics for the product. Conversely, in situations where demand outstrips supply, companies have the luxury of being selective, choosing to activate only their most profitable channels. This careful balancing act ensures that resources are allocated efficiently, maximizing profitability while meeting market demand effectively.

Should the supply exceed demand, it is financially prudent for a company to engage all available value-generation channels to mitigate excess stock, utilizing all avenues of value creation, from high-margin to low-margin options.

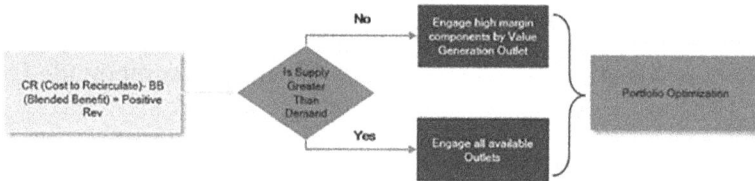

Figure 5.1. The Value Generation Optimization diagram depicts how a company can maximize revenue through strategic engagement with various outlets based on the existing supply and demand dynamics of a product.

In Chapter 3, we discussed how goTRG leverages their AI-powered disposition engine. The case exemplifies an advanced application of the "Value Generation Optimization Diagram," leveraging artificial intelligence, machine learning, and structured data within a WMS. goTRG's AI-powered disposition engine analyzes vast datasets, predicting optimal resale channels and pricing strategies for returned goods, determining both value and velocity of sales. By intelligently processing and learning from historical sales data, market trends, and product conditions, goTRG transforms the complexities of reverse logistics into actionable, data-driven decisions. This system not only streamlines the asset disposition process but also maximizes value recovery, embodying a sophisticated integration of technology for **value generation optimization.**

Fish Market Analogy

Imagine fishing boats returning daily to dock, offloading their catch. The captains are compensated based on the blended yield of their catch. While some high-end restaurants may pay a premium for the best fish, not every fish in the catch can command such a price. This reality means that one cannot expect to sell all the fish at the prices paid by the highest bidders. Inevitably, there will be leftover fish that start to decay, and as new boats bring in fresh catch each day, the need to quickly generate value from the existing catch becomes apparent, much like the challenge with returns. In this scenario, certain fish might be sold to supermarkets at a lower price, others to wholesalers, and the rest processed into products like cat food. The goal is to maximize value from the entire catch, not just the few premium pieces.[2]

Now, let us apply this **fish market analogy** to value generation optimization: if a boat brings in ten tuna, and a sushi restaurant is willing to buy them all at a high price, then selling the entire lot to them is financially sound. But if the restaurant only wants two, it makes sense to find another buyer for the remaining eight. If these eight are not sold quickly and begin to degrade, the value from only the two sold initially is realized, while the potential value of the other eight is lost. Therefore, it is important to have several alternative avenues for generating value, ready to capitalize on the catch before it deteriorates.

The analogy is especially pertinent when considering the blended benefit of returned products. Daily returns are common, like fish being brought to market that lose freshness each day. In sectors like electronics and apparel, the value of products often decreases as newer models are introduced. Acknowledging this depreciation is essential in reverse logistics models as the value of returned goods typically diminishes over time, necessitating swift and diverse strategies to recover value.

5.6 Depreciation

There are various methods of calculating depreciation, but **straight-line depreciation** is the most frequently used method in linear finance. Whichever it is, maintaining consistency in the depreciation method of choice is important for internal financial reporting. Frequently changing methodologies can cause confusion, inconsistency in financial statements, and potential mistrust among stakeholders. Each finance team should establish and stick to controls and methods they believe in and can defend. Let us examine the method of straight-line depreciation over a two-year period using a product worth $100.

Straight-Line Depreciation

Assuming no resale value (value of the asset at the end of its useful life), the formula simplifies to:

- **Depreciation Expense Per Year = Cost of the Asset / Resale Value.**

In a straight-line depreciation, the product depreciates by an equal amount each year, which can be further broken down by month:

- **Annual Depreciation: $100 / 2 = $50/year**
- **Monthly Depreciation: $50 / 12 = $4.17/month (rounded to the nearest cent).**

Here is the monthly breakdown over two years:

- **Months 1–12:** each month, the product depreciates by $4.17, so at the end of the first year, the accumulated depreciation is $50, and the book value is $50.
- **Months 13–24:** each month, the product continues to depreciate by $4.17. At the end of the second year, the accumulated depreciation is $100, and the book value is $0.

Market Value Depreciation

This method gauges depreciation of the product based on market conditions. It is akin to the way stocks fluctuate in the stock market. An asset's value can decline or even appreciate based on demand and supply, technological advancements, or external economic factors. While not as formulaic as the other methods, it is more reflective of the asset's real-world value at any given time.

The value of products (S1 to S2 to S3 etc.) over time is a gradual decline. Depreciation (De) represents the change of value over time. Generally, the value of a used product will decrease as it ages and experiences wear and tear. This decline in value is often steeper during the initial years after the product's release and then levels off over time, as illustrated in the used-equipment supply curve.

For instance, if our $100 product becomes obsolete due to new technology, its market value might drop to $40 in the first year. If market conditions further deteriorate, it might drop to $15 in the second year.

The rate of depreciation for a used product can vary depending on several factors, including the product's age, condition, and overall demand. For example, products that are in high demand and in good condition may depreciate at a slower rate than products that are older or have significant wear and tear. Additionally, certain types of products, such as electronics or vehicles, may experience more rapid depreciation due to rapid technological advancements, the speed of new product releases, or changes in consumer preferences.

Integrating Market Insight into Circular Economy Pricing Strategies

Accurately predicting the market value of a returned product and integrating this prediction into pricing models for programs like leasing or PaaS is crucial for maximizing profit margins in a circular economy. This approach is more effective than applying a standard depreciation schedule because customers are primarily concerned with receiving fair market value for their returns, rather than the specifics of accounting methods.

Developing a sophisticated understanding of the market value of returned products is essential because it enables companies to set more accurate prices for buyback or leasing programs, aligning closer with the actual market value, and ensuring more favorable profit margins. It also enhances customer satisfaction and trust, as customers feel they are receiving a fair deal based on the real-world value of their returned products. Building on this foundation, we will examine the nuances that distinguish straight-line depreciation from market value, shedding light on their unique roles in shaping effective pricing strategies.

Comparison: Straight-Line vs. Market Value and Its Implications for Buyback Programs

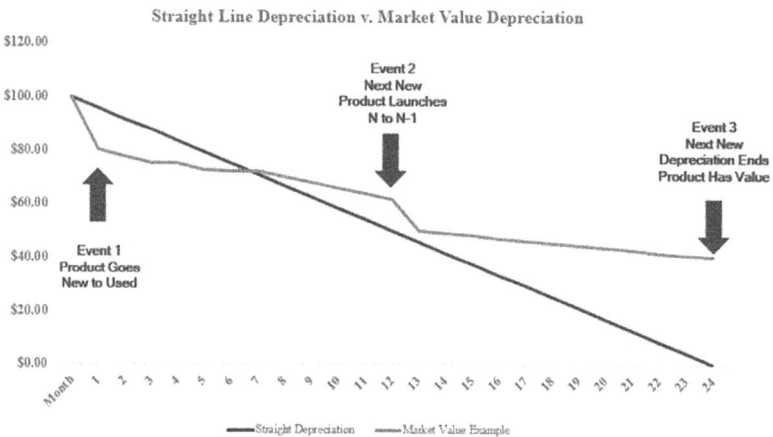

Figure 5.2. Example of a declining market value product versus straight line depreciation.

The straight-line depreciation method and the assessment of market value are two principal ways to gauge this decline.

- **Potential Gaps and Implications for Buybacks.** The disparity between straight-line depreciation and market value can lead to significant challenges, especially when setting trade-in or buyback prices.

- **Perceived Noncompetitiveness.** If businesses set buyback prices based solely on the straight-line depreciation model, they risk being perceived as noncompetitive. Using our example, a customer looking to trade in a product at the twelve-month mark might be offered $49.96 based on the straight-line model. However, if the prevailing market value is $61.83, the customer could feel short-changed.
- **Diminishing Returns Over Time**: As time progresses, the gap between straight-line depreciation and market value can widen. If not addressed, this disparity can undermine customer confidence in the company's buyback or trade-in programs.
- **Risks in Leasing and Product-as-a-Service Models**: Businesses venturing into leasing or offering PaaS need to be wary of the pitfalls of relying solely on depreciation models. Neglecting market value can result in pricing that either undervalues or overvalues the product, leading to potential revenue losses or dissatisfied customers.

In essence, while straight-line depreciation or other accounting depreciation methods offer an organized method for **financial accounting**, it often fails to capture the dynamic nuances of the real-world market. For businesses—particularly those engaged in buybacks, leases, or PaaS models—integrating market value assessments into their pricing strategies is paramount to uphold customer trust and ensure competitive positioning.

The Hidden Costs of Misunderstanding Depreciation in Returned Inventory Management

A misunderstanding of depreciation in returned products can lead companies, particularly those that do not measure value over time, to retain products longer than financially advisable. This issue is often more pronounced in organizations that categorize returned inventory as "free," even assigning it a zero-dollar value in their accounting systems and completely neglecting the opportunity to extract value from these products. Consider a scenario where a company keeps ten returned units each initially valued at $100, amounting now to a total of $1000, in anticipation of a possible future warranty claim. However, if the equipment's value drops to $50 per unit, and only one unit is eventually used for warranty support, the cumulative benefit for all ten units becomes just $5. In such cases, it could be more beneficial for the company to purchase a replacement or upgraded unit when actually needed or offer the customer an upgrade to a newer product instead of retaining the depreciating returned units as a precaution.

Holding on to returned products for too long can also incur additional costs to recirculate the products. As the value of the products declines over time, the cost to manage and store the inventory can become increasingly expensive, especially if space and resources are limited. Since identifying residual value is so difficult and there is a lack of developed software to measure value, many companies are unaware of the leakage that exists in their returns programs.

5.7 Circular Economy Reuse Case Study Three: *Fast Fashion and ACS Clothing*

Fast Fashion

Used to describe a type of clothing production and consumption that focuses on quickly producing inexpensive clothes to keep up with rapidly changing fashion trends, **fast fashion** involves making clothes quickly and cheaply, often using low-quality materials and relying on cheap labor in developing countries. Fast fashion brands release new collections frequently to encourage people to buy more and keep up with the latest trends.

The fashion sector produces an estimated 10 percent of all global carbon emissions.[3] There are several reasons why governments are against fast fashion for sustainability reasons: First, fast fashion relies on the extraction of nonrenewable resources like oil for synthetic fabrics, which leads to resource depletion and harm to the environment. Second, the production, transportation, and disposal of fast fashion items generate a large amount of greenhouse gas emissions, contributing to climate change. Third, the production processes in fast fashion often involve water-intensive activities and the use of chemicals, leading to water pollution and damage to ecosystems.

Figure 5.3. Image taken in 2021 of secondhand clothing dumped in Alto Hospice, Chile.

Governments are considering various legislation and measures to address the negative impacts of fast fashion. One approach is the implementation of **extended producer responsibility (EPR)** policies, aimed at holding fashion brands accountable for the environmental impact of their products throughout their lifecycle, including collection, recycling, and disposal. Governments are also considering limiting or banning the use of hazardous chemicals, protecting both the environment and human health. Additionally, there is a focus on promoting sustainable sourcing and traceability with regulations that require brands to disclose information about their supply chains and encourage responsible sourcing practices.

Legislation may soon be introduced to mandate longer warranties and guarantees for clothing, encouraging brands to produce more durable garments and offer repair services. There is also consideration for the Right to Repair, which would give consumers the ability to repair their clothes and extend their lifespan. All in all, public awareness campaigns are well underway to educate consumers about the environmental and social impact of fast fashion, encouraging more sustainable and conscious consumer choices.

ACS Clothing

In today's world, dominated by the fast-paced churn of trends, the apparel industry stands as one of the most significant contributors to environmental waste. However, Advanced Clothing Solutions (ACS) based in the UK is challenging and changing this narrative with a groundbreaking circular economy model. By addressing the waste challenges typically associated with fast fashion, ACS presents an innovative system that prioritizes and maximizes reuse while significantly reducing waste.[4]

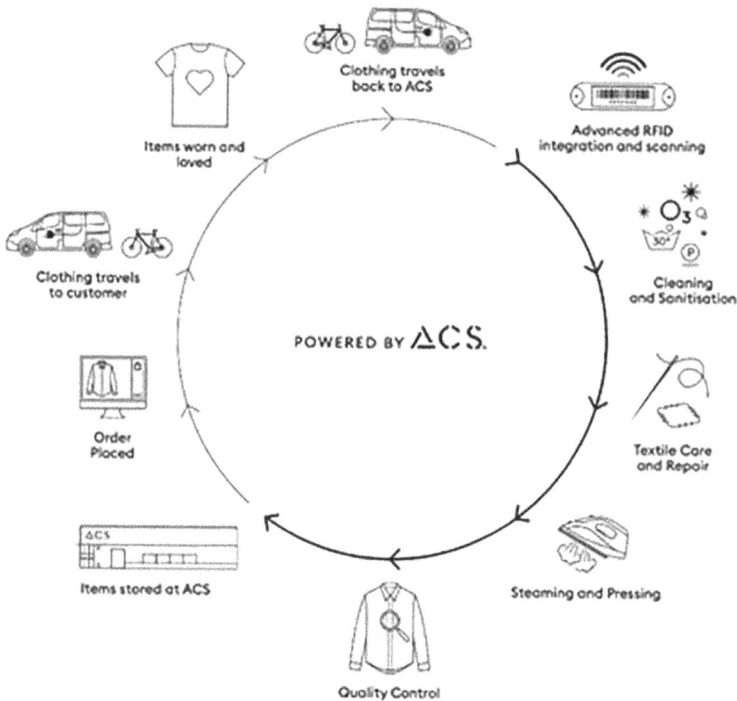

Clothing travels
back to ACS

Items worn and
loved

Advanced RFID
integration and scanning

Clothing travels
to customer

Cleaning
and Sanitisation

POWERED BY ACS.

Order
Placed

Textile Care
and Repair

Items stored at ACS

Steaming and Pressing

Quality Control

Figure 5.4. Above is a high-level overview of the ACS's Sustainability Model.

ACS's key strategy is their acquisition and meticulous assessment process. ACS procures its garments primarily from returned stocks of established brands, then each item undergoes an exhaustive inspection to categorize it as either "new" or "used." The intriguing part of their criteria is that clothes merely tried on, perhaps in a department store fitting room but not bought, still fall under the "new" category, and they have applied similar logic for online purchases. This nuanced differentiation not only allows ACS to optimize their reuse strategy but also provides unparalleled value back to their suppliers.

However, ACS's unique approach does not end there. Unlike other platforms where unsold or returned garments might be quickly resold, ACS has turned the tables with an ingenious model: they do not merely resell these clothes; instead, they rent them out, emphasizing the product-as-a-service model.[5] Through this, ACS astonishingly manages to reuse an item of clothing several times—in some cases up to fifty times—before determining its end-of-life. When it reaches this point, items are either responsibly recycled or removed from production.

Central to ACS's efficient operation is their unwavering reliance on cutting-edge technology. By integrating RFID tags into garments, ACS has achieved a remarkable efficiency in tracking products in terms of both outgoing shipments and returns. This technological foresight ensures minimal picking errors, reduces fraud, and streamlines the logistics process. Although one of the biggest barriers to the adoption of rental or pre-loved fashion is the perception that these clothing items are dirty and carry odors, ACS overcomes this obstacle through its commendable, innovative **green sanitization** approach. They employ a state-of-the-art ozone sanitization chamber that can process up to 45,000 items daily. Impressively, this method ensures 99.8 percent virus removal as well as odor removal, all while conserving water and electricity. Additionally, their **automated cleaning systems**, coupled with advanced analytics drawn from Industry 4.0 principles, ensure that products are not only maintained at high standards but are also dispatched and reused efficiently.

Beyond these operational measures, ACS's quality control systems (marked by a unique ribbon seal on garments) guarantee that products that reach customers adhere to very high standards. Moreover, they have in-house capabilities to repair any damage, ensuring prolonged garment life. In summary, ACS prides itself on being garment-longevity specialists and keeping clothes in circulation. Their process is as follows:

1. **Acquisition and Assessment.** ACS procures returned garments from renowned brands. These items then undergo a thorough inspection to determine whether they are "new" or "used." The labels allow ACS to optimize its processes further and give value back to their suppliers.

2. **Operational Triage.** Any unsold garment or a product returned due to inventory rotation or buyback channels is not simply resold. ACS has implemented a unique model where they rent out the product as a service. Remarkably, ACS can demonstrate that they have rented some items of clothing approximately fifty times before their end-of-life.

3. **Technological Advancements:**

   · **RFID Technology.** By integrating RFID tags into their garments, ACS can accurately track the movement, shipment, and return of products. This tech-driven approach minimizes errors and optimizes the logistics process.

   · **Green Sanitization.** ACS employs a groundbreaking ozone sanitization chamber capable of sanitizing up to forty-five thousand items per day. The chamber removes 99.8 percent of viruses and odors, using minimal water and electricity.

   · **Automated Cleaning System.** An advanced system using steam and conveyance automatically prepares products for reuse.

   · **Automated Sortation of Products.** Products are kept on a conveyor system until use.

   · **Industry 4.0 Intelligence.** Advanced analytics prioritizes the placement of fast-moving products to reduce shipment time.

4. **Quality Control.** Any garment with its ribbon seal removed is treated as unworn unless there is visible evidence of wear. ACS ensures products maintain high-quality standards and can even repair damages within their operations.

ACS is not just content with their internal operations. They are pushing the boundaries, urging governments to recognize the benefits of such models and, in turn, provide regulatory and tax incentives.[6] The hope is that with such incentives, a shift can occur in the fashion industry, making sustainability-driven models both an ethical and economical choice.

Furthermore, ACS has excelled in efficiently managing returned products, ensuring rapid recirculation. Their sales-enablement strategy improves return streams by finding new users for unsold or returned items and allowing some to be resold as new. Cost management is enhanced through automated and sophisticated returns programs, optimizing recirculation costs and efficiency. ACS has also made strides in green logistics, significantly reducing their environmental footprint. Lastly, their approach to circular economy enablement promotes the repeated use of garments, generating revenue multiple times from the same item and mitigating the effects of fast fashion.

With an impressive processing capacity of approximately six million clothing items annually, ACS stands as a testament to how innovative approaches can transform industries.[7] By successfully blending sustainability with profitability, ACS is not only leading the charge against the perils of fast fashion but also demonstrating that with the right strategies, businesses can be both eco-friendly and economically successful.

Chapter 6

The Secrets of the Secondary Market

6.1 How the Secondary Market Works

Capitalizing on the Circular Economy: The Power and Potential of the Secondary Market

The secondary market holds a central position in the reverse supply chain and circular economy, providing a platform where both preowned and slow-moving products—those that were manufactured and distributed but remain unsold—can find new opportunities for liquidation. By leveraging trusted partners, companies may intentionally sell products in bulk into the secondary market through **third parties** and not be a part of the final sales transaction. A world-class secondary-market partner would monetize the processing capability or skill gaps of their supplier's operations. Some companies that choose to not develop a robust reverse supply chain can take advantage of these benefits through strategic relationships.

Secondary market partners provide value-added services such as logistics services, repair, **consignment** of excess products, purchasing of materials that the supplier does not self-consume, and understanding the demands of Customer Two+. Transactions in this market can take place directly between end users or through intermediary firms, generally offering items at prices more affordable than their brand-new equivalents. The use of technology has made it easier to match used supply with used demand, and companies that ignore the potential of these reverse logistics avenues may be missing out on significant revenue streams.

This rapidly growing sector is defined by a variety of platforms and services that assist in the redistribution and liquidation of goods, connecting various users and advancing sustainability by prolonging the lifecycle of products, thereby avoiding waste and encouraging economic gains. It has already demonstrated a vast presence in the global economy and is on track for staggering growth in the coming years.

The secondary apparel sector is one that is hard to ignore. In 2022, the Global Secondary Apparel Market was valued at an impressive $71.2 billion. However, by 2032, it is projected to skyrocket to an overwhelming $282.7 billion. This represents a four-fold increase within just a decade, highlighting not just the market's current size but its immense potential for expansion.[1]

The used smartphone sector is another convincing example of the secondary market's robust growth trajectory. According to the International Data Corporation (IDC), the number of used smartphones shipped globally stood at 209.1 million units in 2022, with a significant 26 percent of these shipments originating from the US. Fast forward to 2026, and this number is forecasted to almost double, reaching approximately 415 million devices. More strikingly, the market value of these shipped smartphones is estimated to touch $99.9 billion by 2026. This not only underscores the sheer magnitude of the secondary market but also signifies its rapidly expanding value proposition.[2]

The numbers speak volumes: the secondary market, already sizable, is on the brink of an explosive surge. From fashion to electronics, consumers globally are increasingly recognizing the value, sustainability, and appeal of secondhand products, driving this active market to unprecedented heights.

The Dual Aspects of the Secondary Market: Navigating the Gray to Green Transition

The secondary market, often referred to as the Gray Market, is a unique avenue for trading returned, refurbished, or previously owned goods. These items, ideal for Customer Two+, might emerge from returns streams or might have been reintroduced via circular economy endeavors. Such goods can be refurbished to nearly new conditions or sold in their existing state.

With its roots in economics and sustainability, the secondary market offers an eco-conscious alternative to handling unused or unwanted items by promoting reuse over recycling or discarding an item. As such, it has also earned the title of the Green Market, with the dual connotation of green implying both its environmentally responsible approach and its potential for financial gains. Customers are frequently attracted to these products because they can find value for unwanted products or acquire an item they desire at a more affordable price point; companies see an untapped reservoir of revenue in matching this supply with the latent demand. Interestingly, some third-party companies have opted to directly acquire these products from consumers, bypassing traditional retail channels, which can lead to reduced acquisition costs and the potential for higher resale margins.

Despite this unprecedented potential, the term Gray Market prevails, largely propelled by manufacturers' and distributors' concerns about it undermining their primary product sales and the perceived lack of control. The word "gray" conveys a somewhat-ambiguous stance, hinting at a market that operates in a nebulous zone that is neither entirely black (illegal) nor entirely white (fully authorized by the manufacturer). Yet, as illustrated in the Circular Economy Puzzle Piece diagram in Figure 2.8, the secondary market can also present an array of opportunities for the original manufacturers and distributors to find value and grow their customer base. The transition in terminology from "gray" to "green." Market suggests a positive evolution in the industry's perspective on this market.

To navigate the Gray Market effectively, it is essential to highlight a few of its characteristics:

1. **Legality.** The Gray Market primarily deals with authentic, legal products and ensures that customers are purchasing genuine items. Each product is correctly classified and labeled upon sale, providing clarity and transparency in transactions.

2. **Warranty and Support.** A significant aspect of Gray Market products is that they are often not distributed through the official channels sanctioned by the original manufacturers. As a result, these products may not come with the original manufacturer's warranty. However, alternative warranty options are frequently available, which can be quite appealing to customers. These alternatives might include third-party warranties or limited guarantees provided by the seller, which, while different from the original warranty, still offer a degree of protection and support.

3. **Pricing.** The pricing structure in the gray market is a major factor that attracts consumers. Products here are typically priced more competitively compared to those in the primary market because of various factors, such as the bypassing of official distribution channels, lower operational costs, and the absence of brand premiums. The pricing advantage is twofold:

   - **Selling Price.** For individuals looking to sell their products in the Gray Market, there is an opportunity to set competitive prices that are attractive to buyers yet profitable for the sellers. This pricing flexibility allows sellers to adjust their rates based on market demand and the condition of the product.

   - **Purchase Price for the Next Customer.** Buyers benefit from lower prices on the Gray Market compared to retail stores or official outlets. These reduced prices make high-demand products more accessible to a broader range of customers, particularly those who are budget-conscious or seeking deals on items that are otherwise expensive in the primary market.

Whether labeled as "gray" or "green," the secondary market serves as a bridge between consumers, corporations, and sustainable practices, underscoring the enduring worth of products beyond their initial purchase. It is a platform for end users to find value, either by selling products they no longer need or by buying items that remain in demand.

Navigating the Distinction: Gray Market versus Counterfeit Products

Counterfeit products are fraudulent imitations meticulously designed to mislead consumers into believing they are procuring authentic items. These deceptions do not just breach intellectual property laws; the counterfeits often pale in comparison to the genuine product's quality and safety standards. On the other hand, Gray Market goods, while genuine, are distributed through unauthorized channels, posing challenges related to brand reputation and pricing variations.

Manufacturers and distributors must remain vigilant and proactive about potential counterfeiting operations. Routing returned products back to the original source through established returns programs provides a strategic advantage. It not only facilitates the identification of counterfeit infiltrations but also enables companies to trace **return data** to pinpoint the origins of counterfeit supplies. By restricting returns, companies might inadvertently blind themselves to the very counterfeit operations they aim to counteract. Embracing returns, in this context, grants clearer visibility into the market's underbelly and the malicious activities they hope to curtail.

Strategic Dynamics of Third Parties in the Reverse Supply Chain

Third-party companies in the secondary market frequently employ strategies similar to those seen in manufacturing and distribution. Their approach is centered on three key principles: (1) acquiring supply at the lowest cost while maintaining quality, (2) streamlining operation costs, and (3) maximizing value by building sales outlets.

For optimal growth, a top-tier secondary market entity should prioritize:

- sourcing closer to the initial supply;
- enhancing operational efficiency to minimize costs and boost net benefits; and
- augmenting value by engaging more closely with the end customer.

Exemplary organizations in the secondary market foster a unified culture and ensure their staff is aligned with key strategies such as securing product returns in a circular economy. Activities that do not directly support these strategies are evaluated for potential cost savings. These businesses will attempt to purchase returned products directly from their point of consumption, bypassing the manufacturer when it leads to a net benefit. This tactic aligns with the customer's inclination to prioritize value over the original place of purchase, and it creates an opportunity for third parties to directly compete for the return of products.

Mainstream secondary market entities often collaborate with manufacturers, distributors, and retailers to obtain supplies either through auctions or strategic contracts. By doing so, they ensure the original source retains some semblance of supply control. Detailed process flows can be charted for these market leaders, outlining product acquisition, processing, and sales methods.

The secondary market for returned products can be lucrative for businesses if properly managed and understood. The following are some secrets to success in this market:

- **Understanding Customer Trends.** Understanding the reasons why products are being returned and the customer's behavior behind the returns helps identify which products are likely to have a strong demand and in what condition when they enter the secondary market.
- **Quality Assessment.** Assessing the quality of returned products and determining their marketability aids in determining their value and potential for resale.

- **Networking.** Building strong relationships with buyers and other stakeholders in the secondary market can help businesses secure the best prices for their returned products.
- **Market Knowledge.** Keeping up to date with market trends and pricing ensures businesses receive the best return on their investment.
- **Efficient Logistics.** Efficient logistics management, including warehousing and distribution, ensures that products are received and processed quickly and efficiently, ready for resale.
- **Effective Data Management.** Accurate and efficient data management is essential in tracking the flow of products, monitoring inventory levels, and managing pricing.

By leveraging these elements, businesses can effectively manage the secondary market for returned products and maximize their returns.

Supply and Demand in the Secondary Market

To navigate the secondary market, companies must comprehend the functions of supply sources and **value generation outlets**. These outlets endeavor to boost the value realized at the end of the reverse supply chain, focusing on minimizing the intermediary steps a product undergoes, consequently reducing costs and increasing the ultimate value derived from sales. Collaboration between supply sources and value generation outlets is imperative, ensuring a smooth transition of products through the reverse supply chain and creating a space that leverages the potential value within the secondary market. This section will offer a deeper analysis of these elements, revealing the complex dynamics and strategies that are the backbone of successful secondary market operations.

Supply Sources

In the secondary market, supply sources are the initial points where products are returned by customers. They could be retailers, distributors, or even third-party entities that were not involved in the original sale of the product. Their primary role is to facilitate the return of products that may have residual value, a process which involves determining the cost-to-recirculate of a product. As a product moves through various stages of the reverse supply chain, involving multiple handlers or processors, the CR escalates. The main desired outcome here is to minimize the stages or entities involved in the process, thereby reducing the overall costs associated with the return and potentially driving down the price.

Companies and third-party entities strive to position themselves as close to the initial supply point as possible to reduce the associated acquisition or processing costs and to potentially maximize the value derived from the returns.

First Tier Supply Sources

At the forefront of this system is the **first tier of supply sources**: the initial nodes where customers choose to redirect their products for various purposes. It predominantly comprises manufacturers, distributors, and retailers who serve as critical points of distribution and return for products circulating within their sales cycles. Under the premise of adhering to customer commitments, these entities might propose incentives for product buyback, especially during customer upgrade cycles.

However, to encourage returns, organizations must provide a market value that appeals to the customer's financial considerations as opposed to merely meeting corporate targets. In this scenario, other organizations may seize the opportunity to embed themselves within the first tier by offering more enticing incentives directly to customers, perhaps offering higher purchase prices for the products. These entities can be categorized as Buyback Companies, Resale Businesses, or Sustainability Partners, frequently enhancing their value proposition through additional services such as decommissioning, data clearing, and detailed reporting.

Moreover, this tier welcomes the participation of Harvesters or Recyclers—organizations committed to dismantling unwanted products to salvage parts or raw materials, a process often yielding higher value recovery compared to recycling. Harvesters and Recyclers reassure customers about the environmentally responsible handling of data and materials, sometimes steering the customers to choose this route over landfill disposal. Donation centers further augment this tier, promising customers that their relinquished products will find new users, thus fostering a positive outlook toward product disposal. Additionally, the integration of peer-to-peer selling platforms facilitated by e-commerce frameworks enables individuals to ship products directly from the initial user to the subsequent, adding another dimension to this tier.

Second Tier Supply Sources

In the second tier of supply sources, there are organizations such as **aggregators** and large wholesalers that primarily acquire products from first tier sources. They specialize in consolidating larger product lots, only to fragment them into smaller batches, catering to organizations willing to pay a premium for lesser quantities. Aggregators and large wholesalers are the second organization to touch a return.

Third Tier Supply Sources

This leads us to the third tier of supply sources, home to niche market wholesalers who may lack the bargaining clout of larger aggregators but engage with a diverse product portfolio. This tier also hosts refurbishers, experts in revitalizing damaged or defective products to enhance resale value, and retailers operating smaller businesses focused on direct sales to end customers, thus completing the secondary market supply chain.

Supply Source Liquidation Strategy and Considerations

1. **Lot Complexity and Cost.** The complexity of a lot and its associated costs are primary determinants of the liquidation approach. Larger lots, although more challenging to sort and expensive, attract players with significant capital and capabilities. For example, a $1 million lot comprising of ten thousand items might only be viable for a few elite players.

2. **Customer Base and Service.** As the lot size decreases and becomes more refined, a broader customer base emerges,

necessitating an uptick in customer service and support. For instance, servicing a single customer buying ten thousand items differs vastly from catering to ten thousand customers purchasing individual items.

3. **Cost of Doing Business versus Willingness to Pay.** While end consumers might demonstrate a higher willingness to pay, reaching them incurs logistical, sales, and support costs. On the other hand, selling to wholesalers may fetch a lower unit price but can ensure quicker liquidation and reduced overheads.

Value Generation Outlets

The end points in the reverse supply chain are value generation outlets, where the products find a new home or usage. These are the points where the refurbished, repaired, or recycled products are eventually sold to end customers, thereby generating value from products that were once considered as returns. The goal of value generation is to maximize the value generated at the end of the reverse supply chain, reducing the number of touchpoints a product passes through before reaching the end customer, thus minimizing costs and potentially increasing the final value realized from the sale.

Value generation outlets closely interact with supply sources to streamline the process and ensure a smoother flow of products through the reverse supply chain. The more synchronized these points are, the better the chances are of deriving maximum value from products in the secondary market.

Two major determinants in the secondary market value chain are: (1) the cost of doing business, and (2) the propensity of customers to pay premium prices. The liquidation strategies adopted by suppliers will determine which third-party partner is best suited for collaboration. For instance, if a business is looking to liquidate a lot with an intricate sorting requirement priced at $1 million, involving ten thousand items spread across ten pallets, only entities with matching capital and the required logistical apparatus can engage.

Such bulk sales to a single partner, who then dissects the product into more refined lots, can expand the customer base and necessitate enhanced customer service. Companies might opt for large-lot liquidations, especially when products demand transportation, compliance with industry norms, or hefty capital outlays. Although this might facilitate swift liquidation, the final sales price offered to consumers might be compromised due to embedded logistical and sales processes.

There are, however, entities that specialize in medium-sized lots, absorbing a few pallets of products, and then grading and selling them—possibly even directly—to end users. At the chain's tail end lie specialized entities, often micro-wholesalers, retailers, or end consumers who might not possess grading or kitting capabilities but require ready-to-use products.

The essence of lot size can be compartmentalized into three categories: (1) large, which comprises vast quantities requiring significant transportation and capital; (2) medium, signified by pallet-sized lots at a moderate price point; and (3) small, representing individual items prepared for immediate sale or use. It is evident that selling a bulk order to one entity demands a distinct effort and post-sale support compared to distributing the same quantity among numerous customers. Despite end users offering the maximum price, reaching them incurs logistical and support costs.

Aggregators or wholesalers, adept at handling vast lots, stand out as partners capable of ensuring liquidity and adherence to corporate guidelines. They might not guarantee the maximum monetary return for suppliers, especially if they are not dealing directly with end users. Some might adopt a hybrid approach, segmenting certain products into smaller lots or selling directly to consumers. Large-scale wholesalers typically possess networks comprising medium-sized wholesalers or smaller partners keen on procuring sorted, graded lots in modest quantities. Medium-sized lots, on the other hand, are the forte of regional distributors, mid-tier distributors, and niche-market distributors. The regional tag suggests geographical specificity, while their distribution capabilities entail product acquisition, grading, and redistribution. Specialists in this bracket have unique expertise and connections, linking suppliers with smaller buyers. **Brokers** also operate in this realm, primarily connecting the dots without adding logistical value. Smaller lots usually find takers among micro-wholesalers with limited store networks, retailers with proprietary sales channels, or direct end users.

Key Players in the Value Generation Supply Chain

1. **Aggregators or Wholesalers.** Primarily dealing with large lots, they possess the capital and logistical prowess to handle bulk quantities of products. Their primary role is to provide liquidity, ensure adherence to industry and corporate standards, and act as a bridge between the primary source and other players in the chain.

2. **Regional, Mid-Tier, and Niche Distributors.** These entities handle medium-sized lots, catering to specific geographical areas, markets, or product types. Their capabilities often encompass acquiring, grading, and disseminating products to smaller retailers or direct consumers.

3. **Retailers, Micro-Wholesalers, and Brokers.** Found at the tail end of the chain, these players deal with small lots or individual items. While brokers connect the dots without adding logistical value, micro-wholesalers and retailers directly influence end consumers' purchasing choices.

Every player or outlet within the reverse supply chain has a unique value proposition and a specific velocity at which they can generate this value. Each entity—be it a distributor, wholesaler, or retailer—serves a distinct purpose, filling a niche that might otherwise remain vacant, thus bringing tangible value especially in scenarios where alternatives are sparse. The symbiotic relationship between the primary supply source and the various entities in the value chain is paramount.

An underlying principle to grasp is the correlation between product handling and associated costs: the more hands a product passes through, the steeper the cost to reuse it. This invariably diminishes the bottom benefit accrued to the original supply source. As the landscape of reverse supply chains grows more sophisticated, businesses inch closer to their end consumers. This proximity, while beneficial in many ways, also means that profit margins are becoming increasingly slender. Consequently, the secondary market, ever responsive to the evolving dynamics, will have to adapt and transform to stay relevant and profitable.

Secondary Market Summary

The secondary market operates within a complex system of various suppliers and intermediaries, each playing a distinct role. Figure 6.1 illustrates the relationship.

Secondary Market Supply Chain

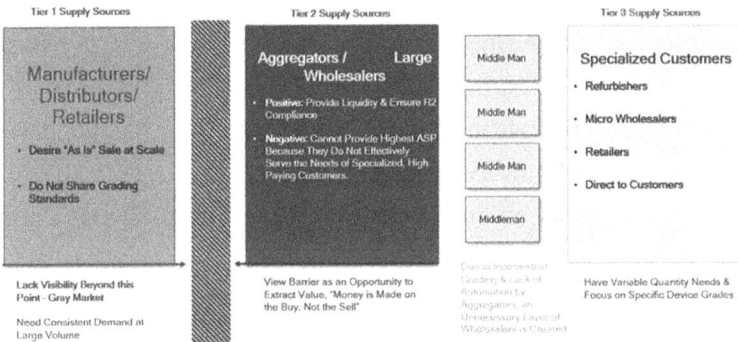

Figure 6.1. This is a high-level architecture of how Product One moves from carriers or manufacturers to through the secondary market into the hands of Customer Two+.

1. **Tier One Suppliers: Manufacturers/Distributors/Retailers**
   a. **Role:** *The return sources from the original owner.*
   b. **Returns:** *Products often get returned to these suppliers for multiple reasons, facilitated by different return stream.*

c. **Challenges:** *Different competitors have varying product grading standards. Many of them do not publish specific grading criteria but offer only general descriptions.*

d. **Liquidity Move:** *With a large inventory to liquidate, they introduce these products into the secondary market through auction-style formats. This implies:*

   i. no guarantees are provided;

   ii. all sales are final; and

   iii. the focus is on a quick inventory turnover with minimal post-sales support.

e. **Barrier:** *At this juncture, the Tier One suppliers lose visibility into where their products end up after the point of sale once they are introduced to the secondary market. However, they benefit by freeing up inventory space and generating revenue.*

2. **Tier Two Suppliers: Aggregators/Large Wholesalers**

   a. **Role:** *The second entities to handle the products, purchasing them in large lots.*

   b. **Value Proposition:**

      i. offer liquidity to the market

      ii. ensure environmental responsibility through their industry certifications

      iii. easier to audit

      iv. can be used to direct supply into or away from key markets.

   c. **Business Model:** *Suppliers add value by capitalizing on the price differential—buying at a lower price from Tier One and selling at a higher price to the next destination. This ensures profitability and sustains their operations.*

   d. **Distribution:** *They break down the large lots into medium or smaller ones, directing them to places that can derive maximum value.*

3. **Middlemen/Brokers**

   a. **Role**: *Occasionally introduced into the reverse supply chain.*

b. **Specialty**: *Their strength lies in their ability to find and connect with customers who have a demand for the specific product in the secondary market.*

4. **End of the Chain: Final Retailers/Consumers**

a. **Role**: *They represent the terminal point in the secondary-market supply chain. Each of these customers may have specific grading or packaging requirements.*

b. **Value Extraction**: *Here, the product achieves its maximum possible value during its final sale.*

The secondary market is a dynamic space where products transition from their initial point of production or sale to various layers, finally reaching the end consumer. The journey entails a series of transactions, grading variations, and value additions, culminating in the optimal utilization of products that might have otherwise been deemed unwanted.

Understanding Price Volatility in the Secondary Market

The used goods market, while governed by the fundamental principles of supply and demand, exhibits distinct dynamics that can lead to pronounced price volatility. Similar to the market for new products, a basic supply curve dictates that an increase in the availability of a used product generally depresses its price and vice versa. However, the used goods sector can be particularly influenced by sudden and diverse changes. For instance, massive liquidations by manufacturers or carriers can inundate the market, swiftly driving prices down.

Additionally, as products transition through their life cycles, the influx of used units from early adopters can further influence price equilibrium. On the demand side, external events, such as the disruptions to global supply chains seen during the COVID-19 pandemic, can elevate the appeal of used goods due to the scarcity of new alternatives. Similarly, economic downturns or the sudden trendiness of vintage items can spur demand. A myriad of factors converges to make the used-goods market notably challenging to predict, emphasizing the need for both businesses and consumers to stay adaptable and well-informed.

Amidst the chaos of the COVID-19 pandemic, one of the most conspicuous examples of volatility in the used goods market could be seen in the automotive industry. As the pandemic raged on, disruptions were not only felt at vehicle manufacturing units but extended deep into the supply chain, affecting areas such as silicone mining and microchip production. This created a long-lasting bottleneck in the production of new vehicles. An unforeseen consequence of these supply chain disruptions was a significant spike in the prices of used cars. As reported by Wayland (2023), with new vehicles in short supply due to these challenges, demand for used cars surged, driving their prices upward. The chip shortage, while prominently affecting the automotive sector, rippled across the entire electronics industry. By September 2023, these challenges were further exacerbated, and the United Auto Workers (UAW) announced a labor strike, promising to plunge the production of new cars even deeper into crisis that would invariably lead to an even more robust demand for used vehicles.[3]

In a contrasting scenario in the same month, the French government took a drastic step, demanding that Apple pull the iPhone 12 from its market due to concerns over electromagnetic radiation exposure. Such a move not only depresses the value of existing iPhone 12s in the French market but also raises questions about potential EU-wide restrictions.[4] An intriguing fallout of this action was the subsequent surge in demand for used iPhone 11s and 13s, models flanking the iPhone 12, as consumers pivot to available alternatives.

The above instances underline the intricate web of factors that influence the used goods market. Whether it is external events like a global pandemic or specific industry disruptions, the resulting price fluctuations make the market landscape incredibly complex and challenging to predict. The ebb and flow of demand in response to such disruptions emphasizes the need for adaptability and a deep understanding of market dynamics for businesses and consumers alike.

Risk of Ignoring the Secondary Market

Manufacturers and wholesalers may choose not to participate in the secondary market because they may not have developed the necessary accounting systems to understand the return on investment. However, there may be other reasons why companies are hesitant to participate in the secondary market, including concerns about cannibalization or the experience needed to possess oversight. Ironically, they are in the best position to control the secondary market but are very limited in their ability to destroy it. Therefore, the best corporate strategy for products with residual value is to be the best in the market, rather than trying to fight back the tide.

While there may be concerns about cannibalization and the desire to move toward a circular economy, there are several advantages to participating in the secondary market, including the cash-to-cash cycle and the intelligence that can be gained about where used products are going. By leveraging the residual-value effect and using strong brands to compete in lower-tier markets, manufacturers and wholesalers can expand their customer base, grow their install base, and strengthen their market position.

Again, it is important to note that customers will only participate in these programs if they offer value. If the offer to return is not greater than what they can get from another outlet, such as a reseller or secondary market, customers will choose the highest offer option. In other words, customers care more about their own financial situation when they participate in the circular economy than they do about a manufacturer's fear of cannibalization.

Therefore, one of the rules of the circular economy is that manufacturers and retailers need to offer attractive returns programs that provide financial and environmental benefits to customers. Only then can they encourage customers to return products for recycling or refurbishing, rather than throwing them away. Ultimately, doing this not only helps reduce waste and conserve resources but it also strengthens customer loyalty and brand reputation.

6.2 Secondary Market Sales Methodologies

The secondary market offers a variety of sales strategies, allowing suppliers to set specific rules and guidelines on how products move through them. The aggressiveness of these strategies largely depends on the supplier's intent to control costs or regulate the flow of products in this market. One major aspect of these strategies revolves around **liquidation methods**. These methods include:

- **Customer Promises.** The assurances a company provides, which can include grading standards, return policies or warranties on products.
- **Transactional Approaches.** The methods a supplier employs when engaging and transacting with their partners.
- **Payment Modalities.** Payment options available to partners, including upfront.

Customer Promises in the Secondary Market: Implications on Pricing and Agreements

In the secondary market where excess new or used goods are traded, the pricing and sale dynamics can vary greatly based on the level of specificity regarding the condition of the products being sold. The process of liquidation, which involves selling off the products in this market, often follows three common methodologies, each with its own implications on pricing and buyer-seller agreements. Let us take a deeper look at these methodologies:

1. **"As-Is" Sales.** In this method, products are sold in their existing condition, with only a general description provided, and it usually does not allow for returns. This method is generally adopted to save on reverse logistics and other resources associated with testing and grading the products.

    a. **Pricing.** *The lack of detailed information about the product's condition often results in a lower price point as buyers are assuming a higher risk regarding the functionality and cosmetic condition of the products.*

     b.   **Suitability.** *This approach is best suited for sellers who do not want to invest time and resources in the grading and testing of products before sale.*

     c.   **Dispute Potential.** *Lower, as buyers are aware of the generalized description and the "as-is" condition of the products.*

2. **"Sort and Sell" or Consignment.** In this method, the liquidation partner takes possession of the products and sells them on behalf of the original seller, usually retaining a percentage of the final sale price as a commission. Payment terms and conditions can vary.

     a.   **Pricing.** *This method has the potential to fetch a better price because the liquidation partner has an incentive to maximize the product value to benefit both parties.*

     b.   **Suitability.** *Best suited for sellers looking for a more hands-off approach, delegating the sales process to a liquidation partner.*

     c.   **Dispute Potential.** *Moderate, depending on the agreement between the liquidating entity and the buyer regarding product conditions and returns.*

3. **Tested or "Direct" Standard.** Here, products are categorized based on functionality status—fully functional, defective, or not tested—and sometimes assigned a cosmetic grade, which allows for more precise pricing.

     a.   **Pricing.** *This method fetches higher prices as the products are tested and graded, providing buyers with more clarity on the product conditions.*

     b.   **Suitability.** *Ideal for sellers aiming to maximize the value of the products by investing in testing and grading before the sale.*

     c.   **Dispute Potential.** *Higher, as buyers have the option to dispute the product's condition if it does not match the described grade or functionality status.*

The secondary market provides diverse opportunities for selling excess new or used goods, depending on the methodology. Generally, it follows that the more detailed the product description, the higher the potential price point. However, this also involves higher logistical investments and a greater likelihood of disputes. Conversely, more general descriptions often entail lower pricing but reduce the potential for disputes and logistical costs. Sellers, therefore, need to weigh the potential benefits against the costs and risks associated with each method when deciding on their liquidation strategy in the secondary market.

1. **Selective Partner Liquidation.** Some companies prefer to liquidate only through large, certified wholesalers like those with ISO or R2 certifications. They may also require buyers to undergo **background checks** or other application processes to ensure that their products are treated responsibly and often helps in averting product cannibalization. Such a strategy makes partner vetting easier through application reviews and compliance audits. For instance, companies might dictate that products be liquidated outside certain geographies. A real-world application of this approach was when Verizon, in the process of sunsetting their 3G network, opted to liquidate products only to partners with overseas outlets. This strategic move reduced the chances of 3G products being reactivated on a soon-to-be-retired network.

2. **Swim-Lanes Strategy:** The concept of "**swim lanes**" is used to describe when suppliers restrict liquidation to a handful of wholesalers, allowing them to manage market segments. This approach counters the "race to the bottom" pricing effect by regulating supply. If numerous players were allowed in one channel, overbidding and undercutting could depress market prices. However, by controlling supply and diversifying across geographies, the secondary market can remain more stable.

3. **Open-Forum Liquidation.** Contrary to the selective approach, some suppliers favor an open forum, permitting a broader range of buyers to register and bid. Although this approach might expose the supplier to a diverse array of smaller buyers, it also

introduces the challenges of managing a larger customer base and potential market price depression if there is an oversupply.

4. **Open Auctions**
   a. **Benefits:**
      i. **transparency**: Everyone knows what the current bid is and can strategize accordingly.
      ii. **increased competition**: The visible prices can spur competitive bidding, potentially driving up prices.
   b. **Weaknesses:**
      i. **overloading issues**: Bots trying to outbid in the last moments can clog the site, potentially causing technical problems or crashes.
      ii. **time sensitivity**: If multiple auctions end around the same time, bidders may miss out on opportunities.

5. **Blind Auctions**
   a. **Benefits:**
      i. **easier management**: With bids being hidden, there is less need for constant monitoring and reaction to ongoing bids.
      ii. **encourages true valuation**: Participants are more likely to bid what they truly believe the item is worth without being influenced by other bids.
      iii. **efficiency**: Bidders can set their maximum willingness to pay without being outbid incrementally.
   b. **Weaknesses:**
      i. **potential for overpayment**: A bidder might greatly overpay for an item if they bid much higher than the next highest bidder.
      ii. **lack of competitive urgency**: Without seeing other bids, some bidders might undervalue items.

6. **Line-Level Auctions**
   a. **Benefits:**
      i. **specificity**: Participants bid on exactly what they want in terms of make, model, and grade. This is particularly

useful for buyers looking for very specific items.

    ii. **efficient clearing of high-demand items**: Fast-moving products can be quickly bought up without having to be bundled with less desirable items.

  b. **Weaknesses**:

    iv. **aging inventory**: Items that are less popular might not get any bids and remain unsold, leading to aging inventory.

    v. **complexity**: It might require more management oversight, especially if there are many lines being auctioned

7. **Lot-Based Auctions**

  a. **Benefits**:

    i. **bulk sales**: Allows for the movement of large quantities of inventory at once.

    ii. **streamlined handling**: Reduces the complexity of managing many individual item sales.

    iii. **velocity boost**: Can potentially speed up the sale of slower-moving inventory by bundling it with more attractive items.

  b. **Weaknesses**:

    i. **potential lower revenues.** Bidders might bid less on lots if they believe there are items they do not want or view as low value within the lot.

    ii. **logistic considerations.** The purchasing party might factor in the potential costs and hassles of sorting, storing, and handling large lots, which could lead to lower bids.

These dynamics all have their unique pros and cons, and the right choice depends on the specifics of the situation, the nature of the goods, the goals of the seller, and the preferences of the buyers in the market. The choice of strategy largely depends on the supplier's desired outcome, market conditions, and desired level of control over the sales process.

6.3 Harmonizing Grading Standards in the Diverse Secondary Market Landscape

In the secondary market, organizations often face challenges stemming from the diverse origins of their products. The inconsistency of grading standards across these sources poses a challenge. Product grading may be standardized within a company, but it is not standardized at scale across industries.

This inconsistency is not static either; it often evolves based on the ebb and flow of consumer preferences and regional inclinations. Third parties, which are crucial players in the secondary market, are at the forefront of this complexity. They source from various suppliers and cater to a range of marketplaces and regions. Consequently, they grapple with a mosaic of grading standards and practices, each unique to its source. The onus is on these third parties to distill this assortment of grades into a singular, consistent format, ensuring they uphold their commitments to their downstream clientele. In addition, the task is not just about standardization; it is about value assessment. The third parties need to discern the potential value of their acquisitions and craft compelling sales strategies to resonate with their customer base.

To illustrate, if we consider three different suppliers, each might bring its own set of grading standards to the table, including aspects like naming conventions, acceptable damage levels, and testing methodologies. These variances need to be meticulously aggregated into marketable categories. The overarching narrative is clear: the broader the supplier base, the more intricate the processes of market understanding, product processing, and grading.

Grading Standard Example

To convey the condition and quality of a product, a variety of grading nomenclatures exist, which can often feel like an alphabet soup. A representative example is the Three-Space Grading System, also called the three-star grading system.

Here is a breakdown:

- The first space provides a classification indicating the source, and how these spaces are filled and what they mean can be done in a variety of methods. For instance, "R" might signify consumer returns, while "W" stands for warranty return and "T" may stand for trade-in product.
- The second space represents the functional status of the product. Again, the way these spaces are filled can vary. Using the preestablished method of letters, "P" can denote that the product passed functional testing and should operate correctly, "N" can suggest it has not been tested and might require further checks, and "F" means the product failed testing.
- The third space relates to the product's cosmetic condition. In the lettering system, "N" can mean it is in new condition, "L" implies a like-new state with minimal use, "A" signifies slight wear, "B" indicates visible wear, "C" stands for substantial wear, and "D" points to significant damage.

By combining the three indicators in a separate-spacing format, the system provides a snapshot of the product's overall condition. However, some products may be sold without this specific grading, essentially as is. An example would be a retail return product that has passed testing in A condition would be graded as R P A, or a warranty return not tested with significant damage may be W N D.

It is worth noting that grading can vary depending on the supply source. Often, products undergo a subsequent round of grading as the reverse supply chain seeks to reevaluate the item, ensuring it is appropriately categorized for its next journey within the chain. There are three data points that secondary market players must grasp in order to assign the correct value to the products they are purchasing and selling.

1. **Understanding Supply Source Composition**. Every supply source classifies its products differently, usually based on a combination of cosmetic and functional conditions. These could be grades like "mint," "good," "fair," or "broken" based on cosmetic appearance and "fully functional," "partially functional," or

"nonfunctional" based on operational capability. It is imperative for a secondary market player to discern the following questions. Answers to these questions can help secondary markets predict the quality and quantity of products they will receive and adjust their expectations accordingly.

    a. What percentage of products from their supply source typically fall under each grade?

    b. How consistent is the grading system of the supply source?

2. **Blended Benefit Analysis.** Once the products are received, secondary-market players will categorize them based on their own grading system. It is possible that their grading criteria differ from the supply source. The blended benefit is a weighted average that reflects the value and volume of products in each grade.

    a. Example: if a majority of received products are in the "good" cosmetic grade but "partially functional," the blended benefit will lean toward this combination. Understanding this blended benefit allows the secondary player to:

      i. price products accurately for their marketplace;

      ii. forecast potential revenue or profitability; and

      iii. determine if the product lot is worth the investment.

3. **Logistical Cost Analysis.** Secondary market players must consider the logistical costs, including:

    a. costs associated with transporting products from the supply source;

    b. inspection, grading, and processing costs; and

    c. costs to repair or refurbish products to meet buyer agreements, local regulations, or their own standards.

Without a clear view of these costs, players could underestimate their expenses and end up overpaying for products.

Historical Data and the Funnel Model

Imagine the product-grading system as a funnel. Products initially face thorough functional and aesthetic examinations at the funnel's entrance, each incurring different costs. This process categorizes products into two groups: those meeting standards, and those falling short. The latter are further classified based on the severity of their aesthetic flaws. The lower end of this **grading funnel**, fed by historical data and market trends, yields essential insights for secondary market buyers. This comprehensive knowledge enables them to refine their buying strategies, ensuring their investments match the expected value and state of the products, thereby maintaining profitability.

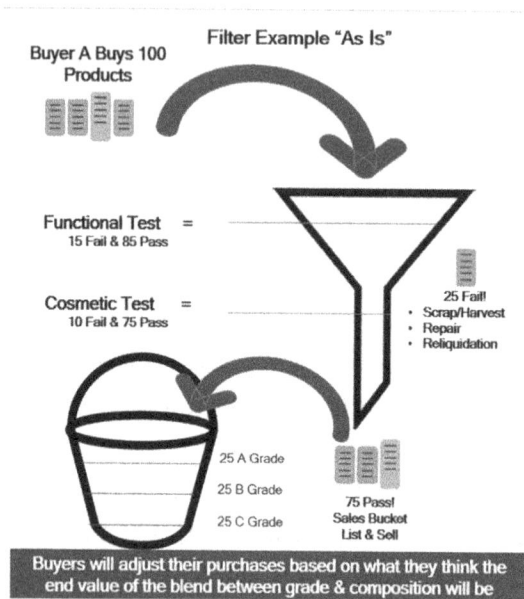

Figure 6.2. The grading funnel is a visual representation of how a post inspection breakout occurs.

6.4 Matching Used Supply to Demand Using E-Commerce

E-commerce, in the contemporary digital age, is not just about selling new products. An evolving dimension of e-commerce is the secondary market where used products, returned goods, and refurbished items find new owners. This is akin to the traditional adage, "One person's trash is another's treasure," but in a much more organized and digital fashion. With the help of e-commerce, suppliers are enabled to efficiently expose used supply across multiple sales channels simultaneously and capture buyer demand.

There are a series of intricacies that a business must factor to support matching used supply to the deal hunter and **green consumer** demand using e-commerce:

1. **Complexity of Matching Supply with Demand.** Unlike traditional e-commerce that primarily deals with new products, the secondary market must match the variable supply of used items with a potentially uncertain demand. Each product is unique in terms of its usage, wear and tear, and even its story.

2. **Shopper Type.** Demand for used supply on e-commerce platforms is primarily driven by two shopper types: deal hunters and green consumers.[5] Understanding buyer intent is crucial for delivering value, as it necessitates tailored product offerings that cater to these distinct shopper profiles.

   · The primary shopper for used supply consists of deal hunters, a significant spending segment. These shoppers— driven mainly by price—form the strongest customer base for used supply, as they often prioritize cost savings over purchasing new products. Deal hunters are typically willing to accept products in various conditions, ranging from "excellent" (like-new) to "fair" (showing signs of wear, such as scratches or dents).[6] In contrast to value shoppers, who may pay more for perceived increased value, deal hunters primarily seek lower prices, even if it means accepting lesser quality.

   · The second-largest shopper type for used supply is the green consumer. These consumers prioritize sustainable purchases but often face a buying intention gap due to higher costs associated with sustainably sourced products. The lower prices of used supply (on average 30 percent off MSRP of new products) help bridge this gap, making sustainable choices more accessible.[7]

E-commerce businesses that effectively connect used supply with these consumer types can leverage social influence to encourage pro-environmental behaviors in consumption. For example, studies have shown that informing online shoppers about others buying eco-friendly products can lead to a 65 percent increase in making at least one sustainable purchase.[8] This approach demonstrates how businesses can drive real conversion by aligning used supply with consumer values and behaviors.

1. **Transition from Reverse to Forward Logistics**. As discussed, when a product is returned, it enters the realm of reverse logistics. It goes through an assessment or "reventory" phase, after which, based on its condition, it is either discarded, refurbished, or listed again for sale. Once listed, the product jumps back into the forward logistics process, waiting to be shipped to its new owner. This seamless transition between the reverse and forward logistics is crucial for meeting demand.

2. **Product Descriptions**. For used products, a mere product description is not sufficient. Sellers must provide additional details about the product's condition. This is where the ambiguity arises. Terms like "good," "better," or "best that indicate the condition of the product are subjective and can differ from one seller or platform to another.

3. **Pricing Challenge**. Pricing used items is not straightforward. While the price needs to reflect the product's condition and usability, it should also resonate with the buyer's perception of its value. Setting a price too high may deter potential buyers, while pricing it too low might result in lost revenue.

4. **Performance Metrics**. In the secondary market, the reputation of a seller or platform is paramount. **Key performance indicators** like on-time shipments, return rates, and seller feedback play a vital role. Any misrepresentation or discrepancy can lead to public negative feedback, which can affect future sales.

5. **Customer Promise**. Unlike primary market players who have standardized warranties and return policies—customer promises pledged by manufacturers or retailers—secondary market players often craft their own promises. These commitments, in terms of warranty, return policy, or customer service, become pivotal in building trust.

Managing an e-commerce platform for used equipment requires a careful balance of transparency, efficiency, and trustworthiness. While the challenges are manifold, the potential rewards in terms of tapping into a growing market segment make it an exciting avenue for businesses. As the secondary market continues to grow, refining these processes and setting clearer standards will be crucial for sustained success.

6.5 Navigating the Complex Terrain of the Secondary Market and Mitigating Bad Behavior

Manufacturers undeniably hold a strategic position with their access to intellectual property, such as schematics, tools, and testing procedures; simply put, they have the upper hand in ensuring both product functionality and authenticity. Moreover, their control over re-registration keys and existing close ties with suppliers and packaging vendors further accentuate their edge in this marketplace.

Leveraging their unique position in the market, manufacturers can exercise greater control and capitalize on the resources and knowledge they have amassed over the years. This section offers an illuminating look into the intricacies of managing the secondary market effectively, highlighting the challenges posed by **unethical practices** and the underbelly of the Gray Market.

Strategies for Choosing Secondary Market Partners

Choosing the right partners can be a linchpin in establishing a successful venture in the secondary market. Manufacturers do not have to go into it blindly, as there are strategies to vet and select partners who align with the manufacturer's vision and standards. By fostering relationships with trustworthy and competent partners, manufacturers can bolster their position and avoid the traps of nefarious elements in the market.

Auction Management: Implementing Best Practices in Supply and Auction Operations

Auctions have perennially been a dynamic and influential component of the secondary market, offering a platform where goods can find a second life and buyers can find products at more competitive prices. However, this sphere also harbors potential for misuse and malpractice, making auction management a critical skill.

The following practices not only ensure a seamless operation but also act as a bulwark against potential fraudulent activities. The following are key strategies to be incorporated:

- setting the ground rules
- onboarding application processes
- monitoring and enforcement
- partnering with reliable auction platforms
- educating the consumers

At the outset, manufacturers need to set clear guidelines that govern auctions. These guidelines should stipulate product warranties, accurate product descriptions, and transparent pricing strategies, which work toward building a trustworthy auction platform. Manufacturers can utilize their deep knowledge and resources to set standards that discourage bad behavior and promote fairness and authenticity.

Effective auction management goes beyond merely setting rules; it also involves regular monitoring and enforcement of these rules to maintain the integrity of the platform. Manufacturers can leverage their existing networks and tools to closely supervise auction proceedings, swiftly identifying and addressing any deviations from the established norms.

In this digital age, technology can be a potent ally in managing auctions efficiently. Manufacturers can implement advanced software solutions that allow for real-time monitoring, data analysis, and even automated rule enforcement to maintain a transparent and fair auction environment. Collaborating with established and reliable auction platforms can be a strategic move for manufacturers. These platforms, with their own experience and resources, can offer a streamlined process, minimizing the risks of fraudulent activities and ensuring that the products reach the right buyers.

An informed consumer base can be the first line of defense against malpractice in auctions. Manufacturers should take the initiative to educate consumers about how to identify authentic products, which will lead to fostering a community that values authenticity and quality.

Bribery and Collusion

A pressing concern is **bribery and collusion**, which can manifest in several ways. For instance, an employee might be compensated based on the number of products directed from a supplier to a specific buyer. This compensation might come directly or indirectly through acquaintances or family members. As the secondary market expands, the disparity between an employee's corporate renumeration and the total revenue present in the market may intensify temptations for collusion.

Money Laundering in the Secondary Market and Safeguarding Measures

The scarcity of knowledge regarding reverse logistics and the secondary market can be a hotbed for illicit activities, particularly when well-intentioned organizations inadvertently leave gaps. Corporate crime occupies a specialized segment within the broader spectrum of criminal jurisprudence.[9] Similarly, the circular economy remains a specialized subset within contemporary business paradigms, and reverse logistics carves out its own distinct space in the supply chain landscape. Consequently, understanding illicit activities within reverse logistics as it pertains to the circular economy is akin to navigating a niche within a niche.

Ill-intentioned actors may:

- **Purchase Products with Illicit Funds.** By using tainted money to buy products, these actors convert their illicit gains into physical assets, which can then be resold—often in other jurisdictions—muddying any paper trails.

- **Overvalued Transactions.** Bad actors might artificially inflate the price of a product. For instance, a product that is worth $100 might be sold for $1000, with an excess of $900 returned to the seller, often minus a commission.

- **Establish Shell Companies.** Bad actors can set up fake companies or use existing ones to conduct transactions on the secondary market. These transactions might appear legitimate on the surface but are merely a ruse to legitimize black money.[10]

Anti-Money Laundering (AML) Safeguards

- **Background Checks.** One of the initial lines of defense is a comprehensive background check on all parties involved. This includes not just the entity purchasing or selling but also the beneficial owners. A thorough check can flag known criminals, entities, or individuals from high-risk jurisdictions or those with known links to illicit activities.[11]

- **Financial Tracking.** Monitoring and recording all financial transactions are pivotal. Special attention should be given to large or repeated transactions from the same source, especially if the pattern seems erratic or without clear business justification.

- **Avoiding Unknown Wire Transfers.** A company should be wary of accepting funds from unknown, third party, or unverified sources. Any wire transfer that appears without prior notice or without a clear link to a legitimate transaction should be flagged for further investigation.

- **Regular Audits.** Regular internal and external audits can help identify discrepancies in the books or suspicious patterns that might have been overlooked during regular operations.

- **Training.** Employees in the secondary market, especially those in finance or in sales roles, should be trained to identify the potential red flags of **money laundering**.

- **Crafting an AML Policy with Legal Guidance.** Given the complexities of **AML** laws, which can vary by jurisdiction, it is crucial to craft an AML policy in consultation with legal experts. This ensures not only compliance but also preventative mechanisms to detect and deter potential money laundering.

By instituting rigorous AML measures, businesses can mitigate risks, protect their reputation, and ensure they operate within the legal grounds, avoiding unintentional entanglement in illicit activities.

Other Unethical Practices in the Secondary Market

- **Bribery to Undergrade Products.** Individuals may receive incentives, often monetary, to assign a lower grade to products than they actually deserve, thereby influencing the products' market value.
- **Intentional Misgrading.** This involves deliberately declaring a product in worse condition than it actually is, reducing its apparent market value.
- **Cherry-Picking.** Here, specific high-grade products are selected from a batch and provided to a buyer, possibly in exchange for kickbacks or other favors.
- **Selling Competitive Intelligence.** Some parties may trade essential business information, like winning bid prices, compromising market fairness.
- **Unrestricted Access to Product Inventory.** Unethically accessing and sharing product inventory information, especially to areas or platforms where the listing company intends to enforce restrictions, seriously undermines trust and violates business confidentiality.
- **Greenwashing.** This is misrepresenting products in an environmentally friendly way when they are not.
- **Counterfeiting Parts in Used Products.** Some unscrupulous dealers may replace genuine parts with counterfeit ones in used products, regardless of safety risks.

- **Use of Bots for Auction Sniping.** Some entities deploy automated bots to outbid genuine bidders in the last moments of online auctions. This not only gives them an unfair advantage but can overload and slow down auction systems, depriving genuine bidders of a fair chance to win.
- **Misrepresentation of Products.** There are cases where products, such as those labeled "certified pre-owned," are falsely marketed as new, misleading consumers about their true condition and value.
- **Violating Contractual Terms.** This could involve selling products in markets or regions where they were contractually not intended to be sold, undermining exclusive deals or regional-pricing strategies.

To navigate these treacherous waters confidently and ethically, companies need to acknowledge the potential for malpractice and fortify their operations with robust mitigation strategies.

Defensive Strategies

While the secondary market does present risks from unethical participants, companies are by no means defenseless. They possess a comprehensive set of tools and strategies designed to align their environmental commitments with prudent business practices. By pro-actively adopting these mitigation measures, companies can safeguard against potential threats and simultaneously enhance their reputation for transparency and ethical behavior. The following are best practices to shield against malicious actors:

- **Enhanced Vetting and Training.** Conduct rigorous background checks for employees involved in secondary-market operations and provide regular training on ethical conduct.
- **Clear Code of Conduct.** Institute a strict code of conduct detailing acceptable behaviors, especially regarding interactions with suppliers and buyers.
- **Transparent Transactions.** Ensure all transactions are transparently recorded and subjected to regular audit.

- **Whistleblower Mechanisms.** Establish anonymous channels for employees to report suspicious activities without fear.
- **Division of Duties.** Distribute responsibilities among multiple employees to ensure a checks-and-balances system.
- **Regular Audits.** Engage external firms to conduct unexpected audits on transactions to detect any inconsistencies.
- **Contractual Safeguards.** Include anti-collusion clauses in contracts with suppliers and buyers.
- **Monitoring Communication.** Use technologies to monitor and flag potentially collusive communications while respecting privacy laws.
- **Performance-Based Incentives.** Reward ethical behavior and policy adherence instead of just meeting sales targets.
- **Limit Employee Turnover.** Reduce frequent personnel changes in crucial roles.
- **Secure Information Systems.** Use top-tier security systems to protect transaction data from unauthorized access or manipulation.
- **Regularly Review Supplier and Buyer Relationships.** Periodically evaluate these relationships to detect potential collusion hints.
- **Engage with Industry Associations.** Actively participate in associations that offer guidelines and resources to combat collusion.
- **Feedback Mechanisms.** Set up a system for suppliers and buyers to provide feedback about employees and transactions.
- **Legal Recourse.** Be ready to take legal action against parties involved in collusion.
- **Sound Corporate Policies on Gifts and Incentives.** Establish clear guidelines about gift or incentive acceptance to prevent potential bribery situations.
- **Electronic Grading Systems.** Utilize digital systems to assess a product's condition, reducing chances of human error or **intentional misgrading**.

- **Electronic POS or Auction Platforms**. Use these platforms to ensure products fetch a fair market prices through transparent bidding processes.
- **IP Address Monitoring.** Monitor the IP addresses accessing business systems to prevent unauthorized access and breaches.
- **Downstream Partner Audits.** Collaborate with recognized standards like ISO, R2, etc., and mandate third-party audits for partners to guarantee adherence to best practices and ethical guidelines.

Managing the secondary market is no easy task, but armed with the right knowledge and strategies, manufacturers can navigate this complex terrain with finesse. By understanding the potential risks and leveraging their inherent advantages, established companies can position themselves in a way that not only complements the primary market but also serves as a testament to their commitment to quality and authenticity.

Chapter 7

Future Trends

Investing in reverse logistics is both an environmentally responsible and business-savvy decision—not to mention it aligns with global trends. As a business scales, an effective reverse logistics system not only prevents revenue loss but also has the potential to positively impact the company's stock price. This chapter reveals emerging trends in reverse logistics.

7.1 Material Shortages and the Birth of New Business Models

The Global Scarcity Landscape

The increasing scarcity of Earth's finite resources is creating growing pressure on companies to take proactive measures in environmental protection. Annually, over 100 billion tons of materials flow into the global market, a number that is difficult to fathom but nevertheless stresses the scale of our consumption.[1] Given the current trajectory, the demand for resources is set to outpace what can feasibly be extracted using present-day technology.[2] This is especially concerning considering the exponential growth of the global population and the corresponding rise in demand for goods, services, and conveniences.

Natural resource scarcity, as it intensifies, will undeniably exert pressure on supply chains. Companies will feel the pinch, not just in the form of increased costs, but also potential disruptions in securing the materials they rely upon. The future may well belong to businesses that preemptively adopt circular manufacturing principles that reintroduce materials into the manufacturing process.

This evolving landscape offers fertile ground for innovative business models.[3] As the demand for sustainable solutions grows, opportunities to provide services related to circular manufacturing, green logistics, and reverse logistics will multiply.

Companies that specialize in collecting, refurbishing, and redistributing products will find a captive market as waste becomes the new raw material for manufacturing products.[4] Similarly, businesses that offer consultancy or technology services to streamline and greenify supply chains will be in high demand.

The challenges presented by global material scarcity are daunting, but they also provide an impetus for change and innovation. By embracing a paradigm shift toward sustainability, circularity, and green logistics, businesses can not only mitigate risks but also discover new avenues for growth and differentiation in an increasingly resource-conscious world.

Resilient Futures: The Convergence of Supply Chain Sustainability and Investor Priorities

The laws of supply and demand are also deeply intertwined with the resource challenge. As these essential materials become scarcer and harder to procure, and as demand either remains consistent or escalates, prices will inevitably surge. Recognizing the writing on the wall, forward-thinking companies are preemptively integrating circular principles into their business models.[5] By doing so, they can both mitigate potential future risks and position themselves advantageously in a competitive landscape increasingly defined by resource constraints and elevated prices.

Further underlining the gravity of this shift toward sustainability and resource-conscious operations is the attitude of the global investment community. According to a survey by Ernst and Young in 2022, nearly 80 percent of approximately four hundred global institutional investors emphasized the importance of companies addressing environmental, social, and governance concerns.[6] This majority believes that companies should make investments targeting ESG issues even if it means compromising short-term profits. This growing sentiment among investors highlights a broader recognition of the long-term value and market resilience that ESG-focused strategies bring to companies. This shift in investor priorities, coupled with the evolving resource landscape, makes it clear that the businesses of the future will be those that prioritize long-term sustainability over short-term gains.

7.2 Government Pressure and Regulation

The Historical Context of Circular Economy Legislation

Historically, technological advancements have often outpaced the development of legislation pertaining to the circular economy. Two sectors that highlight this phenomenon are real estate and automotive. These sectors emerged as pioneers in integrating sustainable practices within the circular economy framework. In response, legislation evolved to support and regulate these initiatives. A notable milestone in this journey was in 2012 when Massachusetts became the trailblazer in upholding the Right to Repair. The state passed the Act Protecting Motor Vehicle Owners and Small Businesses in Repairing Motor Vehicles, a groundbreaking decision that mandated manufacturers to provide parts to independent shops and vehicle owners.[7] This shifted the dynamics for manufacturers. They were now not only responsible for managing repair stock for their warranty needs but also had to cater to the broader Right to Repair requirements.

Today, consumer electronics are at the forefront of the growth of the circular economy. This rapidly expanding sector has highlighted the importance of regulations such as the Right to Repair. States like Minnesota, New York, and California have adopted these regulations, setting a precedent likely to be followed by others.[8] Currently, twenty-seven states are considering legislation that would make it easier to repair or refurbish items containing electronic components.[9] Amid these state-level initiatives, there is debate about federal legislation standardizing the Right to Repair. Across seas, Europe is advancing similar sustainable regulations and reforms. Based on these trends, it is expected that industries like apparel and home goods will see growth in their secondary markets, potentially leading to the introduction of similar legislation.

International Agreements and Global Environmental Consciousness

Platforms such as the World Economic Forum have consistently emphasized the importance of embedding sustainable practices into global business operations. A significant aspect of this push toward sustainability is the development of reverse logistics systems. Expansive government policies have the potential to foster the development of transparent and reliable financial products, facilitating transitions to a circular economy and mitigating environmental impacts.[10] International treaties, like the Paris Agreement, are instrumental in solidifying a global commitment to combat climate change. These agreements bring countries together under shared goals and standards to reduce greenhouse gas emissions and address climate change impacts, which in turn urge businesses to reconsider their supply chains and resource utilizations.

New Instances of Forced Internalizations: Incentives, Penalties, and Local Governance

Successful implementation of environmental legislation can act as a catalyst for change, promoting reuse and sustainability. This is achieved through mechanisms that compel organizations and individuals to internalize the environmental costs of their activities. These "forced internalization" mechanisms make it necessary for businesses and consumers to consider the environmental impact of their actions and incorporate these considerations into their decision-making processes.

In the corporate world, a clear system of rewards and repercussions has surfaced around sustainability. Companies that embrace sustainable norms, especially those that invest heavily in reverse logistics, often reap financial benefits such as tax breaks and grants. Conversely, firms that overlook environmental standards risk facing hefty penalties. Likewise, local governance demonstrates this narrative. As cities worldwide aspire to be more sustainable, reverse logistics integration into waste management and urban planning is increasingly evident. Local governments are harnessing community engagement to educate citizens about recycling, product returns, and refurbishment. Ultimately, as our global society deepens its commitment to the environment, reverse logistics stands out as a fundamental pillar.

7.3 The Empowered Customer: *Savviness in Sustainability*

Adapting to the New Normal: Evolving Returns Policies in the Post-Pandemic Online Shopping Era

The shift from brick-and-mortar shopping to online platforms, though already underway, was dramatically accelerated by the COVID-19 pandemic. The imposition of lockdowns and social-distancing measures resulted in a sudden change in shopping patterns. To adapt to and maintain sales, many companies swiftly introduced customer-friendly policies such as free return shipping and no-questions-asked returns. While these policies enhanced consumer confidence and sales, they also led to an increase in online returns and new forms of fraud, with some studies reporting that fraudulent returns account for 10.6 percent of online.[11]

In reaction to these new purchasing behaviors, businesses started to focus more on cost control, conducting market research to understand the impact of various return promises on sales. This has led to an evolution in return policies, inspiring some companies to reconsider the feasibility of offering free shipping and others to introduce measures like tamper-proof seals to prevent instances of brief product use followed by returns.

Over the next few years, companies are expected to continue adjusting their policies to balance customer satisfaction with cost-efficiency. As consumer shopping preferences evolve, reverse logistics teams and their strategies will also have to change. This ongoing development reflects the dynamic nature of consumer behavior and the need for businesses to adapt to remain competitive and profitable.

Furthermore, there is a likelihood that some companies will adjust their policies to align with the anti-capitalistic sentiments of the new generation of shoppers. An interesting correlation can be observed between reduced returns and the customer's preference to move away from unnecessary consumption of new products in favor of alternatives. Companies will need to take these evolving consumer attitudes into account in their return policies and broader business strategies, potentially leading to innovative practices that resonate with these emerging consumer values.

The Rise of the Informed Consumer

In 2022, ThredUP, a prominent player in the resale market, unveiled a decade's worth of insights into the industry in its tenth annual resale report. A striking revelation from the report highlighted that the fashion-resale sector is anticipated to expand at a rate sixteen times faster than the broader retail clothing industry. Driving this explosive growth is the modern, savvy shopper: individuals adept at navigating online shopping platforms and motivated by a sustainable mindset that prioritizes second-hand first. Notably, the report spotlighted a behavioral trend among Gen Z and Millennials: nearly 46 percent of them actively contemplate the future resale value of apparel before finalizing a purchase.[12] This pronounced inclination not only underscores the burgeoning market for second or subsequent owners but also signals a rising consumer expectation for items to retain value over time. Such trends, while prevalent in fashion, suggest a broader shift in consumption patterns that could reverberate across various industries.

Repairability has emerged as a significant factor influencing consumer choices across various industries.[13] A striking 96 percent of Americans consider repairability important when selecting a car.[14] The high number underscores the fact that vehicles are substantial investments, and consumers seek the reassurance that they can extend their car's lifespan without needing to replace the entire vehicle at the first sign of trouble. This mindset is not restricted to cars: 77 percent of Americans value repairability when choosing a smartphone.[15] Given the central role smartphones play in our daily lives and their escalating costs, it is evident that consumers view these devices as long-term companions rather than disposable gadgets. Moreover, evolving customer perspective on repairability is not limited to the auto, electronics, or fashion industries. It is indicative of a more profound shift toward embracing the principles of the circular economy.

Empowered Consumers: Extending Product Lifecycles in the Digital Age

The rising emphasis on repairability ties directly into the broader **Right to Repair Movement**, which pushes for consumers to have the ability to mend the products they purchase, and by implication, have access to essential components for repair. These components include replacement parts, crucial information in the form of repair manuals or guides, and specialized tools. Traditionally, many manufacturers reserved these resources for their certified repair centers. However, the call for more democratized repair options has been growing louder.

The digital revolution has transformed the way consumers interact with and perceive products. Internet-proficient consumers can easily tap into a vast reservoir of information.[16] Online platforms such as YouTube and TikTok, along with specialized forums, offer an abundance of tutorials, insights, and step-by-step guides. These resources empower users to maintain and upgrade a diverse array of products, ranging from electronics to household appliances, regardless of manufacturer support.

This widespread access to knowledge has significantly amplified self-repair capabilities among consumers.[17] Repairing a product is no longer just a reactionary step to a malfunction: it is a conscious decision to understand a product's lifespan, extend its utility, and minimize wastage. Such self-reliant attitudes reduce the need for traditionally centralized repair hubs, offering a strategic advantage to companies that recognize and leverage this educated consumer base.

However, this newfound consumer capability comes with heightened expectations. As consumers become increasingly skilled at self-repairs, there is concurrent expectation for manufacturers to facilitate this process, whether it is through providing spare parts, proprietary software, or specialized tools. Companies face intensifying pressure to meet these demands with transparency and accessibility. Failure to do so can lead to mounting consumer advocacy for regulatory interventions, such as the Right to Repair legislation.

Ultimately, the digital age has transformed consumers from mere end users to proactive participants in a product's lifecycle. For businesses, this paradigm shift underscores the need for adaptability and responsiveness. Their strategies, product designs, sustainability initiatives, and legislative stances must now cater to an empowered and informed consumer base that is shaping the future of the circular economy.

Transparency and Traceability in Reverse Logistics: Harnessing Blockchain and Advanced Technologies

The modern consumer landscape is characterized by an increasing demand for transparency and traceability in products and services. This shift is especially pronounced in the realm of reverse logistics, where the journey of products, from their return to reentry into the market, necessitates a clear and accountable pathway. Technological solutions, particularly **blockchain** and advanced supply chain tools, are emerging as viable means to address these demands.

Technology-Enabled Transparency in Product History and Quality Assurance

The integration of modern technology in various industries to enhance customer trust and satisfaction is indeed a fascinating and important development. In the automotive industry, CarFax has set a standard by providing comprehensive histories of vehicles, including maintenance and accident records. This approach is now being adapted to the electronics industry and has potential applications across numerous product categories. For example, mobile devices that are sold today by a major third-party resale partner come with a label that plays a crucial role in this process, and the label includes five key features discussed in this book.

1. **License Plate Identification**. Positioned in the top right corner for easy identification and scanning in warehouse operations. This acts as a unique identifier for each device, streamlining logistics and tracking.

2. **Integrated Testing and Erasure**. The integrated erasure and testing technology represents a significant advancement in the process of refurbishing and reselling electronic devices. This technology serves a dual purpose: it simultaneously erases any existing data on the device and conducts comprehensive functional tests. The application of technology automatically generates documentation that verifies the completion and success of both data erasure and functional testing needed to maintain industry standards relating to information security.

3. **Visible Serial Number**. Essential for customers to activate their device. The number is clearly printed, allowing customers to easily reference it during the activation or registration process.

4. **Friendly, Informative Language**. A summary of the testing report and data erasure status that is written in a customer-friendly manner. This part of the label assures customers about the quality and safety of their purchase, highlighting that the device has been thoroughly tested and any previous data securely erased.

5. **QR Code.** Linked to a detailed diagnostic and testing report. This QR code connects customers to an extensive report provided by an industry-leading data erasure and testing solution provider like Mannapov, with their item compatibility engine they have branded (ICE Q) software tool. QR codes offer transparency and detailed information about the device's condition and history.

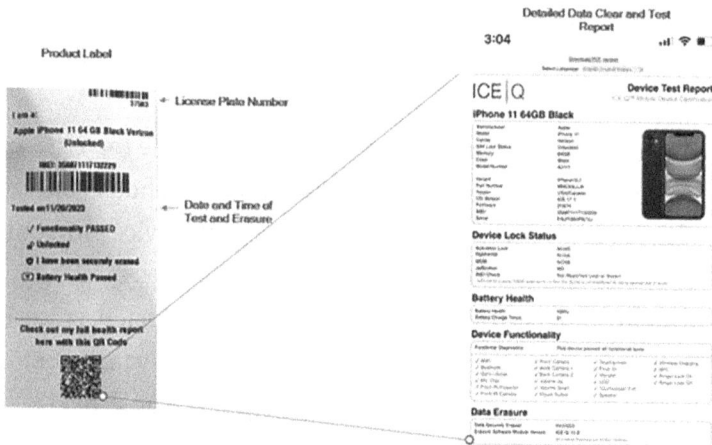

Figure 7.1. This visual depicts a comprehensive product label and detailed report used to inform customers about the data erasure and functionality testing of an Apple iPhone 11 64GB Black (unlocked).

These labels are more than just informative tools; they are a blend of marketing and operational strategy. By providing crucial information in an accessible way, they build customer trust and enhance the buying experience. As technology continues to evolve, we can expect to see more such innovative applications that combine sophisticated marketing with operational efficiency, all aimed at improving the customer experience across various industries.

Blockchain in Reverse Logistics

Blockchain technology offers transformative potential for enhancing the transparency and efficiency of reverse logistics. It could provide a secure and immutable ledger for recording the journey of returned products, addressing key challenges in the industry.[18] With real-time tracking data, stakeholders can ensure that the product's condition, location, and travel history are transparent and tamper-proof.

The concept of "digital passports" for products can concentrate important data such as repair history and touchpoints in the reverse supply chain, similar to a vehicle's Carfax report or the ICEQ testing results. These passports would serve as a comprehensive record of the product's history and status.

E-commerce platforms and marketplaces could assume the role of custodians for these digital passports, ensuring that testing and grading results are recorded on the blockchain before allowing products to be listed for sale. Doing so would maintain a high level of quality and trustworthiness and would eliminate redundant testing and grading at different points in the reverse supply chain, leading to cost reductions and an increase in the speed at which products can be moved and sold. It would also significantly reduce the potential for fraud and misinformation, increasing consumer and secondary market buyer confidence in purchasing used or refurbished items.

Technology-Assisted Supply Chains

Advanced technologies, including IoT and AI, can streamline supply chain processes. They can identify inefficiencies or duplicative processes, such as redundant grading or repeated functional tests on returned products. If a product has already undergone electronic imaging, functional testing, or data clearing upstream, repeating these processes downstream in the secondary market leads to unnecessary time consumption and labor costs. Such inefficiencies impede the goal of the circular economy by increasing the costs and barriers to reusing products.

Integrating advanced-shipment notice files or other information-exchange methodologies is one way to seamlessly pass on the product condition and other vital information from one point to another in the supply chain. This ensures that when a product reaches the secondary market, there is no need for redundant checks or tests. The product can swiftly move through the reverse logistics chain, reducing overhead costs and promoting faster product reuse.

Targeting the Empowered Consumer: The Rise of the Customer Two+ Segment

In today's rapidly evolving marketplace, a new breed of consumers has emerged, defined by their heightened knowledge and proactive behavior. Dubbed Customer Two+, these individuals are characterized by their dual motivation to save—both financially and environmentally. They are not mere end users but active participants in the lifecycle of products, from procurement to maintenance and eventual reuse or recycling.

Some characteristics of Customer Two+ are being:

- **Economically Motivated.** They seek value for their money, often opting for used products that offer similar functionality at a fraction of the cost.
- **Environmentally Conscious.** Beyond financial savings, they are driven by a genuine concern for the environment. Reducing waste and promoting sustainability are more than just buzzwords for them; they are guiding principles.
- **Informed and Skilled.** With a wealth of knowledge at their disposal, they know where to source used products and possess the skills to repair or maintain them, thus extending product lifespans.

The integration of technologies like blockchain and advanced information-sharing mechanisms—which promote transparency, traceability, and authenticity—can be key to approaching this segment.

Harnessing the Potential of Customer Two+ with the Four Desired Outcomes and Reverse Logistics

In essence, the emergence of the Customer Two+ segment of reverse logistics is a testament to the evolving dynamics of the modern marketplace. Businesses that recognize, understand, and tailor their strategies to this segment will not only witness enhanced customer loyalty and satisfaction but also contribute to building a more sustainable and eco-friendly future.

- **Sales-Enablement Programs.** Businesses can tailor their sales strategies to the unique attributes of Customer Two+ by offering certified pre-owned products, DIY repair kits, or loyalty rewards for sustainable practices.

- **Green Logistics.** Businesses can adopt sustainable logistics principles that can further endear customers to this segment. By minimizing transportation emissions, using eco-friendly packaging, or implementing energy-efficient warehousing solutions, companies can resonate more deeply with environmentally conscious consumers.

- **Circular Economy Initiatives.** Businesses can promote programs that focus on product reuse or recycling and align well with the values of the Customer Two+ segment. This approach creates a continuous flow of inventory, becoming available as Customer One's need for their product diminishes. Simultaneously, it helps to develop expanded markets that can effectively match this supply with the demand for used products. This strategy not only taps into the ethos of environmentally conscious consumers but also ensures a sustainable cycle of product usage and availability.

7.4 Employee-Driven Change

The Information Era and the Conscious Workforce

The new era of information has not just **empowered consumers**, it has also nurtured a more informed and conscientious workforce that is characterized by distinct values and priorities, diverging from traditional motivators. Increasingly, the primary factor in their career decisions is shifting away from financial incentives. Instead, there is a growing emphasis on the degree of connection and dedication they feel towards a company's mission and its societal impact. This shift reflects a broader change in work culture, where meaningful engagement and ethical alignment are becoming central to professional fulfillment.

Deloitte's 2023 Survey: An Insight into the Modern Workforce

In the dynamic corporate environment of today, the values and priorities of employees are undergoing a significant transformation. This is particularly true for businesses focused on engaging millennials and Generation Z, the youngest segments of our workforce. For these groups, sustainability has become a critical factor. As members of these generations ascend to positions of leadership, they are fundamentally altering the landscape of corporate decision-making.

The insights from Deloitte's twelfth annual survey of Gen Z and Millennial employees, conducted in 2023, are particularly revealing. This extensive survey—with gathered responses from over twenty-two thousand individuals across forty-four countries—provides a comprehensive view of the attitudes and priorities of these younger employees. The data gleaned from this survey sheds light on the evolving expectations and motivations of this pivotal generation in the workforce.

1. There is a notable sense of cynicism among employees regarding their company's principles. Less than half of the surveyed employees believe that their employer positively impacts society.[19]

2. Environmental consciousness is soaring. Seven out of ten employees are not only aware of their ecological footprint but are actively making decisions to reduce it.[20]

3. There is a burgeoning expectation for employers to equip their workforce with skills and education for a transition to a more sustainable economy.[21]

Building a Hiring Strategy for the Future of the Circular Economy

Developing a hiring strategy targeting professionals skilled in reverse logistics can set your clients or organization on a path that aligns with both sustainability goals and economic efficiencies. In a world where the circular economy is gaining traction, recruiters must be at the vanguard, leading the charge in sourcing talent that will shape the future of business. Companies that integrate reverse logistics into their operations and adapt to the changing landscape will invariably be perceived as more forward-thinking, sustainable, and attractive to potential employees.

The Future of Organizational Design to Support Reverse Logistics

The creation of executive roles like directors and vice presidents of sustainability marks a significant shift in the corporate focus toward sustainability and its essential link with reverse logistics. These roles represent a deep-seated acknowledgment in companies that sustainable practices and effective reverse logistics are crucial not just for environmental responsibility but also for sustained business growth. This shift is prompting organizations to reconsider and possibly reinforce their reverse logistics teams to maximize resource efficiency and achieve their sustainability objectives.

Unlike long-established business sectors such as sales, finance, marketing, manufacturing, and forward logistics, reverse logistics lacks a universally accepted organizational structure. This absence of a standard model opens up opportunities for innovative, customized hiring strategies for reverse logistics. Crafting the ideal structure for reverse logistics is a complex and dynamic challenge in the contemporary business landscape, as the logistics sector exhibits considerable variability across different industries.

Currently, there are relatively few vice president roles specifically dedicated to managing reverse logistics. Nonetheless, the rising significance of the secondary market—expected to outweigh the negative consequences of product returns—combined with the necessity to handle both unwanted and essential returns underscores the growing importance of such positions. As businesses seek to more-comprehensively integrate reverse logistics into their operations, the demand for leaders who possess both logistical acumen and a sales-oriented mindset is increasing. These evolving executive roles are becoming pivotal in guiding companies toward more sustainable and efficient business practices.

7.5 From Linear to Circular: *Mastery in the Era of Reverse Logistics*

Pioneering Ahead: The Expanding $1.5 Trillion Opportunity in Reverse Logistics

The market trends explored in Chapter 1 revealed that unwanted returns pose a serious challenge for retailers, with an impact of $862 billion in 2022.[22] The situation is intensified by new fraudulent threats in online shopping combined with the rapid growth of the US's secondary market for used products, estimated at $664 billion in 2020.[23]

The rise of the circular economy and secondary markets is a response to increasing environmental concerns, influenced by shifts in consumer purchasing behavior. There has been a surge in the purchase of returned products, indicative of changing consumer habits. The secondary market's value has dramatically increased from approximately $309.926 million in 2008 to $644 billion in 2020, more than double in just twelve years. It is projected to exceed around $776 billion by 2023.

The combined negative impact of unwanted returns and the positive impact of the secondary market create a total market opportunity of $1.5 trillion. This continues to grow. This number represents the intersection of the $862 billion cost of unwanted returns and the $664 billion (and growing) value of the secondary market. Both these aspects pass through reverse logistics as products move away from the point of use, thus impacting reverse logistics professionals who need training to manage both negative and positive outcomes effectively.

While the management of unwanted returns has traditionally been viewed separately from managing the circular economy—sometimes considered as different as apples and oranges—the forecasted growth in the positive value of the secondary market is expected to soon surpass the negative impact of unwanted returns. Reverse logistics teams must adeptly manage both the "apples" and the "oranges" combined, addressing the complexities of both traditional returns and the evolving circular economy. Both the reduction of bad returns and the increase of good returns can be achieved through these well-trained teams.

Reverse logistics will play a critical role in both reducing the financial impact of unwanted returns and promoting the growth of circular returns, thus serving both economic and environmental objectives. This is possible while supporting sales-enablement programs and minimizing harm to the environment. The interaction of challenging returns with the growing secondary market, enabled through effective reverse logistics, illustrates the importance of adopting a going-circular approach. Companies are advised to view the outcomes of reverse logistics holistically, utilizing them to achieve a broad range of economic and environmental benefits.

Skillsets Required for Mastery in the New Logistics Era

Training, education, and a realignment of the logistics workforce are vital for the growth and optimization of reverse logistics. It is no longer sufficient to treat reverse logistics as a mere afterthought. The rapidly changing landscape of commerce, characterized by a shift from traditional outlets to online platforms, necessitates an evolution in the infrastructure for returns.

Key skillsets for the new era include:

- **Operational Expertise**. Understanding and managing the complexities of returning products, be it due to defects, dissatisfaction, or end-of-life recycling.
- **Behavioral Analytics**. Grasping consumer's return behaviors and patterns, enabling businesses to predict and plan accordingly.

- **Financial Acumen**. Realizing how to utilize logistics not just as a cost center but as a profit-generating unit.
- **Sales and Marketing Adaptability**. Constantly reevaluating strategies and adapting them to an evolving market, akin to industries like real estate and telecommunications.
- **Regulatory Knowledge**. Understanding governmental regulations and policies on waste management, recycling, and product returns.
- **Innovation and Leadership**. Pioneering new methods, technologies, and strategies to streamline and enhance the reverse logistics process.
- **Holistic Understanding**. Having a comprehensive grasp of how the circular economy functions from the first customer to the subsequent one and the pivotal role reverse logistics plays.

For a company to thrive in this shifting paradigm, it needs an adept workforce that comprehends manufacturing, sales, finance, forward and reverse logistics, and how these can harmoniously coexist. The literature and training modules on this subject will need to expand to cater to the challenges of the future. The vision should be clear—a sustainable, efficient, and profitable way of managing products throughout their entire lifecycle.

Conclusion

This book is not designed to be a definitive or long-term answer to the intricacies and nuances of how reverse logistics should function. Instead, it serves as a compilation of best practices based on contemporary industry norms and trends.

It is important to understand that the landscape of reverse logistics is dynamic. The content of this literature, like the field it discusses, needs to be revisited and revised periodically to stay abreast of advancements in technology, shifts in best practices, and changes in consumer behavior.

The onus rests upon the shoulders of reverse logistics professionals to design, adapt, and innovate programs that resonate with the ever-evolving market demands. Gone are the days when logistics professionals could work behind the scenes and still secure success. In today's fast-paced and interconnected world, reverse logistics teams wield significant influence, and their strategies and execution can drive transformative change, leaving a tangible impact on corporate reputations and valuations. Their role is not just functional but instrumental, steering businesses toward sustainable success in a resource-conscious era.

Glossary

advanced exchange: A repair strategy where a customer is sent a replacement device before returning their defective one, ensuring minimal disruption to the user.

advanced shipping notice (ASN): A detailed accounting of expected return shipments, allowing the creation of expected orders for receipt.

aggregate bulk shipment: Method of shipping where multiple goods are shipped together to streamline transportation and potentially reduce costs.

aggregators: Entities that purchase large lots of products, often from first tier supply sources, to break down lots into smaller batches for resale.

air and water pollution: Contamination of air and water bodies due to emissions and waste materials, leading to environmental degradation and potential health problems.

analytics: The systematic computational analysis of data, which is pivotal in reverse logistics for understanding and optimizing return processes.

anti-money laundering (AML) safeguards: Measures taken to prevent, detect, and report money laundering activities, including background checks and financial tracking.

artificial intelligence (AI): A branch of computer science focused on creating smart machines capable of performing tasks that typically require human intelligence.

"as-is" sales: A liquidation method where products are sold in their current condition without detailed descriptions or the possibility of returns.

asset recovery: The process in reverse logistics that involves retrieving value from used or end-of-life products.

assisted self-repair: A repair strategy where customers are sent replacement parts and instructions to conduct repairs themselves.

augmented reality (AR): Technology that layers computer-generated enhancements atop existing reality to make technology more meaningful through interaction; used in reverse logistics for tasks like identification and repair guidance.

automated cleaning system: A system that uses steam and conveyance to prepare products for reuse in an efficient and environmentally friendly manner.

automated sortation: The process of using technology to sort returned items based on predetermined criteria, such as product mix, category, or condition.

automation: The use of technology to perform tasks with reduced human assistance.

background checks: The process of verifying information (either for businesses or individuals) to ensure they are not involved in illegal activities.

barcode scanning: A method for capturing data from barcodes, used in WMS for tracking inventory and updating system records.

best practices: Guidelines or principles proven effective in a particular industry or field, often codified into policies that serve as rules or standards that organizations should adhere to.

big data: Extremely large data sets that may be analyzed computationally to reveal patterns, trends, and associations, especially relating to human behavior and interactions; crucial for analyzing returns and customer behavior.

biodiversity loss: A decrease in the variety of species, genes, and ecosystems within a particular habitat, usually as a result of human activities, including waste, emissions, and resource depletion.

blended benefit (BB): The combined advantage specific to each product within every value-generation channel.

blockchain: A distributed database or ledger that allows for secure, transparent, and tamper-proof recordkeeping, often used to track transactions and product journeys.

bounce: A scenario where products are returned, refurbished, reshipped, and returned again, leading to inflated costs and decreased customer satisfaction.

brand reputation: The perceived value and image of a company in the market.

brokers: Middlemen who connect sellers and buyers in the secondary market without adding logistical value.

business rules: Directives that dictate the outcome of the return based on post-inspection information.

buyer's remorse: The regret a customer feels after making a purchase, which sometimes leads to product returns.

buyout: A process wherein one manufacturer acquires the entire supply of a competitor's products from a retailer or distributor with the intention of replacing them with their own products.

cannibalization: A potential threat where repaired or refurbished products may compete with new products, potentially affecting brand value or new product sales.

Cannibalization Effect: Refers to a scenario in business and marketing where a fear exists that the promotion or introduction of a reused or refurbished product leads to a decline in the sales of new products; occurs because customers may choose to purchase the reused product instead of a new one.

cash-to-cash cycle: The process that outlines the time it takes for a company to convert resource investments, like inventory, into cash flows from sales, particularly beneficial in a secondary market where products find new life, potentially offering faster return cycles.

centralized warehouse: A single, centralized location where replacement parts or returned products are stored, as opposed to multiple local outlets, aiming to reduce inventory costs.

certified like-new: A term denoting products that have been returned and refurbished to a quality comparable to new products.

certified refurbished: Items that have undergone rigorous functional and cosmetic inspections to ensure like-new quality, complete with verified battery health, original accessories, and the latest software updates.

cherry-picking: Selectively choosing the best items from a lot for personal gain or to provide an unfair advantage to certain buyers.

circular economy: An economic model that aims to eliminate waste and encourage the reuse of resources by moving products backward to their original source, usually involving the recycling, repairing, and refurbishing of products to extend their lifespan and reduce environmental impact.

circular programs: Initiatives designed to encourage customers to return products, possibly as part of a lease return or annual upgrade program, facilitating the migration to new products.

climate change: Long-term shifts and alterations in temperature and weather patterns, primarily caused by human activities and their cumulative impacts on the environment.

closed-loop recycling: A strategy within the circular economy that involves creating a contained system where the components of a product are recycled to create new products within the same company.

closed-loop system: A circular system that facilitates the recollection, refurbishment, and redistribution of products, aiming to create a continuous cycle that minimizes waste and extends the lifespan of products.

closeout: A sales strategy where excess or discontinued products are sold at discounted prices to clear inventory.

cloud-based systems: Systems that use online platforms to store and manage data, facilitating easier access and sharing of information across different stages of the supply chain.

commission chargeback: The practice of reducing or reclaiming commission paid to sales representatives or distributors in the event of product returns.

complimentary recycling assistance: Corporate initiatives that offer help with recycling at no additional charge, aiming to reduce environmental impacts associated with product returns.

condition of packaging: The varying states of packaging when goods are returned, which could be "open," "damaged," or "nonexistent," necessitating different methods of storage or identification.

consignment ("sort and sell"): A liquidation strategy where a partner sells products on behalf of the original seller and retains a percentage of the sale.

consumer data: Personal, confidential, or sensitive information stored on devices such as personal contacts, messages, photos, call histories, financial details, and more.

consumer information (CI): Data stored on a product or package that can identify the previous owner, such as personal contacts, messages, emails, photos, call history, and financial information.

cosmetic condition: The visible state of a product, particularly regarding its appearance and any external damages.

cosmetic grade: A scale denoting the external and aesthetic condition of a product, often ranging from "perfect/new" to "damaged."

cost management: The process of controlling and reducing the costs associated with returns, including direct and indirect expenses.

cost of capital: The opportunity cost of investing resources in the reverse logistics process, which includes the potential interest or revenue foregone from other investments.

cost of goods sold (COGS): The direct costs attributable to the production of the goods sold by a company; this is deducted from revenues to calculate gross profit.

cost to reuse (CR): The operational cost associated with the processes needed to reintroduce returned products into the sales or production cycle.

counterfeiting parts in used products: The unethical practice of replacing genuine parts with fake counterparts in refurbished or second-hand products.

cumulative impacts: The combined effects of direct and indirect environmental impacts over time, which contribute to larger-scale environmental issues such as climate change, pollution, and loss of biodiversity.

customer feedback: The information coming from customers about the satisfaction or dissatisfaction they feel with a product or a service.

Customer One: Term used to mark the original customer who purchased a product.

customer promise: Commitments made by a company to incentivize customers to purchase their products, which may include various benefits such as warranties, return policies, and trade-in programs.

customer relationship management (CRM): A system for managing a company's interactions with current and potential customers; may or may not utilize AI to understand and predict customer behaviors and preferences.

customer returns programs: Strategies implemented by businesses to facilitate the return of products from customers, aiming to enhance customer satisfaction and promote sustainability. These programs encompass various policies like satisfaction guarantees, trade-ins, and recycling salvage.

customer satisfaction: The degree to which a customer's expectations are met or exceeded.

Customer Two+: Term used to identify the next potential customer who might receive the product, either through resale, refurbishment, or recycling.

customer warranty: A warranty provided by a distributor or retailer that allows customers to have a faulty product repaired or replaced. It is usually managed through reverse logistics teams and might involve additional offers like extended warranties.

data clearing: A multi-level system of ridding devices of sensitive information; per NIST guidelines, there are three levels—clear, purge, and destroy—where data is made inaccessible through normal means and makes devices suitable to be repurposed or resold.

data destruction: The highest level of data clearing where a device is physically destroyed and all data made irretrievable; typically applied to devices containing highly sensitive data.

data erasure: The secure removal of sensitive data from devices, preventing unauthorized access and ensuring privacy.

data layer: A layer of information containing details such as RMA number, serial numbers, tracking information, and more.

data security threats: The potential risks associated with data breaches or unauthorized data access when products containing data are reintroduced in the market.

data-driven insights: Information derived from analyzed data that aids in identifying areas contributing to unwanted returns and formulating strategies to mitigate them.

dead on arrival (DOA): A term that denotes products that do not work upon the customer receiving them, necessitating return or replacement.

decision support system (DSS): Computer-based information systems that support business or organizational decision-making activities.

demonstration devices: A program where customers are given items for temporary use or display before making a purchase.

denial criteria: Specific conditions or criteria that were not fulfilled in order to authorize a return (e.g., packaging not intact or failure to return an item within a specified timeframe).

depreciation: The reduction in the value of an asset over time due to factors like wear and tear, obsolescence, and market trends.

Diffusion of Innovation Theory: A theory that seeks to explain how, why, and at what rate new ideas and technology spread through cultures.

direct costs: Expenses that can be directly linked to the return process, including shipping, handling, and storage.

direct impacts: Quantifiable environmental effects resulting directly from return management activities, such as CO_2 emissions and resource usage.

direct liquidation: A process where surplus or returned products are sold in bulk, often through auctions, to various buyers, including those in the secondary market.

direct (tested) standard: A sales method where products are categorized and priced based on their tested functionality and cosmetic condition.

discrepant returns: Situations where a returned product does not match expectations or agreed-upon conditions.

disposal: The act of getting rid of unsellable goods, which could involve methods like landfilling or recycling.

disposition: The methods or strategies employed to manage returned goods, including resale, refurbishment, recycling, or disposal.

distribution centers: Facilities that play a role in aggregating products from different manufacturers for sale.

distribution channel: A network of intermediaries or middlemen that facilitates the transfer of goods from producers to consumers; sometimes involves leveraging other organizations to aid in the sales process.

distribution points: Locations where products are transferred to in large quantities through forward logistics processes, which could be outlets or retailers.

early adopters: Individuals who adopt new products early in the product lifecycle, often willing to pay premium prices and serve as opinion leaders.

early pragmatics: Consumers who purchase new products but do not upgrade immediately with each new release, opting to use products until they no longer meet their needs.

early upgrade: A customer-oriented program where customers, under a contractual agreement, can exchange their current device for a newer one before the end of the contract. The value of the returned device goes toward fulfilling the remaining contractual obligations. This approach fosters customer loyalty and encourages continued engagement by keeping customers updated with the latest releases.

eco-friendly: Term to describe sustainable methods and practices that minimize environmental impact and promote conservation of resources.

eco-friendly logistics: Methods and strategies that aim to minimize negative impacts on the environment, promoting sustainability and conservation.

e-commerce: A method of buying and selling goods and services over the internet.

e-commerce marketplaces: Online platforms where goods and services are bought and sold. The rise of these platforms has facilitated the matching of supply and demand for used products, fostering trade-in and trade-up programs.

edge computing: A distributed computing paradigm that brings computation and data storage closer to the location where it is needed to improve response times and save bandwidth.

electronic data interchange (EDI): The structured transmission of data between organizations electronically.

electronic validation tools: Tools that provide an electronic record verifying that data has been cleared from a device and the device is restored to its original configuration.

empowered consumer: A shopper who uses their knowledge and resources to make informed decisions about their purchases, focusing on sustainability, value retention, and repairability.

end customers: The final consumers who purchase products for usage.

end of life (EOL): The phase in a product's lifecycle when a manufacturer stops production and support, often leading to liquidation of remaining inventory.

end of support (EOS): The point at which a manufacturer discontinues active support and updates for a product.

energy consumption: The utilization of energy during the transportation and processing of returned goods, contributing to environmental impacts like greenhouse gas emissions.

enterprise resource planning (ERP): Integrated management of main business processes, often in real time; mediated by software and technology.

environmental impact: The effect of business operations on the environment.

environmental and regulatory compliance: Ensuring that business practices, especially in reverse logistics, adhere to environmental laws and regulations; facilitated by ERP systems.

environmental stewardship: The responsible management and conservation of the environment through sustainable practices and initiatives.

Environmental Sustainability and Governance (ESG) : Tools and metrics that help to evaluate and emphasize the unique focuses of green logistics and circular economy strategies, aiding in better decision-making processes aligned with environmental sustainability goals.

executive information system (EIS): A type of management information system intended to facilitate and support the information and decision-making needs of senior executives.

extended producer responsibility (EPR): Policies that hold brands accountable for the environmental impact of their products throughout the lifecycle, including disposal.

failure to deliver: A situation where a shipped product fails to reach the customer due to various reasons such as incorrect address or shipping errors.

fast fashion: A model of mass-producing inexpensive clothing rapidly in response to the latest fashion trends; may result in environmental and social issues.

financial accounting: The field of accounting concerned with the summary, analysis, and reporting of financial transactions pertaining to a business.

First Industrial Revolution: The period marked by the shift from manual labor to mechanization in the late 1700s to to mid-1800s.

first tier supply sources: The initial points where products are returned by customers, which can include manufacturers, distributors, or third-party entities.

fish market analogy: A comparison used to describe value-generation optimization in reverse logistics, illustrating how returned products are like fish in a market, with a need for quick and strategic value extraction before deterioration.

forced internalization: A government-introduced regulation that mandates companies to bear the full costs of environmental impacts associated with the production and consumption of their goods and services.

forecasting: The process of making predictions about future events, based on historical data and analysis of trends; used in both manufacturing and reverse logistics.

forward logistics: The movement of products from manufacturers to end users, typically encompassing the processes of manufacturing, distributing, and selling.

forward supply chain: A process that begins with the acquisition of raw materials necessary for manufacturing a product, involving several stages including manufacturing, distribution, and retail.

four desired outcomes of reverse logistics: Core principles or approaches that encompass the desired outcomes a business wants from its reverse logistics teams.

Fourth Industrial Revolution (Industry 4.0): The current era of industrial revolution, characterized by data exchange and automation in manufacturing technologies, including AI and ML.

functional status: An indicator of whether a product is fully functional, partially functional, or non-functional, influencing its grade and value.

General Data Protection Regulation (GDPR): European Union regulations that require businesses to protect the personal data and privacy of EU citizens.

goTRG: A company that provides third-party logistics, software solutions, and re-commerce services for reverse logistics.

grading and assessment process: The process where returned products are inspected to determine their condition and potential for reuse, which might include refurbishment, repairs, or repackaging.

grading funnel: A visual representation of the process where products are inspected, tested, and graded to determine their quality and marketability.

green consumer: Shoppers who prioritize purchasing products that are environmentally sustainable and have a reduced ecological footprint.

green logistics: The planning and implementation of environmentally friendly and sustainable practices in the logistics industry, encompassing efforts to reduce waste, emissions, and resource depletion.

green sanitization: An eco-friendly sanitization process, such as the use of ozone chambers, to clean garments without the heavy use of water or electricity.

greenhouse gas emissions: Gases emitted into the atmosphere as a result of energy consumption during transportation and processing of returns, contributing to global warming.

greenwashing: Misleading consumers by falsely marketing products as environmentally friendly or sustainable.

happy path returns: Successful return processes where the returned product matches original expectations without issues.

harvesting: A strategy involving dismantling a product to use its parts for repairing other devices or selling for residual value.

hidden costs: Costs that are not readily apparent or allocated to returns, often absorbed into the broader financials of the company, making them difficult to track and manage.

holistic approach: A comprehensive method to green logistics management that integrates strategies for reducing environmental impacts across all aspects of logistics operations.

idle inventory: Products that are not being actively sold or used, typically resulting in a net benefit of zero and increasing costs over time due to storage and depreciation.

image capture technology: Technological systems that use cameras to recognize, capture, and process images of returned items for identification and grading.

indirect costs: Expenses that are not directly attributed to returns but are incurred due to the consequences of returns, including lost sales and harm to brand reputation.

indirect impacts: Environmental effects that are secondary or less tangible and harder to measure directly, occurring as a result of managing returns.

Industry 4.0: Also known as the Fourth Industrial Revolution, this term refers to the ongoing automation and data exchange in manufacturing technologies, including the Internet of Things, cloud computing, and artificial intelligence.

information consumption logic: Used to discern subsequent actions in the return process, from issuing refunds to identifying variances.

infrastructure: Expenses for facilities and equipment necessary for reverse logistics operations, like warehouses and repair centers.

innovation: The process of translating an idea or invention into a good or service that creates value or for which customers will pay.

insourced reverse logistics: When a company handles the reverse logistics process internally using its own resources, such as personnel and facilities.

inspection: The process of assessing the condition of returned products and identifying any defects or damages.

intentional misgrading: Deliberately misrepresenting the condition of a product to manipulate its market value.

interface tools: Digital or physical platforms facilitating the returns process. They capture essential return data and streamline product shipment details.

Internet of Things (IoT): A network of interconnected devices that can exchange data without human intervention, used in logistics to track product movements and gather data for decision-making.

inventory: The stock of finished goods or products that a company holds at any given time, including items that have been manufactured or remanufactured and are awaiting sale or distribution.

inventory control: The process of managing the supply, storage, and accessibility of items to ensure an adequate amount without excess.

job-out: A program where products are sold to other parties at discounted rates to fulfill specific orders or contracts.

key performance indicator (KPI): A measurable value that demonstrates how effectively a company is achieving key business objectives; in WMS, this commonly includes inventory turns, order accuracy, and warehouse efficiency.

labor: Work needed to oversee, handle, inspect, and repair returned products.

lease: A customer return program where products can be returned after a period of time, offering customers flexibility and avoiding long-term ownership commitments.

Level One Process Flow: A fundamental tool in business-process management and engineering that provides an overarching view of a system or process.

license plate identification (LPN): A system used in WMS that assigns a unique identifier to items, enabling easier tracking and management of inventory.

like-for-like or like-for-better alternatives: A practice where companies offer replacements that are identical or superior to the returned or defective products.

like-new or excellent-condition product: A product that has been returned but retains a condition that is indistinguishable from a brand-new item.

line-level auctions: Auctions where participants bid on specific items based on make, model, and grade, allowing for precise purchases.

linear finance models: Financial structures associated with traditional linear supply chains, which prioritize product sales and typically view returns negatively.

linear returns: The process that occurs when a customer sends back a product because it fails to meet their expectations.

liquidation: The process of converting assets into cash, often by selling them in bulk to liquidators or through auction platforms.

logistics: Originally referred to the art of calculation in ancient Greece; now pertains to the comprehensive process of managing the movement and storage of products or goods, including activities such as warehousing, resource management, packaging, transportation, and services. It aims to ensure the right product is in the right place, at the right time, in the right condition, to meet the four desired outcomes.

logistics operations: Activities and processes that involve the movement, storage, and flow of goods, materials, and information from the point of origin to consumption points. These operations encompass transportation, warehousing, inventory management, and distribution.

lot complexity: The variety and assortment within a batch of products that affect sorting, processing, and the overall cost of managing the lot.

lot-based auctions: Sales of large quantities of inventory at once, which may include a mix of high- and low-demand items.

machine learning (ML): A subset of AI that involves the use of algorithms that improve automatically through experience and by the use of data.

manufacturer warranty: A guarantee provided by the manufacturer that defective or malfunctioning products can be returned for repair, replacement, or refund within a specified period.

manufacturers: Entities or companies that produce goods in large quantities, which are then transferred to distribution points.

market value: The current sale price of an asset in the open market, influenced by supply-demand dynamics, technological advancements, or broader economic conditions.

market value accounting: An approach that values returned items based on their current market price, considering their condition and market demand.

market value depreciation: A method of gauging depreciation based on real-time market conditions and trends, which can fluctuate significantly.

money laundering: The illegal process of making large amounts of money generated by criminal activity appearing to have come from a legitimate source.

money-back warranty options: Policies that provide refunds to customers, allowing them to purchase their next products, reducing the company's burden of maintaining parts supply.

natural resource scarcity: The limited availability or depletion of vital natural resources due to overconsumption, environmental degradation, or other factors, resulting in an inability to meet the current and future demand of human populations and ecosystems.

New Equipment Product Curve: A model illustrating the lifecycle of a product, including its market entry, pricing strategy, sales volume, and value over time.

omni channel returns programs: A system that allows customers to return products purchased from one channel (like online) through another channel (like a physical store), offering convenience and flexibility in the return process.

omni-channel shopping: A retail strategy that offers a seamless and integrated shopping experience across various channels, including physical stores, online platforms, mobile apps, and social media.

open auctions: Public auctions where the current highest bid is visible to all participants, encouraging competitive bidding.

operational processing: The set of procedures involved in maneuvering the product through various stages of the return process to maximize value and minimize costs.

order fulfillment: The complete process from point of sales inquiry to delivery of a product to the customer, streamlined by WMS.

order issue reduction: Strategies to decrease problems like incorrect item shipment or delivery, leveraging feedback from reverse logistics teams.

outflow methods: The strategies employed to move returned products onto their next use or customer, aiming to realize value from returned goods.

over-repair(ing): The act of unnecessarily repairing or replacing non-defective parts of a product, leading to increased costs.

packing: Preparing products for the next phase, which may include shipment, refurbishment, or recycling; includes the relevant documentation.

partial credit(s): A practice where customers are offered only a partial refund or credit for returned products.

picking: The act of retrieving specific products from storage based on determined criteria or specific orders.

point-of-sale (POS) systems: Systems used for processing sales transactions that can update inventory levels in real time and may integrate with CRM and other functionalities.

post-inspection information: Data regarding the actual condition of the received product after it has undergone evaluation.

pre-inspection information or return data: Information acquired during asset recovery which ensures that the correct device is returned in the specified condition and timeframe.

procurement: The process of obtaining goods or services, typically for business purposes. In the context of new product launches, it involves direct purchasing and budgeting based on sales forecasts.

Product Curve Model: Notations used to describe the lifecycle stages of a product, especially for frequently updated models.

product descriptions: Detailed information provided about a (used) product's condition, history, and specifications to inform potential buyers.

product design: The blueprint of a product's construction, can be refined to decrease return rates and associated costs by enhancing quality; shifts in blueprints may foster sustainability through the incorporation of repairability aspects and the utilization of recycled or recyclable materials in manufacturing.

product identification: The use of unique identifiers like SKUs and UPCs to manage and track inventory in a WMS.

Product Lifecycle Loop: A model that maps out the journey of a product from manufacturing to the hands of first and subsequent users, encouraging continuous use and minimizing waste. This loop includes stages like manufacturing, sales, forward logistics, reverse logistics, repair/refurbishment, and resale, ending in responsible recycling when the product can no longer be economically circulated.

Product One: The first product that is sold to the primary customer, the sale of which initiates a cycle of demand generation and potential reuse or repurposing through upgrade incentives.

Product Two+: A newer model or version of a product that primary customers are encouraged to upgrade to, fostering a cycle of consumption and facilitating the potential resale or repurposing of the first product (Product One).

production schedule: A plan that outlines the timing and quantity of production to align with demand forecasts and sales projections.

promotional trade-in: A return program where the value offered to the customer in exchange for returning an old product exceeds its standard trade-in value. It combines marketing budget with the old product's value to create attractive market offers, aiming to boost customer acquisition, promote upgrades, and persuade customers to switch brands.

quality control: The process of ensuring that repaired products meet the expected standards to prevent negative customer experiences and protect brand reputation.

quick response (QR) codes: A type of matrix barcode that is machine-readable and contains information about the item to which it is attached, used in WMS for detailed inventory management.

Radio Frequency Identification (RFID): The use of radio waves to read and capture information stored on a tag attached to an object, used in WMS for advanced inventory tracking without the need for a direct line of sight.

receiving: Accepting returned products into the reverse logistics system, initiating warehouse tracking, and verifying items against the return merchandise authorization (RMA).

reclamation: The process of reclaiming or recycling components from returned products, often as part of warranty management or green logistics strategies.

re-commerce: The process of selling previously owned or used products, often through online platforms, to give items a second life and promote sustainability.

recycling salvage: A program encouraging customers to return old products voluntarily for environmentally responsible disposal. It ensures that the products undergo proper disposal methods, such as recycling or material reuse, securing data, and preventing landfill disposal.

refurbishment: An extensive process aimed at enhancing a product's aesthetic and functionality, including cleaning, repair, or part replacement.

regional, mid-tier, and niche distributors: Entities specializing in handling medium-sized lots and catering to specific markets or product types in the secondary market.

remote diagnostics: Tools or applications that help identify and resolve product issues remotely, reducing the need for physical returns.

repackaging: The act of packing returned products in new packaging for resale, which can involve costs and resource consumption.

repair: The act of mending or fixing a product to regain its functionality.

repair operations: Processes focused on improving the cosmetic and/or functional aspects of a returned product or packaging to prepare it for resale or support a warranty program.

re-registration: The process where a subsequent user officially registers a used product to access legitimate software or services.

Resale Value Effect: A strategic benefit for companies in promoting the reuse of returned products; includes generating additional revenue from software and warranties, leveraging products' residual value to encourage future purchases quicker, and expanding the market by reselling the same product to new customers.

residual value: The remaining benefit of a product that has become unwanted, which can potentially be reclaimed, reused, or resold in the reverse supply chain.

Residual Value Upgrade Effect: Refers to the increased value perceived by customers when they can trade in a used product and the residual value of that product can be leveraged towards the purchase of a new item; encourages customers to invest more in new product sent or resale.

resistance: In the context of returns management, resistance refers to the strategies and processes employed to reduce the volume of product returns, which can include implementing return windows, charging restocking fees, and establishing denial criteria.

restocking fees: Fees charged to customers for returning products, typically to offset the costs associated with processing returns and restocking products.

restoration: Cleaning and reviving a product to enhance its aesthetics and value.

retailers: Entities acting as distributors collecting products from distribution centers or receiving direct shipments, catering to both other businesses (distributors) and end customers.

return material authorization (RMA): A formalized process ensuring that product or material returns are properly documented, tracked, and managed.

return prevention and cost management (RPCM): A strategic approach in logistics focusing on reducing the frequency and costs associated with product returns, which may involve improving product quality or refining return policies.

return rights: A policy where manufacturers or distributors allow retail outlets to return items that customers no longer want in exchange for credit, thus shifting the risk of customer returns upstream.

return stream: A concept within sales-enablement programs that refers to the processes and paths that returned products follow, which can vary based on a company's return policies and the expectations of value from customers. The strategy may aim to either decrease or increase returns depending on company goals and customer satisfaction priorities.

Returned Equipment Product Curve: A representation of the availability and pricing behavior of returned or used products over time in the circular economy.

return to vendor (RTV): An event where a returned product moves from a point back to its originating supplier or manufacturer.

returns enablement programs: The guidelines which dictate the terms of return to customers.

returns programs: Strategies designed by companies to manage the return of products, offering avenues for recouping value and maintaining positive business relationships in the supply chain.

reuse as new: Introducing returned products that can be restored to a "new" state back into forward distribution channels for resale.

reuse: The practice of using products or materials more than once, rather than discarding them after a single use, to reduce waste and environmental impacts.

reventory: Products that have been sent back to the company through the reverse logistics flow and are awaiting disposition. It represents a phase where the products have been returned and are awaiting further processing.

reverse logistics: The process of moving goods from their final destination back to a collection point for the purpose of capturing value (refurbishment, recycling, and redistribution) or proper disposal; the central mechanism in enabling the goals of the circular economy by minimizing waste and aligning economic operations with environmental sustainability desired outcome.

reverse supply chain: Contrary to being a linear process moving backward from the customer to the manufacturer, it involves various paths where the product can move from the customer back into the hands of the next user, fostering competition to maximize product value through alternative points of return.

reverse value chain: The sequence of activities a company performs to reintegrate returned products back into the market, including repair, refurbishment, or recycling.

Right to Repair Movement: A campaign advocating for consumers' ability to repair the products they own by having access to parts, tools, and information.

rules of engagement: Guidelines or stipulations set by suppliers on how their returned products should be liquidated, including minimum pricing and buyer qualifications.

sales-enablement programs: Initiatives managed often as a marketing function, focused on enhancing the processes and tools that help in selling products efficiently and effectively.

sales outlet: The various channels, both online and offline, where products are sold, influencing customers' buying behaviors and return rates.

Sales Racetrack Model: A model in which the customer is encouraged to continuously consume products, moving from one product to the next. It represents a traditional approach focusing on customer-centric sales and consumption patterns.

sales teams: Groups within organizations that play a central role in marketing products to primary customers, fostering demand for both new and reused products, and contributing to revenue generation.

same-unit repair: A strategy where only the defective part of a product is fixed, reducing the need for complete product replacement.

satisfaction guarantee: A policy where customers have the option to return a product within a specified period if not satisfied with the purchase, ensuring a risk-free buying experience.

Second Industrial Revolution: The period of rapid industrial growth with the emergence of mass production and electrification in the late 1800s to early 1900s.

second tier supply sources: Entities that purchase products from the first tier of supply sources, often specializing in consolidating larger lots into smaller batches.

secondary market: A market where used products are acquired and sold, either by the end customers themselves or through other companies, often at lower prices compared to new products; highlights the growth of platforms and services facilitating the recirculation of products between different users.

seed-stock management: The use of brand-new products to support warranty replacements, eventually transitioning to using refurbished returns to maintain the "like new" promise.

selective partner liquidation: A strategy where companies choose specific, often certified, wholesalers to liquidate their products, ensuring responsible treatment and minimizing cannibalization.

self-service diagnostics: Tools or applications that enable customers to diagnose and potentially fix issues on their own, reducing the need for product returns or in-person repairs.

service level agreement (SLA): A formal documented agreement that outlines the level of service expected by a customer from a supplier, laying out the metrics by which that service is measured, and the remedies or penalties, if any, should agreed-upon service levels are not achieved.

shell companies: Businesses established with no significant assets or operations, often used as a front for illegal activities such as money laundering.

shipping: The process of sending products to their designated destinations after all preceding activities are completed.

software as a service (SaaS): A software-licensing and delivery model where software is licensed on a subscription basis and is centrally hosted.

sort and sell (consignment): A secondary market sales method where products are sorted and sold on behalf of the original seller, who then shares in the proceeds.

sortation: Categorizing returned products based on various parameters, such as product type or condition, for easier processing.

stock keeping unit (SKU): A unique code that identifies each distinct product and service that can be purchased, crucial for inventory tracking in WMS.

straight-line depreciation: A method of calculating depreciation where the asset's value is reduced by an equal amount over its useful life.

strategy: A high-level plan or set of guidelines created to achieve specific goals or desired outcome within an organization. In reverse logistics, strategy outlines the approaches and plans for managing product returns, repairs, and refurbishments effectively.

supply chain: Comprises multiple points and involves the movement of goods and services, with logistics being a crucial component including storage, distribution, and various customer-tailored elements. It facilitates the efficient movement of products between different elements, integral to the overall supply chain process.

supply chain management: The management of the flow of goods and services, encompassing all processes that transform raw materials into final products. It includes a wide range of activities such as procurement, production, distribution, and logistics.

surplus: Products that fail to sell as anticipated, resulting in excess stock with diminished demand. These unsold items need to be removed from the shelves and might be returned to the supplier or disposed of through alternative channels to generate value.

sustainability: The use of resources in a way that meets the needs of the present without compromising the ability of future generations to meet their own needs, typically encompassing environmental, economic, and social dimensions.

sustainable practices: Initiatives and strategies adopted by companies to minimize their negative impacts on the environment, often involving efforts to implement circular economy principles.

swim lanes strategy: A controlled liquidation approach where suppliers restrict sales to a select group of wholesalers to manage supply and market segments.

takeback guarantee: A commitment by companies to accept returns of their products, often bearing all associated costs.

tested (direct) standard: A sales method where products are tested, categorized, and priced based on their functionality and condition.

testing: Evaluating the functionality and performance of returned products to determine their condition and the necessary next steps.

Third Industrial Revolution (the Digital Revolution): The period characterized by the advancement of electronics, computers, and automation in the late twentieth century.

third parties: Entities in the secondary market that source products from various suppliers and cater to different marketplaces and regions.

third tier supply sources: The niche market wholesalers, refurbishers, and smaller retailers that operate at the end of the secondary-market supply chain.

third-party logistics (3PL) providers: An external company hired to handle specific aspects of the reverse logistics process, such as product collection, transportation, sorting, and disposal or resale.

third-party service providers (3PSP): Companies that handle the return, repair, refurbishment, recycling, or disposal of products for other businesses. Their role includes managing return policies, processing returns, and determining cost-effective methods for reprocessing or disposing of goods.

third-party solutions partners: Businesses that collaborate to provide custom reverse logistics solutions. They offer technological and logistical expertise to optimize reverse supply chains, including software for tracking returns and strategies for reducing waste and maximizing recovery value from returned items.

threat asset: An entity with motivation to exploit vulnerabilities, which could be an actor, such as an individual or organization, looking to gain unauthorized access to sensitive information.

tiered re-registration fees: A pricing strategy that adjusts re-registration or relicensing fees based on the product-lifecycle stage to balance new sales with secondary market opportunities.

trade-in: A return process where customers return used products to receive residual value, applicable toward a new purchase or as an alternate payment method. This circular program incentivizes product upgrades and brand switching, potentially generating additional revenue streams through the refurbishment and resale of returned products.

transaction processing systems (TPS): Computerized systems that perform and record the daily routine transactions necessary to conduct business, such as sales-order entry, hotel reservations, payroll, employee record keeping, and shipping.

transfer order: An order or notice that outlines the transfer of inventory between locations, which can be linked to an RMA.

transparency: The practice of reporting costs clearly and accurately to facilitate informed decision-making and efficient management of returns.

transportation (in Forward Logistics): Focuses on moving goods from the point of origin to the point of consumption, involving activities such as selecting appropriate modes of transportation, arranging shipping routes, and coordinating deliveries.

unethical practices: Actions that are dishonest, unfair, or illegal, particularly in business dealings in the secondary market.

universal product code (UPC): A barcode symbol that is widely used in the United States and Canada for tracking trade items in stores, used in WMS for product identification and tracking.

Unrestricted Access to Lists: Illegally obtaining access to business databases, customer lists, or other proprietary information.

value generation: The decision-making process related to the subsequent use of a returned product, be it redeployment for value or responsible disposal.

value generation methods: Strategy employed by companies to maximize the value derived from products through various stages of their lifecycle, including return and recycling processes.

value generation optimization: A strategy that involves using various channels to generate value from returned products, maximizing revenue by engaging the most profitable outlets based on supply and demand dynamics.

value generation outlets: The endpoints in the reverse supply chain where refurbished, repaired, or recycled products are sold to end customers.

value seekers: Customers who are price sensitive and only purchase new products when the price has decreased, typically after newer models are released.

value-stream mapping: A visualization tool utilized in lean manufacturing to depict and improve the flow of production and information.

velocity: The speed at which a returned product is received, and its value realized.

Venn diagram: A diagram using overlapping circles to illustrate the relationships between different sets. In this context, used to illustrate the similarities and differences between forward and reverse logistics.

warehouse automation: The application of specialized equipment and storage and retrieval systems to automate tasks in a warehouse managed by WMS.

warehouse management system (WMS): A software application designed to support and optimize warehouse or distribution center management.

warehousing: The act of holding or storing returned products until their next designated action is determined. In forward logistics, this involves facilities to store products before distribution to customers, where activities such as inventory management and order fulfillment occur, handling new products that are identically packaged. In reverse logistics, it involves facilities to handle returned products, with processes like sorting returned items, assessing their condition, and determining the appropriate disposition (repair, refurbishment, recycling).

warranty management: A critical function in returns management overseeing the application of repair and refurbishment protocols and determining strategies for handling products under warranty.

warranty options: Various forms of guarantees offered by manufacturers to provide repair or replacement services for their products within a specified period; helps foster customer trust and satisfaction.

warranty replacement: The process of replacing a defective product under the company's warranty policy, often involving stringent quality and functional standards to uphold brand reputation and customer satisfaction.

waste generation: The creation of waste due to disposal of defective products that cannot be repaired or recycled, contributing to environmental impacts.

whistleblower mechanisms: Systems that allow individuals to report illegal or unethical activities anonymously within an organization.

wholesale liquidation: The bulk sale of products to the secondary market, transferring the responsibility of distribution to other partners.

Notes

Introduction

1. Dale S. Rogers and Ronald S. Tibben-Lembke, *Going Backwards: Reverse Logistics Trends and Practices* (Reverse Logistics Executive Council, 1999).

2. Dale S. Rogers and Ronald S. Tibben-Lembke, *Going Backwards: Reverse Logistics Trends and Practices.*

3. Bernard J. LaLonde and Baymond E. Mason, "Some thoughts on logistics policy and strategies: Management challenges for the 1980s," *International Journal of Physical Distribution & Materials Management* 15, no. 5 (1985): 5–15, https://doi.org/10.1108/eb014614.

Chapter 1

1. Dale S. Rogers and Ronald S. Tibben-Lembke, *Going Backwards: Reverse Logistics Trends and Practices* (Reverse Logistics Executive Council, 1999).

2. Sun Tzu, *The Art of War*, Amereon Ltd, 1988.

3. Capt. Matthew G. MacDonald and Dr. Robert Neeley, "Supply Chain Management in a Data-Driven World," *Army Sustainment*, June 1, 2022, 60–63, https://www.army.mil/article/254988/

4. Wallace A. Burns, "What is the Difference Between Logistics and Supply Chain?" Inbound Logistics, originally published November 2015, http://www.inboundlogistics.com/cms/article/good-question/.

5. Deborah Dull, *Circular Supply Chain: 17 Common Questions*, September 3, 2021.

6. Fara Alexander (Director of Brand Management, goTRG and VIP Outlet), in discussion with the author, November 2023.

7. Taebok Kim, Suresh K. Goyal, and Chang-Hyun Kim, "Lot-streaming policy for forward–reverse logistics with recovery capacity investment," *The International Journal of Advanced Manufacturing Technology* 68, no. 1–4 (2013): 509–522, https://doi.org/10.1007/s00170-013-4748-9.

8. "Consumer Returns in the Retail Industry 2021," Voice of Retail, 2021, https://cdn.nrf.com/sites/default/files/2022-01/Customer%20Returns%20in%20the%20Retail%20Industry%202021.pdf.

9. "Consumer Returns in the Retail Industry 2021," Voice of Retail, 2021.

10. Danielle Inman, "2022 Retail Returns Rate Remains Flat at $816 Billion," National Retail Federation, December 14, 2022, https://nrf.com/media-center/press-releases/2022-retail-returns-rate-remains-flat-816-billion.

11. Zachary S. Rogers, Dale S. Rogers, and Haozhe Chen, "The importance of secondary markets in the changing retail landscape: A longitudinal study in the United States and China," *Transportation Journal* 61, no. 1 (2022): 18–59, https://doi.org/10.5325/transportationj.61.1.0018.

12. Sender Shamiss (CEO, goTRG), in discussion with the author, November 2023.

13. "U.S. Census Bureau History: Montgomery Ward and the Shop-At-Home Catalog," The United States Census Bureau, 2022, https://www.census.gov/history/www/homepage_archive/2022/august_2022.html.

14. Kannan Govindan and Hamed Soleimani, "A review of Reverse Logistics and Closed-Loop Supply Chains: A Journal of Cleaner Production Focus," *Journal of Cleaner Production* vol. 142, part 1, p. 371–384, (January 20, 2017), https://doi.org/10.1016/j.jclepro.2016.03.126.

Chapter 2

1. Deborah Dull, *Circular Supply Chain: 17 Common Questions*.

2. "Consumer Returns in the Retail Industry 2021," Voice of Retail, 2021.

3. Fara Alexander and Chuck Johnson, "Next Best Practices: Returns Management," *Reverse Logistics Association Magazine, September 2022, 121,*

https://www.rla.org/media/article/view?id=1480.

4. Sender Shamiss (CEO, goTRG), in discussion with the author, November 2023.

5. Siham El Kihal and Edlira Shehu, "It's not only what they buy, but also what they keep: Linking marketing instruments to product returns," *Journal of Retailing* 98, no. 3 (October 2022): 558–571, https://doi.org/10.1016/j.jretai.2022.01.002.

6. Dale S. Rogers and Ronald S. Tibben-Lembke, *Going Backwards: Reverse Logistics Trends and Practices.*

7. Sender Shamiss (CEO, goTRG), in discussion with the author, November 2023.

8. Angela L. Jones, et al., "An examination of the effects of omni-channel service offerings on retailer performance," *International Journal of Physical Distribution & Logistics Management* 52, no. 2 (2021): 150–169, https://doi.org/10.1108/ijpdlm-06-2020-0175.

9. Angela L. Jones, et al., "An examination of the effects of omni-channel service offerings on retailer performance." *International Journal of Physical Distribution & Logistics Management* 52, no. 2 (2021).

10. Jeff Rossen, "Rossen Reports: These retailers will now charge you for returns," *KCRA 3*, June 13, 2013, https://www.kcra.com/article/these-retailers-will-now-charge-for-returns/44189497.

11. Victoria Song, "California passes right-to-repair act guaranteeing seven years of parts for your phone," *The Verge*, September 13, 2023, https://www.theverge.com/2023/9/13/23871712/california-right-to-repair-act-sb-244.

12. "If not now, when (Volume 4)," Climate Impact Partners, 2022.

13. Hervé Corvellec, Alison F. Stowell, and Nils Johansson, "Critiques of the circular economy," *Journal of Industrial Ecology* 26, no. 2 (August 2021): 421–432, https://doi.org/10.1111/jiec.13187.

14. "Environmental Impacts," Adidas, accessed June 12, 2021, https://report.adidas-group.com/2021/en/group-management-report-our-company/sustainability/environmental-impacts.html.

15. "2023 Gen Z and Millennial Survey (report)," Deloitte, 2023, https://www.deloitte.com/global/en/issues/work/content/genzmillennialsurvey.html

16. Hervé Corvellec, Alison F. Stowell, and Nils Johansson, "Critiques of the

circular economy," *Journal of Industrial Ecology* 26, no. 2 (August 2021).

17. Zora Kovacic, Roger Strand, and Thomas Völker, *The Circular Economy in Europe: Critical Perspectives on Policies and Imaginaries* (1ˢᵗ Edition), Routledge, 2019.

18. "Where Does Nike Grind Come From?" Nike Grind, accessed June 22, 2023, https://www.nikegrind.com/about/.

19. "Where Does Nike Grind Come From?" Nike Grind.

20. "Recycling + Donation," Nike, accessed June 22, 2023, https://www.nike.com/sustainability/recycling-donation.

21. "Where Does Nike Grind Come From?" Nike Grind.

22. "A timeline: Notable milestones in the history of iPhone from Apple," Verizon, accessed June 5, 2023, https://www.verizon.com/articles/Smartphones/milestones-in-history-of-apple-iphone/#:~:text=June%202010%3A%20%E2%80%9CThis%20changes%20everything,be%20unveiled%20as%20iPhone%204.

23. "A timeline: Notable milestones in the history of iPhone from Apple," Verizon.

24. "Towards the Circular Economy," Ellen Macarthur Foundation, 2013.

25. Braungart and MacDornough, "Circulate products and materials," Ellen MacArthur Foundation, accessed April 2, 2023, https://ellenmacarthurfoundation.org/circulate-products-and-materials.

26. Nektarios Oraiopoulos, Mark E. Ferguson, and L. Beril Toktay, "Relicensing as a Secondary Market Strategy," Management Science 58, no. 5 (2012): 1022–1037, https://doi.org/10.1287/mnsc.1110.1456.

27. John Reeder, "Cisco's First Closed Loop Plastic Product," Cisco, June 18, 2020, https://blog.webex.com/cloud-calling/ciscos-first-closed-loop-plastic-product/#:~:text=We're%20closing%20the%20loop,an%20exciting%20first%20for%20Cisco!.

28. John Reeder, "Cisco's First Closed Loop Plastic Product," Cisco, June 18, 2020.

29. Nektarios Oraiopoulos, Mark E. Ferguson, and L. Beril Toktay, "Relicensing as a Secondary Market Strategy," Management Science 58, no. 5 (2012).

30. "A timeline: Notable milestones in the history of iPhone from Apple," Verizon, accessed June 5, 2023.

31. Brian Schuchman (Founder of Sector 7), in discussion with the author, December 2016.

32. Brian Schuchman (Founder of Sector 7), in discussion with the author, December 2016.

33. Rishi Iyengar, "Your old iPhone is worth big bucks. Here's why," *CNN*, October 17, 2020, https://www.cnn.com/2020/10/17/tech/iphone-12-trade-in-programs/index.html.

34. Ian Carlos Campbell and Julia Alexander, "A guide to platform fees," The Verge, accessed June 5, 2023, https://www.theverge.com/21445923/platform-fees-apps-games-business-marketplace-apple-google.

Chapter 3

1. Sender Shamiss (CEO, goTRG), in discussion with the author, November 2023.

2. Fara Alexander and Chuck Johnson, "Next Best Practices: Returns Management," *Reverse Logistics Association Magazine*, September 2022, 121.

3. Eugene Cook, "Cold Jet—Carbon Rated," Business Focus, February 7, 2023, https://www.businessfocusmagazine.com/2023/02/07/cold-jet-carbon-rated/.

4. Chad W. Autry, Patricia J. Daugherty, and R. Glenn Richey, "The challenge of reverse logistics in catalog retailing," *International Journal of Physical Distribution & Logistics Management* 31, no. 1 (February 2021): 26–37, https://doi.org/10.1108/09600030110366384.

5. SERI, "The Sustainable Electronics Reuse & Recycling (R2) Standard," version 3.0, p.6, https://sustainableelectronics.org/.

6. SERI, "The Sustainable Electronics Reuse & Recycling (R2) Standard," version 3.0, p.6, https://sustainableelectronics.org/.

7. Sean Magann, "Developing a Comprehensive Program for Data Destruction," *Reverse Logistics Magazine*, August 16, 2023, 126.

8. Richard Kissel, et al., "NIST SP 800-88 Rev. 1: Guidelines for Media Sanitization," National Institute of Standards and Technology, US Department of Commerce, 2014.

9. Richard Kissel, et al., "NIST SP 800-88 Rev. 1: Guidelines for Media Sanitization," National Institute of Standards and Technology, US Department of Commerce, 2014.

10. Richard Kissel, et al., "NIST SP 800-88 Rev. 1: Guidelines for Media Sanitization," National Institute of Standards and Technology, US Department of Commerce, 2014.

11. Fredrik Forslund, "Media Sanitization Standards Are Changing for Data Storage Devices, Data-Driven Organizations & Tech Vendors," International Data Sanitization Consortium, February 4, 2022, https://www.datasanitization. org/device-sanitization-standards-are-changing-iso-27040-ieee-p2883/.

12. Bernard Le Gargean, "New IEEE Data Erasure Standard Fills Technology Gap," *Reverse Logistics Association Magazine*, August 16, 2023, 123.

13. Sean McManus, "Why millions of usable hard drives are being destroyed," BBC, June 6, 2023, https://www.bbc.com/news/business-65669537.

14. Chad W. Autry, Patricia J. Daugherty, and R. Glenn Richey, "The challenge of reverse logistics in catalog retailing," *International Journal of Physical Distribution & Logistics Management* 31, no. 1 (February 2021): 26–37, https://doi.org/10.1108/09600030110366384.

15. Dale S. Rogers and Ronald S. Tibben-Lembke, *Going Backwards: Reverse Logistics Trends and Practices*.

16. Dale S. Rogers and Ronald S. Tibben-Lembke, *Going Backwards: Reverse Logistics Trends and Practices*.

17. Robert Saracco, "Pervasive AI in Industry 4.0," IEEE Future Directions, August 3, 2020, https://cmte.ieee.org/futuredirections/2020/08/03/pervasive -ai-in-industry-4-0/.

18. Sridhar Dharmarajan, *"How industry 4.0 will transform manufacturing as we know it,"* The Times of India, updated September 2, 2022, https://timesofindia.indiatimes.com/blogs/voices/how-industry- 4-0-will-transform-manufacturing-as-we-know-it/.

19. Thomas Maher, "Time to reach 100M users," Reverse Logistics Association Show, June 2023.

20. Ryan Heath, "China races ahead of U.S. on AI regulation," Axios, May 8, 2023, https://www.axios.com/2023/05/08/china-ai-regulation-race.

21. Andrew Dalton, "AI is the wildcard in Hollywood's strikes. Here is an explanation of its unsettling role," AP News, accessed July 23, 2023, https://apnews. com/article/artificial-intelligence-hollywood-strikes-explained-writers-ac- tors-e872bd63ab52c3ea9f7d6e825240a202.

22. "Transaction Processing," IBM, 2022, https://www.ibm.com/docs/en/cics-ts/5.4?topic=overview-transaction-processing.

23. Chi-Yen Yin, "Measuring organizational impacts by integrating competitive intelligence into executive information system," *Journal of Intelligent Manufacturing* 29, no. 3 (2015): 533–547, https://doi.org/10.1007/s10845-015-1135-4.

24. "Industry 4.0, the fourth revolution (A Frost & Sullivan White Paper)," Frost & Sullivan, 2009.

25. Michael J. Coren, "Why you should buy everything used," *The Washington Post,* May 23, 2023, https://www.washingtonpost.com/climate-environment/2023/05/23/buy-resale-store-second-hand-clothes-furniture/.

26. "Transforming Returns for Retailers," goTRG, accessed November 12, 2023, https://www.gotrg.com/retailers.

27. Fara Alexander (Director of Brand Management, goTRG and VIP Outlet), in discussion with the author, November 2023.

28. "Transforming Returns for Retailers," goTRG, accessed November 12, 2023, https://www.gotrg.com/retailers.

29. Sender Shamiss (CEO, goTRG), in discussion with the author, November 2023.

30. Fara Alexander and Chuck Johnson, "Next Best Practices: Returns Management," *Reverse Logistics Association Magazine,* September 2022, 121.

31. Sender Shamiss (CEO, goTRG), in discussion with the author, November 2023.

32. Fara Alexander (Director of Brand Management, goTRG and VIP Outlet), in discussion with the author, November 2023.

33. Sender Shamiss (CEO, goTRG), in discussion with the author, November 2023.

34. Sender Shamiss (CEO, goTRG), in discussion with the author, November 2023.

35. Fara Alexander and Chuck Johnson, "Next Best Practices: Returns Management," *Reverse Logistics Association Magazine,* September 2022, 121.

36. Sender Shamiss (CEO, goTRG), in discussion with the author, November 2023.

37. Fara Alexander (Director of Brand Management, goTRG and VIP Outlet), in discussion with the author, November 2023.

38. Fara Alexander (Director of Brand Management, goTRG and VIP Outlet), in discussion with the author, November 2023.

39. Fara Alexander (Director of Brand Management, goTRG and VIP Outlet), in discussion with the author, November 2023.

40. Fara Alexander (Director of Brand Management, goTRG and VIP Outlet), in discussion with the author, November 2023.

41. Arlene Karidis, "Returned Merchandise Stockpiles as Waste: One Company's Solution," Waste360, 2021, https://www.waste360.com/industry-insights/returned-merchandise-stockpiles-as-waste-one-company-s-solution.

42. Fara Alexander (Director of Brand Management, goTRG and VIP Outlet), in discussion with the author, November 2023.

43. Fara Alexander (Director of Brand Management, goTRG and VIP Outlet), in discussion with the author, November 2023.

44. Fara Alexander and Chuck Johnson, "Next Best Practices: Returns Management," *Reverse Logistics Association Magazine*, September 2022, 121.

45. Arlene Karidis, "Returned Merchandise Stockpiles as Waste: One Company's Solution," Waste360, July 13, 2021, https://www.waste360.com/industry-insights/returned-merchandise-stockpiles-as-waste-one-company-s-solution.

46. Arlene Karidis, "Returned Merchandise Stockpiles as Waste: One Company's Solution," Waste360, July 13, 2021, https://www.waste360.com/industry-insights/returned-merchandise-stockpiles-as-waste-one-company-s-solution.

47. "Transforming Returns for Retailers," goTRG, accessed November 12, 2023, https://www.gotrg.com/retailers.

Chapter 4

1. Nektarios Oraiopoulos, Mark E. Ferguson, and L. Beril Toktay, "Relicensing as a secondary market strategy," *Management Science* 58, no. 5 (2012): 1022–1037, https://doi.org/10.1287/mnsc.1110.1456.

2. Hervé Corvellec, Alison F. Stowell, and Nils Johansson, "Critiques of the circular economy," *Journal of Industrial Ecology* 26, no. 2 (August 2021).

3. Nektarios Oraiopoulos, Mark E. Ferguson, and L. Beril Toktay, "Relicensing as a secondary market strategy," *Management Science* 58, no. 5 (2012): 1022–1037, https://doi.org/10.1287/mnsc.1110.1456.

4. Carla Fried, "Dealers Might Not Profit from Soaring Used-Car Prices," UCLA Anderson Review, February 16, 2022, https://anderson-review.ucla.edu/dealers-might-not-profit-from-soaring-used-car-prices/.

Chapter 5

1. Deborah Dull, *Circular Supply Chain: 17 Common Questions.*

2. Dave Stritzinger (Co-Founder and Operating Partner, Sequoia Solutions Group), in discussion with the author, December 2022.

3. "Second Hand Apparel Market," Future Market Insights, September 2022, https://www.futuremarketinsights.com/reports/secondhand-apparel-market#thankyou.

4. Andrew Rough (CES ACS Clothing), in discussion with the author, October 2023.

5. Andrew Rough (CES ACS Clothing), in discussion with the author, October 2023.

6. Andrew Rough (CES ACS Clothing), in discussion with the author, October 2023.

7. Andrew Rough (CES ACS Clothing), in discussion with the author, October 2023.

Chapter 6

1. "Second Hand Apparel Market," Future Market Insights, September 2022.

2. "IDC Forecasts Nearly 415 million Used Smartphones Will Be Shipped Worldwide in 2026 with a Market Value of $99.9 Billion," IDC, January 9, 2023, https://www.idc.com/getdoc.jsp?containerId=prUS50005523.

3. Jessica Dickler, "Could the United Auto Workers strike affect car prices? 'Inevitably yes,' expert says," CNBC, updated September 22, 2023, https://www.cnbc.com/2023/09/22/could-the-uaw-strike-affect-car-prices-inevitably-yes-expert-says.html.

4. Lauren Chadwick, "Apple ordered to stop selling iPhone 12 in France over

too-high levels of electromagnetic radiation," Euronews.com, accessed September 13, 2023, https://www.euronews.com/next/2023/09/13/apple -ordered-to-stop-selling-iphone-12-in-france-over-high-levels-of-electro-magnetic-radi#:~:text=Next%20Biztech%20news-,Apple%20ordered%20 to%20stop%20selling%20iPhone%2012%20in%20France%20over,high%20 levels%20of%20electromagnetic%20radiation&text=French%20 authorities%20said%20the%20iPhone,lead%20to%20EU%2Dwide%20 restrictions.

5. Jordan Sielaff (Co-Founder and CEO at Gierd), in discussion with the author, October 2023.

6. Jordan Sielaff (Co-Founder and CEO at Gierd), in discussion with the author, October 2023.

7. Jordan Sielaff (Co-Founder and CEO at Gierd), in discussion with the author, October 2023.

8. Christophe Demarque, et al., "Nudging sustainable consumption: The use of descriptive norms to promote a minority behavior in a realistic online shopping environment," *Journal of Environmental Psychology* 43 (September 2015): 166–174, https://doi.org/10.1016/j.jenvp.2015.06.008.

9. Antoinette Verhage, "Anti money laundering complex and the compliance industry," Routledge Taylor & Francis Group, 2011.

10. "Examples of Money Laundering Techniques," Lexis Nexis, May 4, 2023, https://www.lexisnexis.com/blogs/gb/b/compliance-risk-due-diligence/ posts/examples-money-laundering.

11. "Examples of Money Laundering Techniques," Lexis Nexis, May 4, 2023, https://www.lexisnexis.com/blogs/gb/b/compliance-risk-due-diligence/ posts/examples-money-laundering.

Chapter 7

1. Deborah Dull, Circular Supply Chain: 17 Common Questions.

2. "Under pressure: Supply chain strategies that can overcome natural resource scarcity," Strategic Direction 36 (2020): 10–12. https://doi.org/10.1108/ SD-01-2020-0011.

3. "Bolstering your margin of safety against natural resource scarcity," *Strategic Direction* 34, no.7 (July 2018): 29–31, https://doi.org/10.1108/ SD-02-2018-0021.

4. Jean-Marc van Maren, "Logistics in Transition to a Circular Economy 'We can't afford to create more waste in logistics'," *RLA Magazine*, June 7, 2023, 125.

5. C. Robbins, "Cisco Pledge Statement," Cisco, https://www.cisco.com/c/en/us/support/returns/returns-portal.html#myModal22.

6. Anna Mutoh, "Corporate ESG Requirements Are About to Ramp Up. Here's How CFOs Can Prepare," *The Wall Street Journal*, June 2, 2023, https://www.wsj.com/articles/corporate-esg-requirements-are-about-to-ramp-up-heres-how-cfos-can-prepare-1113a8d2?mod=article_inline.

7. Nicholas A. Mirr, "Defending the Right to Repair: An Argument for Federal Legislation Guaranteeing the Right to Repair," *Iowa Law Review* 105, no. 5 (2020). https://ilr.law.uiowa.edu/print/volume-105-issue-5/defending-the-right-to-repair-an-argument-for-federal-legislation-guaranteeing-the-right-to-repair.

8. Victoria Song, "California passes right-to-repair act guaranteeing seven years of parts for your phone," The Verge, September 13, 2023.

9. Arlene Karidis, "Returned Merchandise Stockpiles as Waste: One Company's Solution," Waste360, 2021, https://www.waste360.com/industry-insights/returned-merchandise-stockpiles-as-waste-one-company-s-solution.

10. Paul Dewick, et al., "Circular economy finance: Clear winner or risky proposition?" *Journal of Industrial Ecology* 24, no. 6 (June 18, 2020): 1192–1200, https://doi.org/10.1111/jiec.13025.

11. "Consumer Returns in the Retail Industry 2021," Voice of Retail, 2021

12. "thredUP Releases 10th Annual Resale Report with Insights on a Decade of Resale," thredUP, May 17, 2022, https://newsroom.thredup.com/news/thredup-releases-10th-annual-resale-report-with-insights-on-a-decade-of-resale.

13. Sam Goldheart, "Right to Repair," Reverse Logistics Association, August 2023, https://rla.org/media/article/view?id=1629.

14. Kaveh Waddell, "People Want to Get Phones and Appliances Fixed—But Often, They Can't," *Consumer Reports*, February 28, 2022, https://www.consumerreports.org/consumer-rights/people-want-to-get-phones-appliances-fixed-but-often-cant-a1117945195/.

15. Kaveh Waddell, "People Want to Get Phones and Appliances Fixed—But Often, They Can't," *Consumer Reports*, February 28, 2022.

16. Nicholas A. Mirr, "Defending the Right to Repair: An Argument for Federal Legislation Guaranteeing the Right to Repair," *Iowa Law Review* 105, no. 5 (2020).

17. Nicholas A. Mirr, "Defending the Right to Repair: An Argument for Federal Legislation Guaranteeing the Right to Repair," *Iowa Law Review* 105, no. 5 (2020).

18. Larry Velman, "The Evolution of Returns Management: Harnessing AI and Blockchain in the Modern Retail Landscape," Reverse Logistics Association, October 2023, https://rla.org/media/article/view?id=1664.

19. "2023 Gen Z and Millennial Survey (report)," Deloitte, 2023.

20. "2023 Gen Z and Millennial Survey (report)," Deloitte, 2023.

21. "2023 Gen Z and Millennial Survey (report)," Deloitte, 2023.

22. Fara Alexander and Chuck Johnson, "Next Best Practices: Returns Management," *Reverse Logistics Association Magazine,* September 2022, 121.

23. Zachary S. Rogers, Dale S. Rogers, and Haozhe Chen, "The importance of secondary markets in the changing retail landscape: A longitudinal study in the United States and China," *Transportation Journal* 61, no. 1 (2022): 18–59.

Illustration Credits

Chapter 1

Figure 1.6. Zachary S. Rogers, Dale S. Rogers, and Haozhe Chen, "The importance of secondary markets in the changing retail landscape: A longitudinal study in the United States and China," *Transportation Journal* 61, no. 1 (2022): 18–59.

Chapter 2

Figure 2.5. "Nike Air Zoom SuperRep 2 Nike Next Nature," Nike, September 2, 2021, https://www.nike.com/a/sustainability-superrep-2-next-nature.

Illustration credit: (Nike Air Zoom SuperRep 2 Nike Next Nature, 2021).

Figure 2.7. C. Robbins, "Cisco Pledge Statement," Cisco, https://www.cisco.com/c/en/us/support/returns/returns-portal.html#myModal22.

Figure 2.12. Tim Cook, "Letter from Tim Cook to Apple Investors," Apple, January 2, 2019, https://www.apple.com/newsroom/2019/01/letter-from-tim-cook-to-apple-investors/.

Chapter 3

Figure 3.5. "Understanding the Cyber Threat Landscape," InfoXChange.com, July 8, 2019, https://www.infoxchange.org/nz/au/news/2019/07/understanding-cyber-threat-landscape.

Figure 3.6. Thomas Maher, "Time to Reach 100M Users," Dell Computers, Presentation at Reverse Logistics Association Show (Netherlands), June 2023.

Figure 3.7. Thomas Maher, "Time to Reach 100M Users," Dell Computers, Presentation at Reverse Logistics Association Show (Netherlands), June 2023.

Figure 3.8. Illustration credit: Source: 2022 Gartner Digital Business Impact on the Supply Chain Survey

Figure 3.9. "goTRG's Earth Day Sustainability Report," goTRG, 2020, https://www.gotrg.com/resources/gotrgs-earth-day-sustainability-report#.

Figure 3.10. Parija Kavilanz, "Just keep your returns: Stores weigh paying you not to bring back unwanted items," *CNN*, June 26, 2022, https://www.cnn.com/2022/06/26/business/retail-returns/index.html.

Figure 3.11. Parija Kavilanz, "Just keep your returns: Stores weigh paying you not to bring back unwanted items," *CNN*, June 26, 2022, https://www.cnn.com/2022/06/26/business/retail-returns/index.html.

Figure 3.14. "Transforming Returns for Retailers," goTRG, accessed November 12, 2023, https://www.gotrg.com/retailers.

Chapter 5

Figure 5.3. Michael J. Coren, "Why you should buy everything used," *The Washington Post,* accessed September 30, 2023, https://www.washingtonpost.com/climate-environment/2023/05/23/buy-resale-store-second-hand-clothes-furniture/.

Figure 5.4. "We take care of the entire reverse logistics process," ACS Clothing, accessed September 27, 2023, https://acsclothing.co.uk/.

Chapter 6

Figure 6.1. Image from Nik Raman (CEO of PhoneX Holdings Inc.), "Secondary Market Supply Chain," permission to use given to author, August 2023.

Chapter 7

Figure 7.1. Product label and report provided by Mannopov CEO to the author, November 2022. (unlocked).